T0319797

Pathways in Decentralised Collective Bargaining in Europe

Pathways in Decentralised Collective Bargaining in Europe

Edited by
Frank Tros

Authors of the book chapters:
Ilaria Armaroli, Jan Czarzasty, Thomas Haipeter,
Andrea Iossa, Niels Jansen, Marcus Kahmann,
Ana Belén Muñoz Ruiz, Valentina Paolucci,
Nuria Ramos Martín, Mia Rönnmar, Sophie Rosenbohm,
Frank Tros, Catherine Vincent

Amsterdam University Press

Co-funding for this open access eBook:
European Commission, agreement VS/2020/0111 – CODEBAR.
The European Commission is not responsible for the authors' views in this book, nor for any use that may be made of the information it contains.

Cover illustration: 123rf.com / Captain Vector

Cover design: Coördesign, Leiden
Lay-out: Crius Group, Hulshout

ISBN 978 90 4856 023 3
E-ISBN 978 90 4856 024 0 (pdf)
DOI 10.5117/9789048560233
NUR 825

creativecommons.org/licenses/by-nc-nd/4.0

© All authors / Amsterdam University Press B.V., Amsterdam 2023

Some rights reserved. Without limiting the rights under copyright reserved above, any part of this book may be reproduced, stored in or introduced into a retrieval system, or transmitted, in any form or by any means (electronic, mechanical, photocopying, recording or otherwise).

Every effort has been made to obtain permission to use all copyrighted illustrations reproduced in this book. nonetheless, whosoever believes to have rights to this material is advised to contact the publisher.

Printed and bound by CPI Group (UK) Ltd, Croydon, CR0 4YY

Table of Contents

1. Decentralisation of Collective Bargaining: Comparing Institutional Change and Company Practices in Europe

Frank Tros

Abstract

This chapter addresses different types of institutional change in collective bargaining regimes and the underlying mechanisms. In recent decades, collective bargaining coverage has decreased in liberal market economies like Ireland and Poland. But also in coordinated economies, such as Germany, sectoral bargaining has eroded as a result of employers' strategies. Governments in southern European countries have established opportunities for company bargaining in (complex) *layering* structures. This chapter further addresses beneficial factors for balancing power relations between collective bargaining parties at the decentralised level, based on company case studies. Best cases of "organised decentralisation" are found in manufacturing. Decentralisation in retail is problematic. The chapter concludes with the challenges for trade unions in Europe.

Keywords: institutional change, collective bargaining, decentralisation, social partners

A common approach to studying decentralisation

Introduction to the problem

One of the main trends in labour relations across Europe – started already in the 1980s – is "decentralisation" in collective bargaining at the company level. This involves a shift from multi-employer bargaining to single-employer bargaining with trade unions or other workers representatives (Marginson,

Frank Tros (ed.). *Pathways in Decentralised Collective Bargaining in Europe.*Amsterdam: Amsterdam University Press, 2023

DOI 10.5117/9789048560233_CH01

2015; OECD, 2018; Traxler, 1995; Visser, 2016). This development continued in the last decade, following the Great Recession, sometimes supported by governments in European Union member states, to deregulate wages and enhance labour market flexibility in the 2010s. At that time, there were voices, also within the European Commission, that aimed to (further) decentralisation as an instrument to reduce rigidities in labour regulations and the wage-setting power of trade unions (Müller & Platzer, 2020; European Commission, 2012).

In the field of industrial relations, "decentralisation" is a buzzword that has a plethora of definitions and meanings at several levels. It can refer to less state intervention in the regulation of terms and conditions of employment and less state support in collective bargaining in sectors and companies. It can also refer to less social dialogue and less coordination by peak-level employers' associations and trade unions at the national level. This book focuses on the decentralisation of collective bargaining from the national/cross-sectoral and/or sectoral level to the individual company level (although, as we will show, the state and national social dialogue also play a role in this process). Recent literature lends nuance to the trend of decentralisation by showing variations in national developments regarding the initiating actors and the intensity and patterns of decentralisation processes and the different factors that account for national differences (Leonardi & Pedersini, 2018; Müller, Vandaele & Waddington, 2019). In some countries, decentralisation is initiated by governments or by employers seeking to make trade union negotiations and collective agreements more responsive to the needs and conditions of individual companies. This can be done through *de*regulation or by breaking down traditional structures in collective bargaining. Or this can be done by setting new rules for "tailor-made" dialogue, negotiations, and agreements at decentralised levels. Besides this divide between disorganised and organised decentralisation (Traxler, 1995), there is a third development going on. In the last few years, a great deal of bottom-up social dialogue has been initiated on issues like human resource management, social security, and the impacts of the "green transition" and COVID-19 on companies and labour. Types and degrees of decentralisation processes are the results of the organisational power resources and strategies of the collective bargaining parties at several levels in the context of sometimes eroded or renewed institutions in collective bargaining regimes.

Why is it relevant to study decentralisation in labour relations, and, more specifically, in collective bargaining? Firstly, it is relevant for assessing the (future) position and roles of trade unions and employers' associations at the cross-sectoral and national sectoral levels in European Union member states: do they still have representative voices and collective influence in social dialogue and labour market regulations in societies that often are more diverse and governments that re more neoliberal than in earlier historical periods? Do social partners adapt to new, often more differentiated, realities? Secondly, centralised and more coordinated collective bargaining regimes seem to perform better than decentralised and less organised regimes, in terms of wage equality and employment levels (OECD, 2018; Carnero, 2020). Thirdly, unorganised decentralisation risks a "race to the bottom" if wage levels and other employment terms and conditions are no longer protected by collective agreements. Labour relations are power relations where individual workers are, by definition, weaker than the employer; collective bargaining by independent trade unions can (partly) compensate for this imbalance.

Recently, collective bargaining has received increased and, indeed, more positive attention from European political institutions. In 2022, the European Council and European Parliament reached a political agreement to promote the adequacy of statutory minimum wages and thus help to achieve decent working and living conditions for European employees. Interestingly, as collective bargaining on wage-setting is seen as an important tool to ensure that workers can benefit from adequate minimum wages, the related directive aims to extend the coverage of workers through collective bargaining and to strengthen the capacity of social partners to engage in collective bargaining (including the protection of worker representatives). In some countries, such as Italy and Sweden, this is even more important because there is no national statutory minimum wage: here, the minimum wage levels are defined by the lowest wage groups of the collective bargaining agreements. Decentralisation of collective bargaining, however, might be at odds with the aims of this political agreement. Firstly, decentralisation might lower the overall bargaining coverage in European countries. Secondly, trade unions in European countries might have less capacity to bargain at the company level compared to negotiating at more centralised levels.

Despite its risks, there are also good reasons for organised decentralisation. For example, it provides the opportunity for trade unions to be more connected to the reality of workers' needs in specific companies and to deepen or widen their memberships. It can also facilitate local trade-offs with the needs of individual employers regarding a company's performance.

The approach

This book adopts an interdisciplinary and multi-level governance perspective to address different types of institutional change in collective bargaining regimes and the underlying aims of companies, governments, and subsequent responses of social partners to downward pressures on the locus of collective bargaining. Through literature and document research, and around 30 in-depth case studies of company-level bargaining in the manufacturing industry, retail sectors, and some other economic sectors, the book chapters analyse the backgrounds, practices, stakeholder experiences, and effects of decentralisation and decentralised bargaining at the company level in eight EU member states: France; Germany; Ireland; Italy; the Netherlands; Poland; Spain; and Sweden.

This book is innovative in the field for several reasons. Firstly, many European studies on collective bargaining follow a more national approach, publishing monographs that feature separate chapters on individual countries (see for example Leonardi & Pedersini, 2018; Müller, Vandaele, & Waddington, 2019). By contrast, international studies follow a very global approach that lacks in-depth analysis about the functioning of institutions or practices in collective bargaining (e.g., OECD 2018; Visser, 2016). This book adopts a thematic and sectoral approach from a cross-country perspective, leading to better understanding of the functioning of institutions and variations in actors' strategies and collective bargaining practices. Secondly, the book is based on investigations of around 30 case studies at the company level aimed at enhancing understanding of the power resources and strategies of collective bargaining parties and their effects on decentralisation processes at the *micro level*.

The following questions will be answered in this chapter:
1. What are the backgrounds and aims of decentralisation in collective bargaining at the company level and what are the institutional pathways of decentralisation in the countries examined?
2. What are the institutional and organisational power resources and strategies of employers and trade unions that shape decentralisation and company-level bargaining?
3. What impact has decentralisation had on the balance and scope of company-level negotiations and the quality of agreements made? Do partnerships or conflicts emerge between individual employers and trade unions and, if relevant, between different representative workers' bodies within companies (such as trade unions and works councils)?

I will start by describing the basic institutional characteristics of collective bargaining regimes in the eight selected countries. This will make the points that there is considerable variation in collective bargaining regimes within Europe and that decentralisation can be only understood in national contexts. I will then provide an overview of decentralisation processes in the eight countries in a theoretical framework of institutional change in collective bargaining. In a more explorative way, I will discuss the qualitative findings from company case studies in the eight European countries. Although not representative, the case studies shed qualitative light and lead to better understanding of the interplay between social dialogue and collective bargaining institutions on the one hand, and actors' strategies and practices in decentralised bargaining at the company level, on the other hand. I will focus on sectoral variations within national systems (manufacturing and retail) and I will discuss beneficial and limiting factors for decentralised bargaining with similar power relations and balanced outcomes, based on the qualitative findings in the case studies. I will answer the question of whether decentralisation leads to new relationships between trade unions and works councils (or other employee representation) in dual-channel systems of worker representation. In the last section, the main conclusions are presented, together with some theoretical and stakeholders' challenges related to (further) decentralisation.

Variations in national collective bargaining regimes

The countries that feature in this book represent a variety of production regimes (Hall & Soskice, 2001) and industrial relations traditions (Crouch, 2005). This means that social partners in the European Union member states have quite different power resources in collective bargaining and in coordinating and regulating decentralisation. I will cluster the eight countries that are the subject of this study in the following four groups.

First, Ireland and Poland – despite having different political histories and being based, respectively, in Western and Eastern Europe – both countries today represent a *liberal market economy*, and both also share a *pluralist and fragmented industrial relations regime*. Related to the low numbers of employees under sector bargaining in these both countries, Ireland and Poland are examples of low collective bargaining coverage: 34% in Ireland and around 13–20% in Poland. Employers and trade unions in Ireland voluntarily engage in collective bargaining, so trade unions have no fundamental right to negotiation, and their agreed employment terms and conditions are not legally binding (Paolucci, Roche, & Gormley, 2022). Both countries have weak or no sector bargaining and relatively more company bargaining. In Ireland, the financial crisis in 2008 was the death knell for the long period of centralised tripartite collective bargaining that spanned the period from 1987. As an effect, collective bargaining primarily takes place are the company and the workplace levels. Sectoral bargaining still occurs in a number of low-paid and weakly unionised sectors, in construction and allied sectors, and in public services (Paolucci, Roche, & Gormley, 2022). The collective bargaining regime in Poland is even more fragmented than in Ireland, and even faced a "near-death experience" when the Polish legislator did not promote collective bargaining at all (Czarzasty, 2022). The fragmentation in Poland can be explained in the pre-1989 era of authoritarian state socialism, combined with the bottom-up activities of trade union movements, representing a contrasting concept of union movement (Solidarity and OPZZ). The political reform towards liberalism led to a vacuum in the industrial relations system with a lack of employers' commitments to national and sectoral collective bargaining institutions and a lack of union activities at the sectoral level (Solidarity and OPZZ). Ireland and de facto Poland do not have legal rights for non-unionised employee representative bodies at the company or establishment levels: both countries are characterised as having a *single-channel system* of worker representation, where, as far as management is concerned, unions are the only worker representatives, albeit they are far less established and developed than in, for example, Sweden's single channel system.

Second, Sweden represents the Nordic model of a *coordinated market economy* and *organised corporatism* with high collective bargaining coverage, based on strong autonomous bargaining between social partners without state interventions. This is reflected in the situation that there is no national legal minimum wage and no public extension mechanisms of sector agreements with respect to unorganised employers. Although sector bargaining is dominant, one can characterise the Swedish collective bargaining regime as being "multi-level." There is elaborate company-level dialogue and bargaining, involving trade unions at sector and company levels, with a key role for sector agreements. Moreover, it takes place in a stable and coordinated industrial relations system (Rönnmar & Iossa, 2022). In Sweden, strong participation and co-determination rights are carried out within a single-channel system of worker representation where trade unions participate in information, consultation and co-determination processes at the workplace level (Pietrogiovanni & Iossa, 2017; Rönnmar & Iossa, 2022).

Third, Germany and the Netherlands both represent a model of a *coordinated market economy* and *social partnerships*. The dominant level in collective bargaining is at the sector level. A key difference with countries like Ireland, Poland, and Sweden is that Germany and the Netherlands have a *dual-channel system* of worker representation. Trade unions are the legally recognised workers representatives in collective bargaining, but at the company level works councils are also legally established workers representatives involved in the implementation of collective agreements and dealing with issues that are not regulated by trade unions. Trade unions and works councils each have their own legal positions and rights, namely, collective bargaining versus co-determination. Collective bargaining coverage has become more differentiated between the two countries: 54% in Germany and 76% in the Netherlands. The role of the state in labour relations in Germany is slightly less intertwined than in the Netherlands. The statutory minimum wage is relatively new in Germany, having been introduced in 2015, and the instrument of extending sector agreements towards unorganised businesses is used less in Germany (Haipeter & Rosenbohm, 2022). The stability of the Dutch collective bargaining regime and its scope is supported by the high use of the public extension mechanism in sectors where employers' associations represent 60% or more of the employment in the sector (Jansen & Tros, 2022). In the Netherlands, once collective bargaining takes place at the sector level, then trade unions do not, generally, exploit activities at the company level (legally they can, and in some company cases, they do). Meanwhile, in Germany, trade unions have bargaining rights at the company level if derogation clauses in sectoral agreements foresee such rights. In Germany, works councils in larger companies (at least in some sectors, like manufacturing) are involved in negotiating workplace-related working conditions or "employment pacts," including pay above the wage norms of collective bargaining. In the Netherlands, works councils have strong legal consultation rights in internal organisational areas, but do not have negotiation rights on topics like wages and other issues already covered by collective agreements. Although the basic institutions in both countries are roughly similar, we see substantially different degrees and patterns of decentralisation , and also different relationships between trade unions and works councils.

Finally, we can cluster the Southern European countries – France, Italy, and Spain – which are characterised as having *statist market economies* and *polarised/state centred* industrial relations. All three countries have high collective bargaining coverage, multi-layered collective bargaining systems, and the state still maintains relatively high involvement in collective bargaining. This includes extension mechanisms towards unorganised businesses, but also state regulation in decentralisation. It is important to note here that France has a longer tradition of state intervention in stimulating and even obliging company-level bargaining (already in the 1980s), in addition to dominant sector-level bargaining practices (Kahmann

Table 1.1. **Characteristics of collective bargaining regimes in eight European countries**

Country industrial relations traditions	Collective bargaining coverage (1) (2000–2020)	Dominant level in bargaining regime (2)	Status works council or other structure for employee representation within firms (3)	Involvement works councils in wage negotiations	Trade union density (2000–2020)
Ireland pluralist/ fragmented	44%–34%	Company	Voluntary	Rare	36%–26%
Poland pluralist/ fragmented	25%–13%	Company	Voluntary (some legal base from 2006)	Very rare	24%–13%
Sweden organised corporatism	88%–88%	Sector	Not existing (Only channel of unions)	–	81%–65%
Germany social partnership	68%–54%	Sector	Embedded by law/ social partners (obligation when workers want)	Informally (wages above the general pay scale)	25%–17%
Netherlands social partnership	82%–76%	Sector	Embedded by law/ social partners (obligation when workers want)	Rare	22%–15%
France polarised/state centred	98%–98%	Sector	Embedded by law/social partners	Yes; if no, union is present	11%–11%
Italy polarised/state centred	100%–100%	Sector	Embedded by law/social partners, but no obligation	Yes	35%–33%
Spain polarised/state centred	85%–80%	Sector	Embedded by law/social partners	Yes	18%–13%

(1) Years 2000–2002 – years 2017–2020. Proportion of employees covered by collective (wage) agreements in force among employees with the right to bargain (based on combined administrative and/or survey data sources).
(2) Years 2018–2020. The dominant level at which wage bargaining takes place in terms of coverage of employees.
(3) Years 2018–2020.
(4) Years 2000–2002 – years 2017–2020

Source: OECD/AIAS ICTWSS database (March 2023). https://www.oecd.org/employment/ictwss-database.html + literature references in the text.

& Vincent, 2022). Furthermore, all three countries have a more complex and mixed type of dual-channel system for worker representation. In Italy and Spain, more or less unionised works councils or mandated representatives can formally negotiate collective agreements alongside, or instead of, trade unions. In France, collective bargaining rights for non-unionised employee representatives are legally embedded if no union is present. In Southern European countries, trade unions can also have seats on consultation and co-determination bodies.

Table 1.1. provides an overview of the characteristics of the main collective bargaining regimes in the eight selected European countries.

Pathways in decentralisation

Theoretical framework for institutional change

This book shows different forms of institutional change in collective bargaining regimes after the economic and financial crisis of 2008/2009 and their different results. We see a breakdown of collective bargaining structures in Ireland and no resurrection of previously broken-down institutions in Poland. Specifically, we see mechanisms aimed at regulating collective bargaining set aside in favour of arrangements that re-impose the discipline of the market (see Chapter 4; Paolucci et al., 2023). In other European countries, we see a tendency towards gradual and incremental decentralisation. However, as Streeck & Thelen (2005) have argued, incremental institutional change can lead to real, in-depth changes over time. Streeck & Thelen (2005) distinguish the following types of gradual institutional change associated with the issue of collective bargaining and its assumed transformation towards decentralisation:

(1) *displacement*, in which dominant institutions gradually lose ground to increasingly important "subordinate" institutions. In the context of the decentralisation of collective bargaining, this occurs when (cross-)sector bargaining structures are replaced by company bargaining structures. Or, in its disorganised form, when sector- or company-level bargaining with trade unions is replaced by single-company arrangements that involve established trade unions being replaced by "yellow unions" or non-unionised workers representatives within the company (e.g., works councils in dual-channel systems of worker representation).

(2) *layering*, in which new elements are added to existing institutions. In relation to our topic, this occurs if the state adds more formal opportunities for company-level bargaining by changing national legislation on collective bargaining (Rehveldt & Vincent, 2018; Vincent, 2019). In addition, social partners in sector agreements can add more competences to individual employers and trade unions or other workers representatives in company bargaining (Marginson, 2015). Chapter 3 of this book distinguishes several types of layering or "articulation" between sector- and company-level bargaining, such as additional wage bargaining, negotiations on additional topics at the company level, and opening clauses and derogation options at the company level within higher-level frameworks (see Chapter 3; Haipeter et al., 2023). Increased intensity of or widening social dialogue and collective bargaining at the company level as a result of autonomous, bottom-up initiatives by local actors with continuing institutional involvement at the centralised levels can also be interpreted as "layering," albeit less centrally coordinated.

(3) *drift*, in which existing institutions are not maintained and not adapted to changing environments, leading to less scope, meaning, and function of the institution. In a context of decreasing membership of trade unions and employer associations, and more neoliberal and individualistic ideas in politics and society, it is theoretically possible that traditions such as collective bargaining may gradually fade away. National and sector bargaining can lose a grip on local realities when it fails to respond to the involvement and needs of (new) companies and (new generations of) workers. "'drift, may also occur when collective bargaining institutions remain in place only for a core of employees (or certain sectors) but are not available beyond this core (or to other sectors), as in trajectories of "dualising liberalisation" (see Chapter 4; Paolucci et al., 2023). The development of less compliance to collective agreements can also be put into this.

(4) *conversion*, in which institutions formally remain unchanged but actors interpret and use them to to achieve different results. For example, if employers become more powerful in industrial relations and use collective agreements as management instruments for efficient HRM and to further company interests, instead using collective agreements as social contracts to balance workers and employers interests (see e.g., Keune, Been, & Tros, 2020). This shifting of focus towards the needs and conditions of individual companies can lead to decentralisation in the setting of employment terms and conditions. Already more than a decade ago, Baccaro and Howell (2011) showed that, in some European countries, centralised bargaining has been

converted to "fit the common imperative of liberalisation" (i.e., in Ireland, Italy, and Sweden) through giving more employer discretion in the period 1974–2005.[1]

Evidence of types of decentralisation in eight countries

In this section, I will give an overview of the most evident trends and pathways of decentralisation in the eight case-study countries with respect to the theoretical categorisation of institutional change.

Breakdown

Collective bargaining institutions in Poland and Ireland have faced the most structural and disruptive changes in recent decades. In Poland, the number of collective agreements is low and falling, and collective bargaining is almost dead, with less than 50 new collective agreements in both 2020 and 2021 (just 14,000 and 20,000 workers, respectively, are covered by these new agreements). Despite the ratification of the ILO Convention 98 and the European Social Charter, the Polish state neither promotes nor supports collective bargaining (Czarzasty, 2022). Employers fear obligations that can hinder their competitive powers. The Polish Trade Union Act promotes a fragmented and establishment-centred trade union movement that cannot overcome liberal and flexible business strategies. In Ireland, following the financial crisis, employers withdrew from the social partnership in 2009, which led to a further drop in collective bargaining coverage from 41% to 34% in the period 2009–2017 (OECD/AIAS database). The breakdown of collective bargaining structures in Ireland had already started before the 2010s but in 1985, collective bargaining coverage was at the far higher level of 70%.

These finding mirrors the literature, which characterises both Poland and Ireland as countries with a liberal market economy and with a pluralist and fragmented industrial relations regime.

Displacement

There is little evidence in the eight countries of the direct replacement of sector bargaining with company bargaining. This type of decentralisation assumes unidirectional changes in a hierarchy of collective bargaining levels, which is mostly not the case. In the countries where sector bargaining is

---

1   Streeck & Thelen (2005: 29) distinguish a fifth form of institutional change, "exhaustion," in which institutions gradually fade away. But as the authors themselves already acknowledge, this is not about institutional change but rather about institutional breakdown.

dominant, we see more multi-level bargaining practices where decentralised parties might be given more bargaining rights or might be more involved in company policies, but with a continuation of sectoral structures. This is clearly illustrated in Chapter 5 in the context of France and Spain (Muñoz Ruiz, Ramos Martín, & Vincent, 2023). However, some displacement does happen when more collective agreements are signed by non-representative ("yellow") unions or works councils instead of established and independent trade unions, e.g., in the retail sector in Italy and the Netherlands (Armaroli & Tomassetti, 2022; Jansen & Tros, 2022). A final, albeit indirect example of displacement is found in Ireland, in the 2010s, where, in response to and as compensation for their lost power in national social dialogue, trade unions transformed their strategies towards company-level bargaining with horizontal coordination through "pattern bargaining."

Layering
Institutional layering in collective bargaining regimes is a common state of affairs or trend in all countries where (cross-)sectoral bargaining is dominant. This holds true for the Nordic model, the social partnership model of Germany and the Netherlands, and the Southern European model. Decentralised elements have been added to existing institutions, but the effects of this in terms of the erosion of the importance of centralised institutions varies between the countries.

Sweden has a long tradition of a multi-layered collective-bargaining regime, tightly coordinated by social partners (Rönnmar & Iossa, 2022). Swedish companies negotiate with trade unions over extra wages or other remuneration elements. There is no hard evidence of growing decentralisation in Sweden, so layering is more a state of affairs. More emphatically, Rönnmar & Iossa (2022) observe greater focus on the *limits* of decentralisation in current debates. For example in the public sector, social partners express a need for a more normative and binding collective bargaining regulation at national, sectoral, and/or regional levels. Interestingly, we see variations between workers groups in Sweden: centralised patterns are implemented for blue-collar workers in production and decentralised patterns are seen as more appropriate for professional, white-collar workers (Rönnmar & Iossa, 2022).

Although Germany and the Netherlands are categorised together in the group of coordinated market economies and social partnerships, we see a divergence between the two countries regarding decentralisation. Collective bargaining parties in Germany have initiated many forms of institutional layering, such as additional wage bargaining by works councils, additional topics in company bargaining agendas, opening clauses for works councils, and derogations from sector agreements in company-level bargaining with trade unions (Haipeter & Rosenbohm, 2022). It is estimated that around 20% of all companies in Germany have used some kind of opening clause in consultations with their works councils. This can be seen as part of an established process of *verbetrieblichung* in German labour relations, where works councils now play a bigger role than in the past (Haipeter & Rosenbohm, 2022). In the Netherlands, however, we see far less layering and far fewer trends of organised decentralisation. Trade unions are rarely given (wage or other) bargaining rights at the company level when these companies are covered by sector agreements (Jansen & Tros, 2022). Since the 1980s, in some sectors, works councils have been given extra co-determination in the field of working hours (Tros, 2000) and these rights still exist. Furthermore, there are stable numbers of company agreements in the Netherlands, but these are not part of sector bargaining; in other words, negotiations occur on one level or the other. Unions are quite weak at company level and employers do not want to "double" negotiations. Works councils in the Netherlands have no bargaining tradition in the area of employment terms and conditions, and have no opportunity to consult (and, consequently, have no "burden" in this regard) on opening clauses in collective agreements, because no such clauses exist (see further Chapter 6; Rosenbohm & Tros, 2023).

The decentralisation developments in the Southern European countries reflect a tradition of state intervention in industrial relations. To start, we see the most broadly regulated form of articulation between the levels in France, as a result of earlier reforms in the 1980s and the Macron laws from 2017. Also in 2017, the government added new decentralised topics to the company bargaining list. In this new collective bargaining architecture, coordination between levels is no longer based on the "favourability principle," but rather on the complementarities of bargained topics (Kahmann & Vincent, 2022: 13–16). Since the 1980s, the topics for compulsory negotiation at the company level have increased over time. Following the last reform, this list now includes: (i) remuneration, working times, and the sharing of added value (e.g., profit-sharing); (ii) professional equality between men and women and the quality of working life; and (iii) strategic workforce planning, subcontracting, or temporary employment. All remuneration rules are now solely governed by a company agreement, with the exception of agreed minimum wages, classifications, and overtime premiums. It is now also possible to adapt the methods and frequency of these compulsory negotiations by company agreement. A second addition is that the government extended the possibilities for non-union representatives to negotiate with an employer in non-unionised workplaces. This broad reform in 2017 has undoubtedly led to increased social dialogue and negotiations at the company level in France. The number of agreements in companies grew from around 31,000 in 2017 to around 50,000 in 2019 (these figures include SMES). Nevertheless, sector bargaining continues to be important and companies' derogations from sectoral agreements remains limited to cases of "economic survival" (Kahmann & Vincent, 2022). In addition to new topics in decentralised bargaining, sectoral agreements in France still leave room for additional wage bargaining at the company level (mostly used among bigger companies regarding variable forms of pay like profit-sharing schemes (Kahmann & Vincent, 2022).

In Spain, large firms negotiate additional wages with trade unions. After the financial crisis, the Spanish government unilaterally stimulated collective bargaining at the company level, especially on issues of flexibility in wages and working hours (Ramos Martín & Muñoz Ruiz, 2022). This is in the context of aiming for deregulation and supporting employers' interests in difficult economic times. Such company agreements could deviate from the labour standards set at sector level, and, indeed, this has been the case since 2012, when a number of companies traded off lower wages/hours for fewer layoffs. Trade unions saw this state-imposed decentralisation as an undermining of their position, which also led to strikes and unrest in social dialogue at national and sectoral levels. Spanish unions have a weak position at the decentralised level, especially in smaller firms, and (therefore) want to keep their relatively strong positions at the sector level. Similar to other Southern European countries, the newly created possibilities for derogation have had little impact on the structure of bargaining. Or, to frame it in our theoretical model: this *layering* –by adding decentralised elements – has not led to *breakdown* or *displacement*. Interestingly, in 2021, the Spanish government restored the primacy of sectoral collective bargaining by preventing company bargaining aimed at avoiding sectoral collective agreements, for example with non-representative employee representation at the local level.

Italy is characterised by widespread bargaining at the company level on additional wage components over and above the wage levels set at national and sectoral levels (Armaroli & Tomassetti, 2022). Such secondary bargaining takes place in about 20% of Italian workplaces, mostly in bigger companies. Furthermore, it is not just the state, as in France and Spain, but also the social partners themselves that have initiated processes of organised decentralisation. Since the 2009 economic crisis, opening clauses have increased the scope for company bargaining to derogate from standards set under sectoral agreements. Cross-sectoral collective agreements have opened up a process of organised decentralisation: the scope of decentralised bargaining continues to be defined by national collective labour agreements, yet opening clauses entitle decentralised bargaining to deviate from standards set by these national agreements, provided that the derogatory agreement is approved by sectoral trade unions (Armaroli & Tomassetti, 2022: 10–11). Moreover, the Italian government has sought to stimulate so-called productivity agreements at the company level, enhancing flexibility in payments and working hours and direct employee participation. However, these new articulation regulations in the Italian collective bargaining regime have resulted in little change in practices. In the last five years, decentralised bargaining practices in Italy seem to have grown as a result of an intensification of (bottom-up) autonomous dialogue in large companies with respect to health, supplementary pensions, social benefits, skills, and smart (mobile or tele-) working during COVID-19 (Armaroli & Tomassetti, 2022).

Drift
A kind of "institutional drift" has developed in Germany. Although employer associations continue sector bargaining, it is no longer automatic and self-evident that their members follow the sector agreement co-signed by their association. This is a societal change leading to less employer support in the meaning and functioning of sector bargaining and making agreements with trade unions. Companies' needs for increased price competition and more flexible business strategies are also visible in other countries, but the German case is noteworthy insofar as some employer associations have created "opt-out" opportunities in which companies can remain members but without being covered by sector bargaining. Between 2000 and 2019, collective bargaining coverage fell from 68% to 52% as a consequence. This, in turn, has big consequences in Germany because of the limited use of public extension mechanisms in Germany. Non-membership of German employers easily can lead to no binding to any collective agreement at all. In most sectors in the Netherlands and in Southern European countries however, non-membership among companies has less effects on collective bargaining coverage because of the continued use of the public extension mechanism where sectoral agreements become binding for all employers in the sectors (including non-members). The exception in the Dutch case is the IT sector, where the same kind of opt-out option is visible for the employers' association (but it is important to note that employment relations in software companies in the Netherlands were never centralised in the past).

Another example of institutional drift is found in Poland, where collective bargaining practices are "ritualistic," with no substantive outcomes for the fragmented, workplace-centred practices (Czarzasty, 2022). In many more countries – including the coordinated market economies of Germany and the Netherlands and statist market economies in Southern Europe – we see that unions in the retail sector have been unable to retain control over the decentralisation process and to play an important role at the company level, leading to high fragmentation in scope and meaning of collective bargaining (see Chapter 4; Paolucci et al., 2023).

Conversion
By definition, decentralisation leads to more trade union consultations and involvement in the economic, business, and HR strategies of individual companies. In Italy, France, and Spain, governments aimed at decentralised bargaining as an instrument to enhance companies' productivity and competitiveness. Nevertheless, close involvement in company policies might relegate the basic function of trade unions, i.e. representing and defending workers interests, to second place, as can be seen in large French firms (Kahmann & Vincent, 2022). Here, company-level bargaining has proven to be ambivalent for trade unions. On the one hand, they get better information and are more involved, and the employees have increased opportunities to participate in career planning. On the other hand, however, company bargaining offers the opportunity for a company to use it as a cost-cutting instrument and to reduce the workforce (Kahmann & Vincent, 2022). Another example can be found in Germany where employers ask for derogations from sector agreements and unions play the role of the employer, demanding productivity increases so that the company can return to the collective bargaining norm (Haipeter & Rosenbohm, 2022).

Another form of institutional conversion occurs when trade unions are replaced by employer-friendly "yellow unions," as we see in Italy (*pirate contracts*), or that large trade unions are excluded from collective bargaining and replaced by a small non-representative one (Armaroli & Tomassetti, 2022; Jansen & Tros, 2022).

Table 1.2. provides an overview of the types of institutional change in collective bargaining towards decentralisation, as evidenced in our eight European countries.

Table 1.2. Types of decentralisation and institutional change in eight European countries

	Uncontrolled decentralisation (*breakdown*)	Replacement: From sector to company level (*displacement*)	Adding decentralised elements (*layering*)	Losing grip (*drift*)	Other use of collective bargaining (*conversion*)
Ireland	Collapse social dialogue central levels + bottom-up union mobilisation				
Poland	Low and falling collective bargaining			Fragmentised, workplace-centred practices	
Sweden			Decentralisation options in multi-layered frameworks		
Germany	Decline collective bargaining coverage *Opted-out* employers' associations	Shifts to works councils	*Opening clauses* Derogations	Circumvent collective agreements informally	Productivity bargaining
Netherlands			Decentralisation provisions in sector agreements		Non-representative unions
France	-	less topics for sectors More topics for companies	More topics in company bargaining Opportunities non-union representation		Instrument for HRM
Italy			Derogations *Productivity agreements* Autonomous bargaining in large companies		Productivity bargaining *Pirate contracts*
Spain			Derogation options at company level		

Similarities and differences in decentralisation pathways

From a theoretical point of view, we can distinguish disruptive and structural changes in collective bargaining institutions from incremental changes that can change the meaning, scope, and impact of collective bargaining institutions. The dominant trend in most of the European countries that have been studied can be labelled as gradual "layering": more company bargaining "on top of" and within national and sectoral structures. Nevertheless, the liberal market economies of Ireland and Poland lack social dialogue at the national and sectoral levels. Pathways in initiating and shaping decentralisation and flexibility at the company level are dependent on legislation on collective bargaining, governmental policies, and the strategies and power of trade unions and employers' associations. Across some countries there are some similarities in the way decentralisation is organised through articulation in multi-layered bargaining systems based on the "favourability" and "complementarity" principles. Degrees of layering and the use of decentralised opportunities are dependent on legislation, initiatives by social partners, and the power of trade unions to maintain (cross-) sectoral guarantees and to shape (new) regulations and practices in decentralised bargaining.

Sectoral variations in decentralised bargaining

Decentralisation of collective bargaining has different impacts in industry sectors depending on company characteristics, labour markets, workers' characteristics, and the different power resources and strategies of collective bargaining parties in these sectors. Sectors show their own developments in business structures, technological developments, working populations, and labour relations. In other words, national institutional contexts might be less significant than is often assumed (Bechter et al., 2012; Keune & Pedaci, 2020). It is, therefore, important to look to sectors, as I will do here below for manufacturing and retailing.

Case studies in manufacturing

There are many reasons why we would expect more organised forms of decentralisation in manufacturing sectors. One reason is simply because there *is* more to deregulate and to decentralise, compared to service sectors. Trade unionism and collective bargaining in Europe grew over decades of industrialisation, and the manufacturing sector played a leading role in the development of labour relations in the 20th century in Europe. In the 21st century, the manufacturing sector is also an important arena for change in collective bargaining. Export-exposed manufacturing companies in Europe face increased global competition, increased diversification in the digital technology that they use, and the continuing need to restructure jobs and workplaces. All this increases the need for more "tailor-made" responses in labour strategies and related demands for flexibility in labour costs, working hours, and worker qualifications. It is commonly assumed and, indeed, it has been confirmed that the shift to post-Fordist production, with an emphasis on flexibility, has unleashed pressures for bargaining decentralisation (Traxler & Brandl, 2012). Lower numbers of blue-collar workers and higher numbers of white-collar workers tend towards less unionisation and more individualisation. Furthermore, manufacturing firms in Europe need to adapt to the consequences of the global COVID-19 pandemic and must also accelerate their "green transitions," both of which are having a great impact on employment, job quality, and the organisation of work. In the global competition on prices and quality, employers might ask for (temporary) derogations from national and sector regulation. For sure, continuing innovations in technology and organisation demand continuing social dialogue with employee representatives in HR issues as well. Compared to other sectors, the relatively high membership levels among trade unions and more established bodies of employee representation in manufacturing companies could lead to more willingness among trade unions to decentralise, and could lead to intensified interactions between unions and individual employers.

Collective bargaining patterns in Europe's manufacturing sector reflect the Polish variations in national industrial relations traditions and production regimes. From company bargaining in Ireland and Poland, to advanced multi-level bargaining in Sweden and Southern European countries, to coordinated decentralisation in Germany. In sector-level dominated countries, employers are trying to make sectoral standards less strict and to leave companies more elbow room to deviate or to opt out. Another common trend is the growth of autonomous social dialogue at the company level, in addition to national and sectoral agreements. Whereas, in Fordist times, social partners in manufacturing were innovators in collective labour relations, today, they seem to be the initiators of organised decentralisation (Chapter 3; Haipeter, Armaroli, & Iossa, 2023).

Integrated bargaining
Case studies in manufacturing show collective bargaining and social dialogue on a wide range of topics, with higher quality in the processes and

outcomes of negotiations than in retailing. Interests of individual employers and trade unions might overlap in "integrated bargaining" practices to produce "win-win" results in issues like labour productivity, sustainable worker employability, and job protection.[2] It is important to note that the "best cases" in company bargaining, with higher levels of pay and other employment terms and conditions, are to be found in "high-end" chemical, pharmaceutical, and electronic companies that demonstrate high labour productivity. Nevertheless, local trade unions in many countries sometimes lack innovation capacity, competence, independence, or early involvement in the case of restructuring. Promising practices in company bargaining have been adopted recently in manufacturing, related to issues of the COVID-19 pandemic and its impact on organisations, such as teleworking, mobile work, or other "smart working" practices (even in liberal market economies). Cooperation and negotiation at the local level led to the finalisation of thousands of local collective agreements on handling the effects of the pandemic at the workplace level in Sweden. Also in the Polish manufacturing case, trade unions participated in various COVID-19 task forces and crisis teams; remedial measures were mutually agreed and jobs guaranteed until 2023. Sometimes, the pandemic context strengthened social dialogue at company level or the connections between trade unions and the participation of employee bodies within companies. In the Dutch manufacturing case, the trade unions found a place in tripartite dialogue with the employer and works council to make new regulations in the organisation and to compensate for teleworking during the crisis, but also for the near future, with the aim of achieving a better work-life balance for the employees.

Employee representation
Co-determination and consultation through non- or partly unionised employee participation have grown in at least the manufacturing sector in the coordinated market economies of Germany and the Netherlands. In Germany, works councils are actively involved in additional bargaining on wages, other topics, and opening clauses in collective agreements. In the Dutch manufacturing case, too, we see significant and strong performances with respect to works councils' consultation practices in HR and organisational issues (including restructuring, acquisitions, and transfers), but their involvement does not yet extend to those areas where trade unions are active in collective bargaining on employment terms and conditions (see

---

2   *Integrated* bargaining with positive sum results can be disentangled from *distributive* bargaining with zero-sum results (such as on wages).

Chapter 6; Rosenbohm & Tros, 2023). The manufacturing case in Sweden presents a (traditionally) stronger mutually reinforcing and synergetic relationship between collective bargaining, on the one hand, and information, consultation, and co-determination, on the other hand (Rönnmar & Iossa, 2022). This can be explained by the Swedish single-channel system of trade union representation where no or fewer tensions exist between the systems of collective bargaining, on the one hand, and employee representation, information, consultation, and co-determination, on the other hand. The findings with respect to employee representation are more mixed in the Southern European countries.

Case studies in retail

Although, formally, collective bargaining parties in the retail sector have the same national institutional power resources as collective actors in manufacturing, the organisational power of trade unions is far lower. The weak collective and individual positions of workers relates to the many low-paid jobs, atypical employment contracts, and short-term commitments. In cases of earlier established sectoral structures, we might assume less need among trade unions to organise decentralisation in order to prevent fragmentation in a context of low membership. However, any attempt by employers to break down sector institutions would meet trade unions with little power to resist. In the case of company-level bargaining, we might assume an employer-driven bargaining agenda.

Fragmentation

This book shows fragmented and unstable collective bargaining structures in the retail sectors. In many countries, retailers miss the pressure of trade unions as a reason to coordinate, leading to a fragmented structure of employers' associations and non-organised retailers (with the exception of Sweden). The relatively low "threat" of trade unions combined with the "low productivity road" are reasons for retailers not to organise. More than manufacturing companies, retailers go their own way, as we see with *pirate contracts* in Italy or exclusion of the largest trade union FNV in collective bargaining in the Dutch retail sector. In the German retail sector, the major trend is "wild" and uncontrolled decentralisation to a greater extent than in the German manufacturing sector (Haipeter & Rosenbohm, 2022).

Nevertheless, national institutions can limit fragmentation in collective bargaining in the retail sector. Sector agreements, also in retail, can be supported by public law that extends to retailers who are not members of employer associations. In Sweden, the retail sector shows quite centralised wage-setting mechanisms compared to other sectors in the country (Rönnmar & Iossa, 2022). There might be a structural reason for centralisation in retail, namely, the high number of SMEs. In general, many small companies in the sector might explain business preferences for centralisation (Bulfone & Afonso, 2020). In the Netherlands, sectoral collective agreements in retail are used by SME companies as an "HR manual," because retail companies are mostly too small to produce their own HR policies (Jansen & Tros, 2022). Retailers and trade unions might have a common interest in setting a level playing field in the sector regarding wages and other labour costs (albeit at a low level) in order to prevent the real risk of a "race to the bottom" with respect to employment terms and conditions.

Employee representation
Lower levels of union representation in the retail sector do not mean that alternative bodies of non-unionised employee representation fill the gap. On the contrary, works councils in, e.g., Germany, the Netherlands, and France, are much less established in retail than in manufacturing, and are generally weaker than their manufacturing counterparts as well. In Italy, too, we see a combination of factors that lead to lower representation of workers in retail companies by (non-unionised) employee representation: lower union density; smaller company sizes; geographically dislocated shops belonging to large retail companies; and greater presence of "atypical" workers groups, such as migrants, young workers, and flexible contracts (Armaroli & Tomassetti, 2022).

Nevertheless, revitalising experiences have emerged in retail companies in Ireland and Germany. A fashion discounter in Germany successfully carried out the consecutive steps to establish a works council, the unionisation of its staff, recognition of the trade unions in collective bargaining, and, finally, strategic cooperation between unions and the works council (Haipeter & Rosenbohm, 2022: 68–70). Although not representative, this case shows the potential to organise workers in the context of bad working conditions – and bringing individual companies (back) into collective bargaining regimes – which can then be replicated in other companies.

Union power resources
The unions' power resources are low in the retail sector due to the earlier mentioned fragility in collective bargaining structures, low degrees of consultation and co-determination activities in the workplace, and because of low trade union membership (with the exception of Sweden).

Low membership is related to workers' characteristics. In all European countries, many employees in retail are young, female, low skilled, and have small part-time and other flexible labour contracts (see Chapter 4; Paolucci et al., 2023). The trade unions' lack of a fundamental social base has effects, firstly, on low acceptance or sometimes even hostility among employers towards unions. This factor has strong implications in Ireland and, in particular, Poland, where the majority of retail employers do not recognise unions for collective bargaining within its highly voluntarist system. The two Polish retail cases show that even if trade unions are recognised, in practice, there are barriers to them developing activities, which limits their affective influence in improving employment terms and conditions (Czarzasty, 2022). All retail cases across the countries suggest an imbalance in bargaining processes and quite limited outcomes in negotiations. The lack of power of the established trade unions in the retail sector in the Netherlands, for example, led to agreements signed only with smaller or "yellow" unions (Jansen & Tros, 2022). The Dutch retail case points to deteriorating labour standards as evidenced by, for example, trade unions no longer being welcome at the bargaining table in negotiations with the distribution centres of a large supermarket. A positive exception is Sweden, where institutional and organisational power resources compensate for low structural power among retail workers (Chapter 7; Rönnmar et al., 2023).

Case-study conclusions

Comparing the case studies in the two sectors leads to the conclusion that there is more organised decentralisation in manufacturing and more wild decentralisation in retail, linked to the different structural characteristic of companies and workers, and different institutional and organisational power resources of trade unions in the sector. Sectoral analyses in this book confirm the statement that "sectoral differentiations in industrial relations do not replace national differentiations in industrial relations" (Bechter, Brandl, & Meardi, 2012), because national institutions matter insofar as they can prevent collective bargaining in the retail sector from falling "too deep" and in order to maintain sector institutions. But we see cross-country variation in Europe. In Sweden, national characteristics in terms of high trade union memberships and multi-layered collective bargaining produce less sector differentiation than other countries. In Germany, however, the difference in unionisation between the two sectors has led to the erosion of sector bargaining in retail. In the Netherlands and Italy, it leads to agreements with fewer representative unions and lower labour standards in collective agreements in retail. In both countries there is also an employer strategy to bypass the legal extension of sector agreements that are made with larger and stronger trade unions. In the context of generally bad working conditions in the retail sector, trade unions across Europe are seeking to organise and activate workers in large retail companies to build up company level bargaining (Ireland, Germany) or to fight for the continuation of their position at company level (Netherlands, Poland). In manufacturing, trade unions have more established positions from which to bargain on "higher end" topics like productivity, restructuring, and competitiveness.

Nevertheless, our research makes clear that there are more "divisions" than sectors. Especially in Italy, sector differentiation seems to play a less dominant role than company size and position in the value chain. The Italian report concludes that the two-tier model of organised decentralisation no longer fits the large companies at the top-end of the value chain or small companies at the lower positions of the value chain. The first group prefers fully decentralised bargaining at the company level, and the preferences of the second group leads to a centralised – though highly "perforated" – bargaining model, for example using loopholes within traditional collective bargaining and signing *pirate contracts* with non-representative unions (Armaroli & Tomassetti, 2022: 60–62).

Beneficial factors and barriers in balanced decentralised bargaining

Company-level bargaining is not something that is by definition good or to be preferred above multi-employer bargaining. It has to be balanced and fair in its intention, its dialogue and negotiation processes, and its outcomes. Indicators for *balanced* company bargaining are:
–   embeddedness in a legal framework and broader collective bargaining regime with employers' commitments
–   access of established, representative, and independent trade unions to the bargaining table at company level
–   relatively equal power positions between individual employer and worker representation in professional negotiation processes
–   scope of bargaining agendas that is broader than wages and working hours (and includes job protection, education, co-determination, consultation in HR and business strategies), or to frame it using game theory: not only distributive bargaining (trade-offs, zero-sum game) but

also integrated bargaining with win-win outcomes (Walton & McKersie, 1965)
- bargaining outcomes that are not only beneficial for the employer and the company, but also beneficial to employees

Labour relations and collective bargaining are based on power relations between employers and employees and between collective bargaining parties. Trade unions are central in organising and representing the less powerful stakeholders: the workers. In this study, we also focus on the power vested in the position and strategies of trade unions in collective bargaining, specifically in their responses to state- and employer-initiated decentralisation, but also to their own initiatives to represent employees at the company or workplace level.[3] Literature distinguishes four different dimensions of trade union power resources (see e.g., Müller & Platzer, 2018; Müller et al., 2019).[4] The first dimension is *institutional power dimensions* relating to the trade unions' legal recognition in collective bargaining at several levels and the rights and obligations of the bargaining parties, again at several levels. Institutional factors also relate to legal and regulative support for employers in multi-employer bargaining and its (legal) extension to unorganised employers. Chapter 7 elaborates on institutional and legal factors at the national and supra-national levels (Rönnmar et al., 2023). The second dimension concerns *organisational power resources*, sometimes also called "associational power." This is the capacity of trade unions to organise and participate in social dialogue and collective bargaining, and, more specifically, also in controlling decentralisation and influencing company-level bargaining. Chapter 7 distinguishes the numerical strength of membership together with other factors like coordination, social partnerships, and activism (Rönnmar et al., 2023). Here, it is important to note that workers' organisational power depends not only on union factors, but also on the support provided by employers and the state for allowing and facilitating union organising and union activities to increase their membership (Müller et al., 2019: 634–635). The third dimension concerns *societal power resources* or "communicative power resources," such as the ability of unions to take part in public discourses, to shape public opinion, and to forge alliances with other civil society actors, such as NGOs, political parties, and social

---

3   Employers' associations also have the distinguished power resources dimensions but they are beyond the focus of this study.
4   While trade unions are central to this study, as previously stated, these dimensions of power resources might, theoretically, be broadened to employers and their associations.

movements (Müller & Platzer, 2018: 305). Countries where trade unions are involved in tripartite social dialogue with the government and business associations or are in networks with employers' organisations do give trade unions social support and recognition, also at the level of individual companies. Dialogue with unions can be part of a company's socially responsible strategy, in the same way as dialogue with NGOs in environmental issues can bolster a company's social image. Academic literature also presents a fourth dimension, namely, *structural power resources* (Schmalz, Ludwig, & Webster, 2018). Structural power refers to the position of wage earners in the economic system, in the production process, and in the labour market. It is a primary power resource as it is available to workers and employees even without collective-interest representation. In Chapter 7, Rönnmar et al. (2023) find (potentially) interchangeable relationships between these forms of power resources.

In this chapter, in addition to examining the first and second dimensions of power resources, I will use evidence from the case studies in our research to produce a more in-depth picture of the influences on decentralisation and the quality of company-level bargaining.

Institutional factors

Many authors have concluded that it is necessary to maintain multi-employer agreements in order to shore up bargaining coverage and to set safety nets and norms for company-level bargaining (see also Visser, 2016; Ibsen & Keune, 2018). The positive effects of national and sectoral institutions on coordinating decentralisation can be clearly seen in France, Italy, the Netherlands, Spain, and Sweden. Furthermore, individual employers need to recognise unions as a representative bargaining party for workers. In more elaborate multi-layered models – such as those found in Sweden, Italy, and France – trade unions have greater access to (additional) collective bargaining at the company level. Clear and supportive regulations about the conditions for company-level bargaining and its relationship to national and sectoral collective bargaining is needed. From a legal perspective, France regulates the most details in this regard, including topics to be regulated at the company level and the conditions set for unions and non-unionised worker representation when representing employees. Italy and Spain also have elaborated institutional frameworks by law and national and sectoral agreements for regulating the articulation between the levels. In Sweden, only social partners regulate centralisation and decentralisation in employment relations.

Within multi-layered frameworks, vertical coordination practices among employers (associations) and among trade union representation are relevant on several levels. Most country reports point to the need for national or sectorial union representatives to assess (proposals for) local agreements, combined with fallback clauses of minimum standards set at national and/or sectoral level. This is to prevent the inclusion of non-beneficial ingredients in local agreements for trade union members and other employees that may result from potential inequalities in bargaining power at the local level. The exceptions are Ireland and Poland, where sectoral and national bodies have almost disappeared and decentralised bargaining is not conditioned by national or sectoral regulation. Filling the gap left by a lack of vertical coordination, trade unions in Ireland have initiated new forms of informal horizontal coordination.

A major advantage of single-channel systems is that the labour counterpart to management at company level has a broader mandate that is anchored in collective bargaining, and in multi-level structures there are also better means of communication and articulation with higher-level actors (Nergaard et al., 2009). The Swedish cases illustrate that clear national and sector regulations on employee representation and information, consultation, and co-determination at the local level is enhancing successful negotiation and the implementation of local collective bargaining. Dual-channel systems are extra challenged by the need for clear demarcations in jurisdictions for trade unions and for works councillors or other representatives in employee participation.

Institutional barriers
Poland and Ireland show the most institutional barriers in decentralised bargaining. Irish and Polish unions lack the support of social dialogue and collective bargaining at the national and sectoral levels. Trade unions here are also confronted with low bargaining rights, making them extra vulnerable to an employer's unwillingness to accept them as a worker representative party. Especially the Polish report – and to a lesser extent – the Irish report – show highly fragmented and highly workplace-centred employment relations despite the existence of cross-sectoral confederations of trade unions. As earlier stated, the fragmentation in Poland can be explained by the long-existing vacuum between the state and workplaces and a lack of employers' unions' activities at the sectoral level. Furthermore, in Poland, collective agreements are concluded for unlimited duration, which discourages employers from entering into collective bargaining if there are no possibilities to adjust or renegotiate

agreements. The Irish cases show more success in company-level bargaining, but also in a context of eroded institutions at the national and sector levels. Polish trade unions seem to enjoy less success in terms of establishing "compensating" practices at the company level compared to Irish unions.

Established trade unions can also meet closed doors in less voluntarist models of employment relations, for example when "yellow unions" take such a position in Italy or in the Netherlands. Sector bargaining can also be a strategic instrument for companies seeking to avoid talking to or negotiating with trade unions: essentially, they have "outsourced" this to an external party (read: employers' association) and use this to legitimise their refusal to interact with trade unions at the company level.

In Germany, the lack of legal extension of sector agreements to unorganised employers is a barrier for German trade unions to control decentralisation processes and to establish alternative positions at the company level. The unorganised company is free to choose whether it bargains with unions or not and trade unions can partly compensate for the holes that have been made in collective bargaining coverage.

Organisational factors

It is clear that a company's trade union membership rate is crucial in decentralised bargaining. This relates to *access* to the bargaining table as a representative party, relatively equal power relations between employer and trade unions in *negotiation processes*, and bargaining *outcomes* that are beneficial for employees. Let us not forget that memberships are the biggest source of financial resources for trade unions. Decentralisation is expensive because of the high number of negotiation tables at the decentralised level and the related effort required to collect local information, to build up a broad range of skilled local negotiators, and to maintain internal coordination.

Where trade unions at company level are relatively weak in terms of membership (such as in Spain and the Netherlands), they have little to gain from diffusing their activities at the company level. In other words, they need to focus their limited resources at higher collective levels. But where trade unions have high membership in companies – within or without the framework of sector agreements – they can profit from a robust social base in their negotiations with management (see also Toubøl & Strøby Jensen, 2014). The case studies in Sweden confirm the importance and benefit of high trade union membership and long traditions in bargaining and social dialogue structures, also when new challenges emerge, such as the corona pandemic or teleworking.

Another beneficial factor is the competence of trade unions in social dialogue and collective bargaining at the company level. This is partly related to the earlier-mentioned factors, but these factors are not enough; bargaining rights and trade union membership do not guarantee a high degree of competence. The Italian cases show that high unionised levels among employees do not automatically lead to strong capabilities in defining positions and organising effectiveness in decentralised bargaining. The trade unions' competence in decentralised bargaining is linked to company specific knowledge, bargaining and dialogue skills and experience, as well as the capacity to translate individual workers' needs into a coherent collective approach. The case study in the manufacturing sector in Poland makes clear that, despite the country's minimally supportive institutional structure, the strong position of trade unionists in companies is the result of proactive and decisive trade union practices.

Interestingly, some case studies consist of innovative actions by trade unions to (re-) engage with workers and workplaces through decentralised bargaining. The Irish cases reveal proactive unions re-engaging their union base through company bargaining with management (Paolucci et al., 2022). At the same time, they mobilise their members, develop shop stewards' negotiating skills, and try to follow a strategy of pattern bargaining towards other individual companies in the sector. The best cases have inspired other Irish unions to see decentralised bargaining as an opportunity to reconnect with members and to demonstrate the unions' effectiveness in gaining pay rises (Paolucci et al., 2022; Rönnmar et al., 2023) Also in Germany, union strategies of (re-)connecting with the rank and file and workplaces, for example, by starting new cooperations with works councils to recruit new members, strengthens existing union involvement and creates new opportunities in company bargaining (Hai-peter & Rosenbohm, 2022). The success of German unions in establishing and continuing decentralised bargaining is largely dependent on whether works councils are able and willing to collaborate with unions, for example in concession bargaining when companies in manufacturing are in crisis. Local derogations from sector agreements in the German metalworking industry and concessions from trade unions in wages and working hours go hand in hand with improvements in employment protection, investment promises, and the extension of co-determination responsibilities. The case of the German fashion retail company can be read as a success story in local organising: after the union helped the employees to install a works council, the council helped the union gain recognition from the employer as a negotiating party. From another point of view, the Dutch case of an e-commerce firm is also innovative, in the sense that the trade union started an experiment with new direct forms of individual worker participation in collective bargaining (referendum, voting) in order to engage with non-unionised individual employees and to increase its representation. Chapter 7 of this book points to the interesting conclusion that countries that have the tradition of a "participative relationship" between union negotiators and members, i.e. that see members as potentially active participants in collective bargaining alongside professional union staff, have been less prominent in redefining trade union strategies in relation to decentralised bargaining (Rönnmar et al., 2023). It seems that re-engaging with workers and bottom-up approaches in decentralised bargaining are more common in countries that experience a more serious decline in bargaining coverage.

Less unidimensional are the conclusions about the benefits of cooperation between trade unions at sectoral level and those at company level. In the well-developed multi-layered Swedish regime, there are rather tight vertical communications in trade union organisations that appear to work well. Also in other countries, local trade unionists are supported by sectoral representatives. But the French and Dutch manufacturing cases show that union delegates have quite autonomous positions and functions at company level. Support does not always appear needed and too much sectoral interference can hinder autonomous bargaining at the company level.

Employers' support
The organisational power of trade unions is not only dependent on a union's characteristics, such as memberships and competence, but also on an employers' commitment to collective bargaining structures and a company's support for trade unions' positions and actions in decentralised bargaining. Generally, the well-established and professional relations between individual employers and trade unions in negotiating wages tend to be broadened by trade unions' involvement in other issues, such as working hours, job security, education, etc. In these practices, the scope of "distributive bargaining" with zero-sum results is growing towards "integrated bargaining" in win-win situations with positive sum results (Walton & McKersie, 1965). This is made clear in all cases in Sweden and some manufacturing cases in Italy, Germany, the Netherlands, France, and Ireland. Related to this is that many case studies concern large companies characterised by high labour productivity where quality matters with

respect to both competitiveness and price. The quality of such relationships and bargaining processes is mostly characterised as being mutually trustful, collaborative, professional, and continuing/sustainable. Here, management uses trade unions strategically to gain social support for their policies regarding competitiveness, technology, digitalisation, HR management, and sometimes environmental issues as well. In turn, trade unions gain established positions, broader involvement, and, when smart, they can also reconnect with workers, workplaces, and employee representative bodies. In short, when social dialogue and collective bargaining agendas at the company level go beyond the classical topics of wages and working hours, integrated bargaining with win-win results can strengthen decentralised bargaining. Nevertheless, there is a limit when an employer sees collective bargaining simply as an efficient and effective HRM tool for creating social support and worker motivation (as some of the case studies in Ireland, Italy, and France suggest). There is also a limit when trade unions become (too) dependent on an employer's financial resources, which can hinder a trade union's autonomous agenda-setting and independent power in the long-term.

Case studies in France, Italy, and the Netherlands reveal the development of (re)centralisation within large manufacturing companies, where collective bargaining at the corporation level enhances harmonisation between departments and workplaces with respect to labour contracts and HRM policies and prevents competition on wages between different establishments or departments. (Re)centralisation is also in a large employers' interest in terms of efficiency in bargaining processes and contract formation. In these cases, workers' participation continues to be at the decentralised workplace level, strengthening the observation that collective bargaining by unions and (non-/partly) unionised employee participation are parallel practices within large companies.

Organisational barriers
Low union membership is definitely a barrier in decentralised bargaining. This is illustrated, for example, in the weaker and less balanced bargaining that we see in the retail sector, where "pirate" bargaining with "yellow" unions is more common due to the lack of strong, organised, and established trade unions in the sector. Lower membership also means there are limited financial resources for building up trade union competences in company-level bargaining.

The unions' lack of engagement and knowledge about workplaces, jobs, and employees within companies is another barrier to decentralisation and decentralised bargaining. Dual-channel systems of worker representation put trade unions at a structural disadvantage in terms of connecting to workplaces, but they might give trade unions a power resource if both unions and works councils are open to partnership constructions. German manufacturing cases demonstrate the opportunities that arise when trade unions' cooperate with works councils. At the same time, one must be cautious about assuming this is the case for all companies and sectors in Germany. The share of companies and employees without representation by a works council is quite high (Haipeter & Rosenbohm, 2022: 16–17). On the on hand, this limits the power of trade unions in structural collaborations with works councils. On the other hand, it also means that when a company is no longer covered by collective bargaining, this decentralisation is "deep" and lacks the "buffer" that a works council provides. In general, across the studied countries, the majority of the cases show low levels of relationships between collective bargaining bodies and employee representation bodies at workplace level.

In all European countries, there is evidence of some hostile, non-committal, or non-supportive employers in decentralised bargaining. We see the most non-committed employers in the case studies from Poland (except for the Polish company that is part of a multinational with a German mother). Sometimes, hostility manifests in the form of not allowing a trade union to be established or refusing to communicate with trade union representatives. Sometimes, it occurs with a minimum level of social dialogue or consultation but without collective bargaining. The Polish cases can be understood in the context of an national model of pluriform industrial relations with traditionally low union activities in collective bargaining. However, there are non-institutional factors in play. In Ireland, also a pluriform model, the cases describe more willing employers that find a link with their company strategies. In the Netherlands, with its overall institutional stability, we see a retail case of an employer that no longer has faith in collective bargaining with the trade unions. Its decision to exclude unions from the bargaining table means it risks new conflicts with established trade unions while breaking a long tradition of decentralised bargaining.

We must not forget that, in addition to trade unions, employers can also "lose" or "risk" something when they introduce decentralised bargaining. Companies that start making collective agreements worry about losing competitiveness in comparison to other companies that are not bound by collective bargaining at all or that are covered by (cheaper) sector agreements.

Towards new relations between unions and other employee representatives?

Single- and dual-channels in workers representation

Patterns of decentralisation are influenced by single or dual channels of worker representation within companies. In single-channel systems, where workplace representatives are elected and/or delegated by trade unions, unions can keep substantial control over decentralisation processes (Ibsen & Keune, 2018). In dual-channel systems, where employees are represented by works councils, the relationships between sector and local negotiators are often weaker and more fragile, reducing the control of unions over decentralisation (Nergaard et al., 2009). This control depends on the extent to which works council members in these dual-channel systems are members of trade unions, and the extent to which works councils and trade unions cooperate at the workplace and company levels. It can therefore be assumed that trade unions in dual-channel systems are more hesitant and cautious about decentralisation, because of the risk of their control and powers being diffused. On the other hand, when works councils are more unionised or have partnership relations with unions, trade unions might be more willing to confer the rights to derogate from sector agreements on works councils. At least in theory, trade unions in dual-channel systems might use works councils as a power resource in collective bargaining at the company level. Trade unions can use the institution of works councils as part of their strategy for better engagement with workers and their needs within companies, to recruit more members, and, indeed, to unionise the councils (Haipeter, 2020). Decentralised bargaining on derogations can give unions and works councils the opportunity for revitalisation and for cooperation between the two bodies of worker participation (Haipeter, 2021).

The Swedish case studies confirm the theory that single-channel systems are characterised by stronger, collaborative relationships between sector and local negotiators in collective bargaining. They lead to higher trust and willingness among trade unions at the national, sectoral, and multi-employer levels to decentralise towards company level (Rönnmar & Iossa, 2022). Workers representatives at several levels are from the same "party" and there is no risk of involvement from competitive, non-unionised worker representatives.

Germany and the Netherlands are examples of countries with an elaborated, legally established dual-channel system of worker representation. In both countries, collective bargaining between employer(s) and trade unions is legally demarcated from the consultation and co-determination rights of works councils within a company (see further Chapter 6; Rosenbohm & Tros, 2023). These are fundamentally separate legal fields. These fields only partly overlap when collective bargaining parties give jurisdiction to works councils, or if works councils are supported by trade unions.

Italy and France have a more mixed-channel model of worker representation, something in between a pure single-channel and a pure dual-channel system. In Italy, there are two channels for workplace representation. The unionised *Rappresentanze Sindacali Aziendali* (RSA), only for organisations under sectoral and/or company collective agreements, and *Rappresentanze Sindacali Unitarie* (RSU) with both unionised and non-unionised elected representatives (Armaroli & Tomasetti, 2022: 11–12). In practice, both channels are not that different and both have links with sectoral trade unions. Interestingly, the Italian findings suggest processes of decoupling between collective bargaining on the one hand, and shop floor representation on the other. First, among large and geographically dislocated companies that prefer uniform labour conditions across their many establishments, the focal point of decentralised bargaining is shifting from individual workplaces to the group or corporate level. Second, the Italian report points to a weakening role of workplace representation and difficulties for unions in bridging shopfloor workers' organising and collective bargaining when trade unions are passive in organising new elections for the RSU and/or are focusing on collective bargaining procedures at the more centralised company level (Armaroli & Tomasetti, 2022: 62).

The French case is an interesting one. On the one hand, unions can set up a union section and appoint one or more union delegates as soon as they obtain at least 10% of the votes in workplace elections (Kahmann & Vincent, 2022). On the other hand, to offset the fact that non-unionised companies, mainly SMEs, cannot bargain, because of a lack of union delegates, successive legislation has extended the possibilities for non-union representatives to negotiate in non-unionised workplaces. Contrary to Germany and the Netherlands, French legislation is guiding the decisions about unionised and non-unionised bargaining parties and signing bodies – in Germany and the Netherlands these factors are generally in the hands of companies and factual power relations between employers, trade unions, and works councils. Furthermore, in France the scope of decentralised bargaining is guided by legislation relating to "obligatory issues," be it in negotiation with union delegates or with non-union representatives. Theoretically, this might work as an incentive in the collective bargaining system for trade unions to present themselves as the best representative body for negotiating. However, it is not clear that this has led to higher membership rates in France.

Changing relationships between unions and works councils?

Relationships between the institution of works councils and the institution of trade unions are effected by the trend of decentralisation in collective bargaining. The legal demarcation of "functions" in co-determination versus collective bargaining and rights and powers between channels and stakeholders can be called into question. Indeed, it can be coordinated by social partners themselves. In Germany, trade unions have the formal lead in negotiating sectoral "opening clauses" at the company level and case studies in the German manufacturing sector show the importance of cooperation between trade unions and works councils in these areas. Unions can offer flexibility to individual employers in Germany through joint activities and collaborations with works councils, while at the same time revitalising their rank and file (Haipeter, 2021). In the Netherlands, trade unions maintain more distance from works councils and are very strict in their strategy of regulating minimum levels set at the sector level without any option of derogation (Jansen & Tros, 2022). However, this strategy means that Dutch trade unions miss the opportunity to (re-) connect with workplaces and their rank and file (see further Chapter 6; Rosenbohm & Tros, 2023).

Germany and the Netherlands show similarities in the wider topic of working hours and restructuring. This can be understood by the assumption that trade unions bargain for "hard money" in distributive bargaining processes (say, wages and other payments), while works councils bargain in issues where the interests of the employer and workers are overlapping. The aim of co-determination legislation in both countries is not only to represent worker interests, but also to enhance the working of the company's organisation (this is the so-called dual aim of the Act on Works Councils in both countries).

Conclusions and future challenges

Decentralisation beyond national institutions

The decentralisation of collective bargaining is not new. Already since the 1980s, collective bargaining institutions have been decentralised in European countries. The main initiators are employers that aim for greater flexibility and deregulation in collective terms and conditions of employment. "Tailor-made" social dialogue at the company level gives employers more opportunities to adapt wages and other labour regulations to their company's competitive and strategic needs and their changing (specific) environments. After the financial crisis, in the 2010s, governments in Southern European countries installed new legislation to (further) stimulate company-level bargaining with trade unions, and in other countries employers adopted decentralisation with trade unions and sometimes works councils. Types and patterns of decentralisation in labour relations can be partly explained by the characteristics of national institutions: the strategies of social partners, trade unions' power resources, and company policies all play an important role. National labour law has less uniform power than is often assumed (see further Chapter 2; Jansen, 2023) and theoretical classifications in industrial relations regimes are partly explained by emerging pathways and trade union responses in the field of decentralisation. In the pluralist model of industrial relations, employers' preferences led to a further collapse in social dialogue and collective bargaining in the 2010s. But in parts of the Irish economy, weak institutional power resources have been compensated by the organisational power resources of trade unions, which found innovative ways to (re-) start negotiations with individual employers (see also Chapter 7; Rönnmar et al., 2023). Trade unions in Poland were not able to do that. Although categorised in the same model of coordinated market economies and social partnerships, Germany and the Netherlands show divergent patterns in decentralisation. Sectoral bargaining structures in Germany have partly eroded, while in the Netherlands collective bargaining coverage continues to be high. German unions in manufacturing responded by organising strategic partnerships with works councils, while Dutch unions did not. In the southern part of Europe, French legislation goes into far more detail regarding company-level bargaining than the Spanish version (see Chapter 5; Muñoz Ruiz, Ramos Martín, & Vincent, 2023). The Nordic model profited in times of decentralisation from the strong coordination (Sweden) in its already established flexible multi-level system. Furthermore, in many countries, there are multiple decentralisation pathways occurring simultaneously. The decentralisation pathway of "institutional layering" in collective bargaining – by organising opportunities to derogate from national and sectoral regulations or to add topics in company bargaining – is now visible in all countries that are dominated by multi-employer bargaining – in the Nordic model, in the Rhineland model, and in the Southern European model. For a sector like manufacturing, innovations in collective bargaining have led to coordinated decentralisation with a strengthening of unionised or non-unionised employee representation in larger firms. Decentralisation trends in the European retail sector have also led to less clear demarcation of national industrial relations regimes. Collective bargaining in retail is increasingly fragmented, liberalised, deregulated, and uncoordinated in almost all countries. This leads to declining collective bargaining coverage, and to lower quality of the remaining social dialogue and collective agreements (see further Chapter 4; Paolucci et al., 2023). Within national regimes, uncoordinated decentralisation in retailing and in other low-paid private sectors have led to more dualisation. Also here, the Swedish collective bargaining model showed more robustness across sectors.

Case studies in company bargaining provide several lessons. To reach balance in negotiations at the company level, it appears to be important to have supportive institutions at national and sectoral levels that facilitate bargaining rights for trade unions and safety nets in terms of wages and other labour standards. Other beneficial factors include higher union membership rates in companies, union competence in local negotiations, and innovative actions to re-engage with workplaces and workers within companies. Of course, employers' commitments to regulating decentralisation and company bargaining practices are essential. Institutional and organisational power resources for collective bargaining are more present in sectors like manufacturing than in sectors like retail. But enabling factors are not simply separated by sectors. Highly productive firms and larger companies are more engaged in decentralised bargaining practices and with more powerful trade unions in more balanced negotiations. Low price competitors and small- and medium-sized enterprises experience fewer beneficial conditions in decentralised bargaining.

Challenges for trade unions and other stakeholders

Neoliberal policies of governments and businesses in the 2010s often put trade unions in a defensive position regarding the push towards further deregulation and flexibility in labour. Following the gradual erosion of collective bargaining structures, it is difficult to establish new bargaining practices. Furthermore, union membership levels are in serious decline in almost all European countries (Vandaele, 2019). It is the challenge of the unions to organise and represent new generations of workers and to show that they are competent partners in terms of discussing innovative sectoral and company strategies, as well as defending decent employment terms and conditions and working conditions. Many trade unions worry about membership, social involvement, and "attitudes" among younger generations of workers in trade unions and works councils' activities. Another related challenge is the shift in employment over sectors. Manufacturing is in decline and as are the numbers of blue-collar workers. Service-oriented sectors are still growing, while they have less established structures in collective bargaining at sector and company level and are usually weaker bodies of employee representation within companies. It is evident that in sectors such as retail, with more vulnerable and low paid workers, it is even more difficult for trade unions to combat fragmentation in collective bargaining and a race to the bottom in employment terms and conditions. The structural power resources of workers cannot always be compensated by institutional and organisational the power resources of trade unions (see further Chapter 7; Rönnmar et al., 2023). Maintaining the position of trade unions in sector bargaining and in large firms seems to be challenging enough within the limited capacities evident in many countries. Trade unions face a dilemma in terms of investing more effort in collective bargaining for workers that are harder to reach. It is promising that some positive experiences have emerged in innovative trade union actions to re-engage with workplaces and workers, also in retail companies.

Today, many of the collective bargaining systems in Europe are truly multi-level systems that can no longer be so clearly framed as "vertical hierarchical" regimes, but rather as coordinators of fragmented autonomous levels of social dialogue and regulations. Experiences in some countries illustrate that updating bargaining agendas can help to preserve trade union involvement in social dialogue and collective bargaining at the company level. Several cases report new topics, such as COVID-19, teleworking, organisational developments with respect to more sustainable and "green" production, the digital transformation of work, and job-to-job transitions in cases of unemployment threats. Less mentioned is the topic of flexible work and atypical labour contracting, despite these issues being highly relevant for attracting new generations of workers to trade union activities, at least in countries with high numbers of flexible workers, such as the Netherlands.

Do trade unions have to bridge the gap between collective bargaining and employee representation at lower levels? It is clear that trade unions must always have an eye on the specific working conditions and needs of workers in r relation to their jobs and the organisation in which they work in order to provide better representation and to motivate workers to become trade union members. More or less unionised works councils and other employee representation bodies at the workplace level might help unions to provide information agenda-setting in collective bargaining. It is also clear that unions should have a task in strengthening voice options for workers in organisations and bottom-up consultation in collective bargaining processes (see e.g., Mundlak, 2020). It is less clear if that also includes partnerships with works councils or other workplace representatives in bargaining. Is it realistic in terms of position and skills to ask non-unionised employee representatives to bargain with their own employer about wages? Collective bargaining and workplace consultation and co-determination are different fields and have different legal backgrounds and legal aims. Interesting in this regard are the best practices in cooperation between trade unions and works councils in the German manufacturing sector. But these practices are not easily transplanted to other German sectors or other countries because of the lack of union positions at the decentralised levels or weak or non-existent co-determination bodies.

Employers' commitments to organising decentralisation and decentralised bargaining practices are essential. Fragmentation in the representation of employers might lead to erosion of sectoral collective bargaining and cooperation with less representative unions. Employers' disengagement with collective bargaining suggests that some employers' organisations are becoming more like business associations, which might lead to less social partnerships with trade unions and further individualisation in employment relations.

Time to re-centralise?
In researching and discussing decentralisation, it is important to focus on its opposite. How far can you go with decentralisation? Recent re-centralisation of collective bargaining in European countries is an evident sign of the limits of decentralisation. At the end of 2021, social partners in France's metal industry signed a national sectoral agreement to replace the existing 78 territorial agreements in the country from 2024 (Kahmann & Vincent, 2022: 28). In Spain, earlier reforms aimed at decentralisation were reversed by the national government in 2021 in order to better guarantee the primacy of sector agreements with representative, established trade unions that were never in favour of derogation options (see Chapter 5; Muñoz Ruiz, Ramos Martín, & Vincent, 2023). In Sweden, social partners started discussions about the limits of decentralisation (Rönnmar & Iossa, 2022). It is clear that the recent EU call to stimulate collective bargaining coverage in member states to provide for better minimum wages – and to make national action plans for this – will be better met by national and sectoral bargaining than by only company level bargaining. A European target of 80% collective bargaining in member states is a big challenge for many countries and might only be reachable with new sector agreements and legal mechanisms of extension towards non-organised businesses. To achieve this aim, it not only makes sense to maintain (cross-) sectoral collective bargaining structures, but also to organise new forms of centralisation in the countries that are dominated by single-employer

bargaining or by no collective bargaining at all. Although centralisation is important for collective bargaining coverage and for securing decent wages and working conditions for all (independent of specific companies and workplaces), it is also realistic to assume that the call for company bargaining will never end, in order to meet employers' needs with respect to competitiveness, productivity, and flexibility in the field of labour. At the same time, workers will continue to have needs in social dialogue, co-determination, and (added) collective bargaining, tailored to their specific labour market and working environments. This book shows that decentralised bargaining can go hand in hand with collective bargaining at (cross-) sectoral level.

References

Armaroli, I. & Tomassetti, P. (2022). Decentralised bargaining in Italy: CODEBAR-project. https://aias-hsi.uva.nl/en/projects-a-z/codebar/codebar.html

Amlinger, M. & Bispinck, R. (2016). Dezentralisierung der Tarifpolitik. Ergebnisse der WSIBetriebsrätebefragung 2015. *WSI-Mitteilungen*, 69(3), 211–222.

Baccaro, L. & Howell, C. (2011). A common neoliberal trajectory: The transformation on industrial relations in advanced capitalism. *Politics & Society*, 39 (4), 521–563. https://doi.org/10.1177/0032329211420082

Baccaro, L. & Howell, C. (2017). *Trajectories of neoliberal transformation: European industrial relations since the 1970s.* Cambridge University Press.

Bechter, B. & Brandl, B. (2015). Measurement and analysis of industrial relations aggregates: What is the relevant unit of analysis in comparative research? *European Political Science*, 14(4), 422–438.

Bechter B, Brandl B., & Meardi, G. (2012). Sectors or countries? Typologies and levels of analysis in comparative industrial relations. *European Journal of Industrial Relations*, 18(3), 185–202.

Been, W. & Keune, M. (2019). The Netherlands: Decentralisation and growing power imbalances within a stable institutional context. In T. Müller, K. Vandaele & J. Waddington (Eds.), *Collective bargaining in Europe: Towards an endgame* (pp. 445–464). ETUI.

Brandl, B. & Traxler, F. (2011). Labour relations, economic governance and the crisis: Turning the tide again? *Labor History*, 52 (1), 1–22.

Bulfone, F. & Afonso, A. (2020). Business against markets: Employer resistance to collective bargaining liberalization during the Eurozone crisis. *Comparative Political Studies*, 53 (5), 809–846.

Carlos J., Rodríguez, F., Ibáñez Rojo, R., & Martínez Lucio, M. (2019). Spain: Challenges to legitimacy and representation in a context of fragmentation and neoliberal reform. In T. Müller, K. Vandaele, & J. Waddington (Eds.), *Collective bargaining in Europe: Towards an endgame* (pp. 563–582). ETUI.

Carrieri, M., Concetta Ambra, M., & Ciarini, A. (2018). The "resistible" rise of decentralised bargaining: A cross-country and inter-sectoral comparison. In S. Leonardo & R. Pedersini (Eds.), *Multi-employer bargaining under pressure. Decentralisation trends in five European countries* (pp. 93–66). ETUI.

Crouch, C. (2005). *Capitalist diversity and change: Recombinant governance and institutional entrepreneurs.* Oxford University Press.

Czarzasty, J. (2019). Collective bargaining in Poland: A near-death experience. In T. Müller, K. Vandaele, & J. Waddington (Eds.), *Collective bargaining in Europe: Towards an endgame* (pp. 465–482). ETUI.

Czarzasty, J. (2022). Decentralised bargaining in Poland: CODEBAR-project. https://aias-hsi.uva.nl/en/projects-a-z/codebar/codebar.html

European Commission (2012). *Labour market developments in Europe 2012*, European Economy 5/2012, Luxembourg, Publication Office of the European Union.

Geppert, M., Williams, K., Wortmann, M., Czarzasty, J., Kağnicioğlu, D., Köhler, H. D., & Uçkan, B. (2014). Industrial relations in European hypermarkets: Home and host country influences. *European Journal of Industrial Relations*, 20(3), 255–271.

Glassner, V. (2012). Transnational collective bargaining in national systems of industrial relations. In I. Schömann, I. et al. (Eds.), *Transnational collective bargaining at company level. A new component of European industrial relations?* (pp. 77–116). ETUI.

Haipeter, T. (2011). Works councils as actors in collective bargaining: Derogations and the development of Codetermination in the German chemical and metalworking industries. *Economic and Industrial Democracy*, 32(4), 679–695.

Haipeter, T. (2020). Digitalisation, unions and participation: The German case of industry 4.0. *Industrial Relations Journal*, 51(3), 242–260.

Haipeter, T. (2021). Between industry and establishment: Recent developments in German collective bargaining and codetermination. *Labour & Industry: A Journal of the Social and Economic Relations of Work*, DOI: 10.1080/10301763.2021.1901333

Haipeter. T. & Rosenbohm, S. (2022). Decentralised bargaining in Germany: CODEBAR-project. https://aias-hsi.uva.nl/en/projects-a-z/codebar/codebar.html

Haipeter, T., Armaroli, I. Iossa, A., & Rönnmar, M. (2023). Decentralisation of collective bargaining in the manufacturing sector. In F. Tros (Ed.), *Pathways in decentralised collective bargaining in Europe* (pp. 73–112). Amsterdam University Press.

Hall, P. A. & Soskice, D. (Eds.) (2001). *Varieties of capitalism: The institutional foundations of comparative advantage.* Oxford University Press.

Ibsen, C. & Keune, M. (2018). Organised decentralisation of collective bargaining: Case studies of Germany, Netherlands and Denmark. OECD Social, Employment and Migration Working Papers, No. 217, OECD Publishing, Paris. http://dx.doi.org/10.1787/f0394ef5-en

Jansen, N. (2023). Decentralised bargaining and the role of law: Decentralisation of collective bargaining in the manufacturing sector. In F. Tros (Ed.), *Pathways in decentralised collective bargaining in Europe* (pp. 53–71). Amsterdam University Press.

Jansen, N. & Tros, F. (2022). Decentralised bargaining in the Netherlands: CODE-BAR-project. https://aias-hsi.uva.nl/en/projects-a-z/codebar/codebar.html

Kahmann, M. & Vincent, C. (2022). Decentralised bargaining in France: CODE-BAR-project. https://aias-hsi.uva.nl/en/projects-a-z/codebar/codebar.html

Keune, M. (2011). Decentralising wage setting in times of crisis? The regulation and use of wage-related derogation clauses in seven European countries. *European Labour Law Journal*, 2(1), 86–96.

Keune, M., Been, W., & Tros, F. (2020). Ongelijkheid: Ontwikkelingen op de arbeidsmarkt en in de arbeidsverhoudingen. *Tijdschrift voor HRM*, 2020 (4), 46–63.

Keune, M. & Pedaci, M. (2020). Trade union strategies against precarious work: Common trends and sectoral divergence in the EU. *European Journal of Industrial Relations*, 26(2), 139–155.

Kjellberg, A. (2019). Sweden: Collective bargaining under the industry norm. In T. Müller, K. Vandaele, & J. Waddington (Eds.), *Collective bargaining in Europe: Towards an endgame* (pp. 583–604). ETUI.

Kjellberg, A. (2021). The shifting role of unions in the social dialogue. *European Journal of Workplace Innovation*. 6 (1–2), 220–244.

Leonardi, S., Concetta Ambra, M., & Ciarini, A. (2018). Italian collective bargaining at a turning point. In S. Leonardo & R. Pedersini (Eds.) *Multi-employer bargaining under pressure. Decentralisation trends in five European countries* (pp. 185–224). ETUI.

Leonardi, S. & Pedersini. R. (2018). *Multi-employer bargaining under pressure: Decentralisation trends in five European countries.* ETUI.

Maccarrone, V., Erne, R., & Regan, A. (2019). Ireland: Life after social partnership. In T. Müller, K. Vandaele, & J. Waddington (Eds.), *Collective bargaining in Europe: Towards an endgame* (pp. 315–336). ETUI.

Marginson P. (2015). Coordinated bargaining in Europe: from incremental corrosion to frontal assault? *European Journal of Industrial Relations*, 21 (2), 97–114.

Mias, A. & Béthoux, E. (2020). How does state-led decentralisation affect workplace employment relations? The French case in a comparative perspective. *European Journal of Industrial Relations*, 27(1), 5–21.

Müller, T. & Platzer, H. (2018). The European trade union federations: Profiles and power resources – Changes and challenges in times of crisis. In S. Lehndorff, H. Dribbusch, & T. Schulten (Eds.), *Rough waters: European trade unions in a time of crises* (pp. 303–329). ETUI.

Müller, T. & Schulten, T. (2019). Germany: Parallel universes of collective bargaining. In T. Müller, K. Vandaele, & J. Waddington (Eds.), *Collective bargaining in Europe: Towards an endgame* (pp. 239–266). ETUI.

Müller, T., Vandaele, K., & Waddington, J. (2019). Conclusion: Towards an endgame. In T. Müller, K. Vandaele, & J. Waddington (Eds.), *Collective bargaining in Europe: Towards an endgame* (pp. 583–604). ETUI.

Muñoz Ruiz, A., Ramos Martín, N., & Vincent, C. (2023). Interplay between state and collective bargaining, comparing France and Spain. In F. Tros (Ed.), *Pathways in decentralised collective bargaining in Europe* (pp. 143–178). Amsterdam University Press.

Nergaard, K., Dølvik, J.E., Marginson, P. Arasanz Díaz, J., & Bechter, B. (2009). Engaging with variable pay: A comparative study of the metal industry. *European Journal of Industrial Relations*, 15(2), 125–146.

OECD (2018). The role of collective bargaining systems for good labour market performance. In *Employment Outlook 2018*, Chapter 3. Organisation for Economic Co-operation and Development.

OECD (2019). Facing the future of work: How to make the most of collective bargaining. In *Employment Outlook 2019*, Chapter 5. Organisation for Economic Co-operation and Development.

Paolucci, V. & Marginson, P. (2020). Collective bargaining towards mutual flexibility and security goals in large internationalised companies: Why do institutions (still) matter? *Industrial Relations Journal*, 51(4), 329–350.

Paolucci, V., Roche, B., & Gormley, T. (2022). Decentralised bargaining in Ireland: CODEBAR-project. https://aias-hsi.uva.nl/en/projects-a-z/codebar/codebar.html

Paolucci, V., Czarzasty, J., Muñoz Ruiz, A., & Ramos Martín, N, (2023). Decentralisation of collective bargaining in the retail sector. In F. Tros (Ed.), *Pathways in decentralised collective bargaining in Europe* (pp. 113–142). Amsterdam University Press.

Pedersini, R. (2018). Conclusions and outlook: More challenges and some opportunities for industrial relations in the European Union. In S. Leonardo and R. Pedersini (Eds.), *Multi-employer bargaining under pressure: Decentralisation trends in five European countries* (pp. 291–298). ETUI.

Pedersini, R. (2019). Italy: Institutionalisation and resilience in a changing economic and political environment. In T. Müller, K. Vandaele, & J. Waddington (Eds.), *Collective bargaining in Europe: towards an endgame* (pp. 337–360). ETUI.

Pernicka S. & Stern S. (2011). Von der Sozialpartnergewerkschaft zur Bewegungsorganisation? Mitgliedergewinnungsstrategien österreichischer Gewerkschaften. *Österreichische Zeitschrift für Politikwissenschaft*, 40 (4), 335–355

Pietrogiovanni, V. & Iossa, A. (2017). Workers' representation and labour conflict at company level: The Italian binary star in the prism of the Swedish ternary system. *European Labour Law Journal*, 8(1), 45–66.

Ramos Martín, N. & Muñoz Ruiz, A. (2022) Decentralised bargaining in Spain: CODEBAR-project. https://aias-hsi.uva.nl/en/projects-a-z/codebar/codebar.html

Rehfeldt U. & Vincent, C. (2018). The decentralisation of collective bargaining in France: An escalating process. In S. Leonardo & R. Pedersini (Eds.), *Multi-employer bargaining under pressure: Decentralisation trends in five European countries* (pp. 151–184). ETUI.

Rocha, F. (2018). Strengthening the decentralisation of collective bargaining in Spain: Between the legal changes and real developments. In S. Leonardo & R. Pedersini (Eds.), *Multi-employer bargaining under pressure: Decentralisation trends in five European countries* (pp. 225–262). ETUI.

Rönnmar, M. & Iossa, A. (2022). Decentralised bargaining in Sweden: CODEBAR-project. https://aias-hsi.uva.nl/en/projects-a-z/codebar/codebar.html

Rönnmar, M., Kahmann, M., Iossa, A., Czarzasty, J., & Paolucci, V. (2023). Trade union participation and influence in decentralised collective bargaining. In F. Tros (Ed.), *Pathways in decentralised collective bargaining in Europe* (pp. 211–238). Amsterdam University Press.

Rosenbohm, S. & Tros, F. (2023). Does decentralisation lead to new relationships between trade unions and works councils? Germany and the Netherlands compared. In F. Tros (Ed.), *Pathways in decentralised collective bargaining in Europe* (pp. 179–209). Amsterdam University Press.

Sapulete, S., Behrens, M., Brehmer, W., & Van Witteloostuijn, A. (2016). Gebruik van invloedtactieken door de OR: Duitsland en Nederland vergeleken. *Tijdschrift voor Arbeidsvraagstukken, 32* (2), 157–176.

Schmalz, S., Ludwig, C., & Webster, E. (2018). The power resource approach: Developments and challenges. Global labour journal, 9 (2), 113–134.

Schulten, T. & Bispinck, R. (2018). Varieties of decentralisation in German collective bargaining. In R. Pedersini & S. Leonardi (Eds.), *Multi-employer bargaining under pressure. Decentralisation trends in five European countries* (pp. 105–150). ETUI.

Streeck, W. & Thelen, K. (2005). Introduction: Institutional change in advanced political economies. In W. Streeck & K. Thelen (Eds.), *Beyond continuity: Institutional change in advanced political economies* (pp. 1–39). Oxford University Press.

Toubøl J. & Strøby Jensen C. (2014). Why do people join trade unions? The impact of workplace union density on union recruitment, *Transfer,* 20 (1), 135–154.

Traxler, F. (1995). Farewell to labour market associations? Organized versus disorganized decentralisation as a map for industrial relations. In C. Crouch & F. Traxler (Eds.), *Organized industrial relations in Europe: What future?* (pp. 3–19). Avebury.

Traxler, F., Arrowsmith, J., Nergaard, K., & Molins López-Rodó, J. (2008b). Variable pay and collective bargaining: A cross-national comparison of the banking sector, *Economic and Industrial Democracy,* 29 (3), 406–431.

Traxler F. & Brandl B. (2012). Collective bargaining, inter-sectoral heterogeneity and competitiveness: A cross-national comparison of macroeconomic performance, *British Journal of Industrial Relations*, 50 (1), 73–98.

Tros, F. (2002). Decentraliserende arbeidsverhoudingen: de casus arbeidstijden. *SMA*, 57 (1): 57–70.

Tros, F. (2022). Innovating employee participation in the Netherlands. *Industrielle Beziehungen*, 29 (1), 3–23.

Vandaele, K. (2019). *Bleak prospects: Mapping trade union membership in Europe since 2000*. ETUI.

Van den Berg, A., Grift, Y., Sapulete, S., Behrens, M., Brehmer, W., & Van Witteloostuijn, A. (2019). Works councils in Germany and the Netherlands compared. An explorative study using an input-throughput-output approach. *WSI-Studien*, 2019 (17), 1–36.

Van Gyes, G. (2006). Employee representation at the workplace in the member states. In *Industrial Relations in Europe 2006* (pp. 57–77). Office for Official Publications of the European Communities.

Van Gyes, G. (2016). Employee representation regimes in Europe. Do they exist in practise?, Paper in the 28th Annual Meeting conference of the Society for the Advancement of Socio-Economics, UCLA, Berkeley.

Vincent, C. (2019). France: The rush towards prioritising the enterprise level. In T. Müller, K. Vandaele, & J. Waddington (Eds.), *Collective bargaining in Europe: Towards an endgame* (pp. 217–238). ETUI.

Visser, J. (2013). *Wage bargaining institutions:– From crisis to crisis*. European Commission. europa.eu

Visser J. (2016). What happened to collective bargaining during the great recession? *IZA Journal of Labour Policy*, 5 (9), 1–35.

Walton, R. & McKersie, R. (1965). *A behavioral theory of labor relations*. McGraw Hill.

2. Decentralised Bargaining and the Role of Law

Niels Jansen

Abstract

Legal systems in European countries differ greatly, and so does the legal design of collective bargaining. These differences manifest in the importance of constitutional principles, the balance between legislation and collective bargaining, the degree of state influence or voluntarism, the degree of trade union organisation and collective bargaining coverage, and forms of employee representation. But what relationship exists between the law, existing structures, and the methods and mechanisms used in the context of decentralisation? The author finds that structures of collective bargaining are mainly determined by non-legal factors, but the legal form of collective bargaining can help to create and maintain a certain structure and can therefore determine how the process of decentralisation occurs and what instruments and mechanisms are used.

Keywords: legal framework, decentralisation, state influence, trade union strategies, voluntarism, conflict rules

Introduction

This book is a study of the status and development of decentralised bargaining in several European countries, which represent the different legal systems that exist within Europe. In general, decentralised bargaining means the development from (more) centrally conducted or controlled collective bargaining about employment conditions to bargaining at lower levels. Decentralised bargaining can refer to various developments. Firstly, decentralisation is referred to when the decision-making power in existing consultations or decision-making is spread over several actors and groups. In

Frank Tros (ed.). *Pathways in Decentralised Collective Bargaining in Europe.* Amsterdam: Amsterdam University Press, 2023

DOI 10.5117/9789048560233_CH02

administrative law, this can include the transfer of powers from the state to
the provinces or municipalities. In negotiations on employment conditions, it
generally relates to a decline in the importance of collective bargaining due
to a reduction in the scope of collective agreements, or a decrease in sectoral
collective agreements and an increase in consultation at the company level
(see e.g., Haipeter & Rosenbohm, 2022: 19 ff.). Related to but not the same
as this form of decentralisation is a situation when existing national or
sectoral agreements create more room for the specific needs of companies
and employees in the form of deviation possibilities. Examples include
different options or alternatives within collective agreements or so-called
opt-out regulations, but also deviation possibilities and forms of coordination
between different levels. This currently occurs in many European countries.
Finally, decentralisation can refer to the involvement of works councils in the
setting of employment conditions (Jansen & Tros, 2022: 21 ff.). In this case,
the decision-making power is not necessarily distributed among actors, but
consultations are held with stakeholders who are less centrally controlled.
At its core, decentralisation always involves changes in the existing system
that entail the reduction of central control or coordination in consultation.
In countries where there is no central consultation structure, it is difficult
to speak of decentralisation, because decentralised consultation in those
countries is usually the existing consultation structure. Poland and Ireland
are cases in point (Czarzasty, 2022; Paolucci, Roche, & Gormley, 2022).

It is true that the moment decentralisation appeared on the political
agenda (and, indeed, whether decentralisation remains on the agenda)
varies somewhat from country to country, but it also true that the motive
for decentralisation is similar in different countries. That motive is, in the
main, strongly economic in nature. In Sweden, the Netherlands, Germany,
and France, it was (and still is) considered necessary, because of increased
international competition. That is to say, it was needed to ensure that companies are able to adapt more easily to economic developments in order to
remain sufficiently competitive. Decentralised bargaining can be helpful
in this respect, at least that was (or still is) the idea (see e.g., Kahmann &
Vincent, 2022). In countries such as Italy and Spain, the 2009 crisis seems to
have been a key driver of decentralised bargaining (Armaroli & Tomassetti,
2022; see also Chapter 5; Muñoz Ruiz et al., 2023). Companies should be given
more space to respond to economic changes that threaten their survival.
Although the motive for decentralisation is relatively similar, the same
cannot be said about the extent and manner in which decentralisation has
been or is being pursued and who initiates it (employers, social partners,
legislator, government). The decentralisation process differs widely from

country to country and the question is what role the national legal framework regarding collective bargaining plays in the decentralisation process (see also Chapter 7; Rönnmar et al., 2023). It is interesting, firstly, to explore which specific elements of the legal framework of collective bargaining actually influence or force the level at which collective bargaining is conducted and, secondly, which legal methods and mechanisms are used to shape decentralisation and what role the existing legal structures play in this process.

Legal systems differ greatly at the level of detail, and so does the legal design of collective bargaining (hereafter also referred to as collective bargaining law). As Rönnmar et al. (2023) point out, these differences manifest in the importance of constitutional principles, the balance between legislation and collective bargaining, the degree of state influence or voluntarism, the degree of trade union organisation and collective bargaining coverage, and forms of employee representation.

In this contribution, I explore whether there is (some kind of) a relationship between the law (legal framework) and the process of decentralisation (in terms of existing structures, outcomes and methods, and mechanisms used). In order to explore the role of law in the decentralisation process and to compare countries, I have selected four aspects of collective bargaining law that (may) influence the emergence of the existing consultation structure and therefore (may) also influence changes to that structure as a result of decentralisation. These four aspects are: i) the bargaining and contractual freedom of collective bargaining parties; ii) the possibility of declaring collective agreements generally binding; iii) the relationship between the sectoral collective agreement and the company collective agreement and the relationship between collective agreements and legislation; and iv) employee representation in collective bargaining. The choice of these topics is open to debate because other aspects of collective bargaining law may also affect the (existing) structures of collective bargaining. Nevertheless, these aspects form the core of collective bargaining law and a comparison between countries on these core elements therefore seems valuable to start with in any case.

I will begin by discussing above-mentioned aspects in more detail. In the subsequent section, I will analyse the decentralisation process. This is not about analysing outcomes, but rather it is about analysing the legal instruments or mechanisms that are used in the context of decentralisation. More specifically, I will discuss the role of the legislator in the decentralisation process and the use of different legislative instruments and the coordinating or non-coordinating role of social partners.

An analysis of the legal design of collective bargaining

Introduction

The right to collective bargaining is aimed at making a significant contribution to social justice by compensating for an inequality of powers. In addition, collective bargaining in the form of collective agreements offers the business community the opportunity to act in a self-regulatory way. This allows it to respond to market developments more quickly and with greater focus than if it had to wait for the legislature to act, which often occurs in a rather protracted and complicated political process. Legislation and regulations can remain limited, particularly by means of sectoral collective agreements that can be declared universally binding. Collective agreements also contribute to cost reductions for employers, reduce uncertainty about wage costs, and exclude competition on employment conditions so that employers can make better forecasts. In short, collective bargaining and collective agreements can be useful for positive socio-economic developments, labour peace, stable labour relations, and proper functioning of the labour market.[1] The collective agreement is an important outcome of collective bargaining. The law applicable to collective agreements varies greatly from country to country. While international and European treaties recognise the right to collective bargaining (Chapter 7; Rönnmar et al., 2023)[2] those treaties simultaneously take into account the national context of collective bargaining and collective bargaining law.[3]

---

1   On the benefits of collective bargaining, see: *Communication Concerning the Application of the Agreement on Social Policy Presented by the Commission to the Council and to the European Parliament* (Commission of the European Communities, COM(93) 600 final 14 December 1993), Brussels; HvJ EG 21 September 1999, case C-67/96 (Albany); International Labour Conference, 101st Session, ILC.101/ III/1B, Giving globalization a human face (General Survey on the fundamental Conventions concerning rights at work in light of the ILO Declaration on Social Justice for a Fair Globalization, 2008), Report III (Part 1B)), pp. 17–18; and, more recently, *Proposal for a Directive of the European Parliament and of the Council on Adequate Minimum Wages in the European Union* {SEC(2020) 362 final}, pp. 2–3.

2   ILO Conventions nos. 87 and 98; article 11 Convention for the Protection of Human Rights and Fundamental Freedoms; article 28 EU Charter of Fundamental Rights.

3   See e.g., Article 4 ILO Convention 98: *Measures <u>appropriate to national conditions</u> shall be taken, where necessary to encourage and promote the full development and utilisation of machinery for voluntary negotiation between employers of employers' organisations and workers' organisations, with a view to the regulation of terms and conditions of employment by means of collective agreements*; Article 28 EU Charter: *Workers and employers, or their respective organisations, have, <u>in accordance with Union law and national laws and practices</u>, the right to negotiate and conclude collective agreements at the appropriate levels and, in cases of conflicts of interest, to take collective action to defend their interests, including strike action.*

There are major differences with regard to, for example, the importance of constitutional principles, the balance between legislation and collective bargaining, the degree of state influence or voluntarism, the degree of trade union organisation and collective bargaining coverage, and forms of employee representation. For this study, I analyse the different systems in terms of four aspects that (might) influence the formation of the existing structure in practice, and which are therefore also important when changing that structure as a result of or due to decentralisation. I also examine to what extent these structures affect the process of decentralisation. The four aspects in question are: i) the bargaining and contractual freedom of collective bargaining parties; ii) the possibility of declaring collective agreements generally binding; iii) the relationship between the sectoral collective agreement and the company collective agreement and the relationship between the collective agreement and the law; and iv) employee representation in the process of employment conditions formation.

Freedom of collective bargaining: Freedom to contract and negotiate

In many of the countries studied, there is no (basic) legal obligation for employers to enter into either collective bargaining or a collective agreement. These systems are based on voluntarism. Freedom of collective bargaining implies that social partners have the freedom to decide whether to negotiate a collective agreement, what to negotiate about, and whether to conclude a collective agreement. Whether a collective agreement is concluded depends, to some extent, on the willingness of employers and the power of trade unions. Employers have two possibilities in this matter: firstly, they have the freedom to conclude a collective agreement or not; and secondly, they have the freedom to join or not to join an employers' association that can conclude a collective agreement at the sector level. If employers do not join an employers' association they are not bound by its agreements, unless and in case the agreement has a generally binding effect. The extent to which employers have the freedom under the law to participate in collective bargaining (and at what level) does not appear to be a decisive factor in shaping collective industrial relations in a country. The emergence of a particular bargaining structure seems to depend more on historical, political, and cultural factors (as well as trade union power resources) and less on the extent to which an employer's freedom to bargain collectively has been limited by the legislature, i.e., that it has some obligation to bargain and it is not entirely voluntary. I will elaborate on this.

In Poland, the absence of consultation at the sectoral level seems to be largely related to reforms of the political system and the circumstance that employers do not see the benefit of sectoral negotiations (Czarzasty, 2022). In Ireland, there was a period when wages were negotiated at the central level, but the 2009 crisis put an end to that as employers stopped central-level consultation. After that period, however, consultations at company level became more coordinated. In this context, we can speak of pattern negotiations in Ireland (Paolucci et al., 2022). Poland and Ireland lack any constitutional right to collective bargaining by workers and some obligation to do so by employers.

Like Poland and Ireland, the Netherlands and Germany also lack a constitutional right to collective bargaining by workers and obligation to do so by employers. In the Netherlands and Germany, however, the sector model developed after World War II as a result of the circumstance that employers and employees tended to organise themselves on a sectoral basis.[4] As a result, collective agreements also came into being at the sectoral level, and, although the importance of sectoral collective agreement has declined in Germany in recent decades, sectoral consultation remains dominant in the Netherlands and Germany. It should be noted, however, that in the Netherlands and Germany there is a solid legal framework regulating collective bargaining agreements. In the Netherlands, the sector model has been an important foundation of the further design and development of the labour market and its regulation. The Dutch consultation model is known as the "polder model" in which social partners share responsibility for socio-economic policy. In Italy, the sector model is mostly the result of the idea, which has prevailed since the 1980s, that – similar to the Dutch polder model – employers and employees should play an important role in shaping labour market policies and social laws and regulations (Armaroli & Tomassetti, 2022: 8–10). This is also called "responsive regulation" and tripartite consultation and delegation of regulatory powers are important components of this concept in the Italian context. As a result, a consultative system of several layers of collective consultation has emerged in which central consultation and sector bargaining play an important role.

In France, the freedom of employers within the framework of collective bargaining is limited by law, in the sense that French employers are obliged to negotiate with unions on certain topics at the sector level. As a result, sectoral consultation also has a legal basis. In Sweden, employees have a

---

4   Sector bargaining emerged in the first decades of the 20th century as a way for individual employers not to have direct contact with trade unions (Tros et al., 2006).

strong right to enforce collective consultation and this has helped to create a strong national and sectoral consultation system. This is also undoubtedly the result of a strong trade union position.

As mentioned before, the emergence of a particular bargaining structure seems to depend mainly on historical, political, and cultural factors (as well as trade union power resources) and much less on the manner in which the right to collective bargaining is shaped in law. As a result, a fully liberal system, based on voluntarism, with a lot of freedom for social partners to conclude collective agreements, does not necessarily lead to the absence of a centrally (national and/or sectoral) driven consultation system and the lack of strongly embedded social partners. The legal design of collective bargaining can, however, contribute to the preservation of existing structures. From the country reports of the countries with a less liberal system, such as France, the limited freedom of employers to enter into a collective agreement or not, and with which unions and at what level, does seem to have a direct influence on the emergence of certain bargaining structures. In these countries, the limited freedom of employers seems to have led to highly institutionalised collective bargaining in which the sectoral collective agreement plays a more important role than the company collective agreement. The degree to which collective bargaining is centralised (nationally or sectorally) seems to be mainly determined by non-legal factors, while the legal form of collective bargaining can help to create and maintain a particular structure.

The declaration of collective agreements as generally binding

Many European countries have a system of declaring collective agreements to be generally binding. The declaration of the binding nature of collective agreements is often seen as an act of substantive legislation and means that the binding collective agreement applies to all employers and employees who fall within its scope. The declaration of the binding effect extends the scope of the collective agreement, but its significance for the collective bargaining process is broader than just the widening of the scope of the collective agreement. A numerical approach to the declaration, in the sense that the declaration ensures that the collective agreement applies to a larger percentage of workers, does not do the instrument justice. This is because the extension not only has direct consequences for the scope of regulation of current collective agreements, but also influences the conclusion of collective agreements and the form of collective bargaining. After all, the possibility of being declared binding appears to be an important incentive for collective bargaining, because it excludes wage competition by unaffiliated employers. A major goal of declaring an agreement binding is therefore the stimulation (or maintenance) of collective bargaining. The possibility of binding agreements not only encourages collective bargaining in general, but also that collective bargaining is conducted particularly at the sectoral level, since, as a rule, only sectoral collective agreements are eligible for binding agreements. By declaring them binding, collective agreements can include agreements on, for example, wages, which can then apply to the entire sector. As a result, coordination at a central level means that legislation can be dispensed with, and, in that sense, the extension contributes to self-regulation of the social partners (Jansen, 2019).

The possibility of declaring collective agreements binding is not necessarily a guarantee of centrally directed consultation at the national and/or sectoral level. Polish collective bargaining law provides for the possibility of extending collective agreements, but this possibility is not used and sectoral consultation is almost non-existent in Poland (Czarzasty, 2022: 9). In this sense, the mere presence of the possibility of binding agreements does not say much about the extent to which collective bargaining is centrally controlled. This is confirmed by developments in Germany. German law includes the possibility of declaring collective agreements binding, and this possibility was frequently used. In recent years, the instrument has been used less, and this is mainly due to the declining degree of organisation on the employers' side. As a result, the instrument of the declaration of binding effect in German law has been adapted, in the sense that the criterion for declaring it binding has been relaxed. However, this change has not resulted in more collective agreements being declared binding. The importance of sectoral collective agreements is decreasing in Germany, while it has become easier to declare collective agreements generally binding (Haipeter & Rosenbohm, 2022: 19). In the Netherlands, too, it is possible to declare collective bargaining agreements generally binding, and although that legal system is almost a century old, until ten years ago hardly any changes were visible in the coverage ratio of sectoral collective bargaining agreements. In the last decade, there has been a decline in that coverage ratio. What is causing this decline is the subject of research.

Furthermore, the absence of the possibility of making an agreement generally binding does not seem to be decisive for the extent to which there is sectoral collective bargaining. Irish, Italian, and Swedish law do not allow for the possibility of generally binding agreements, and whereas in Ireland there is hardly any sectoral consultation, in Italy and Sweden sectoral consultation is an important pillar of the existing bargaining model.

The absence of the possibility of generally binding agreements seems to be compensated in Sweden by agreements at the national level.

Many European countries have the possibility of making collective agreements generally binding, but this possibility does not seem to be decisive for the design of collective bargaining and the extent to which there is central control through consultation at the national or sectoral level. After all, Polish law does provide for the possibility of declaring a collective agreement binding, but Polish collective bargaining is characterised by decentralised consultation at the company level. Swedish law, on the other hand, does not allow for the possibility of making generally binding agreements, but Swedish collective bargaining is centrally controlled and the sectoral collective agreement is an important pillar of collective bargaining. The possibility of declaring collective agreements generally binding can make an important contribution to centralised control of the negotiations. The system of declaring collective agreements binding can contribute to the self-regulation of social partners and is therefore a suitable instrument in systems that involve social partners in the formation of socio-economic policy and legislation, such as France and the Netherlands.

Conflict rules and deviation options

Discussions or issues inherent to the collective bargaining process are those related to the overlap of the scope of collective agreements, as a result of which two collective agreements may apply to an employment relationship. The applicability of two collective agreements often leads to problems, because the employment conditions agreed in both collective agreements may not correspond thus raising the question of which collective agreement or which collective agreement provision has priority. Rules in collective bargaining law that determine which collective bargaining agreement or which collective bargaining provision takes precedence in the event of concurrent and conflicting collective bargaining agreements can be referred to as "conflict rules." In countries where sectoral consultation is an important pillar of collective bargaining, most collective bargaining law contains rules that give precedence to the sectoral collective agreement in the event of clashing collective agreements. How these conflict rules are shaped, however, differs from one legal system to another.

In the Dutch and German systems, the consequence of declaring a collective agreement generally binding is that it becomes a form of public law that takes precedence over (purely) private collective agreements. The clash between two collective agreements that have both been declared universally applicable is avoided as much as possible by not declaring one of the collective agreements universally applicable where there is an overlap in their scope (Jansen & Tros, 2022: 8–11). It is then up to the social partners to resolve the overlap in scope. If there is an overlap between two collective agreements, neither of which have been declared generally binding, the problem is, in principle, solved by the binding effect of collective agreement law. An employer has the power, via collective labour agreement law, to prevent his employment relationships from being governed by two different collective labour agreements (Jansen & Tros, 2022: 8–11). If a company in the Netherlands falls within the scope of a sectoral collective agreement that has been declared binding and it wishes to apply its own company collective agreement, this is only possible if: i) the sectoral collective agreement leaves room for this; ii) parties to the sectoral collective agreement grant permission; or iii) the minister asks for dispensation from the sectoral collective agreement.

Under Polish law, it is not possible to deviate from a sectoral collective agreement to the detriment of the employee through a lower regulation. Derogations in favour of the employee are therefore possible. Given the fact that Polish employers like to be as competitive as possible, the lack of deviation possibilities from the sector collective agreement could mean that the sector agreement is anything but popular in Poland. Polish employers appear to be afraid of competition from other employers who are not bound by a collective agreement and do not see the benefits of a level playing field with regard to employment conditions (Czarzasty, 2022: 9).

In France, until the major reforms of the 21st century, the principle of the most favourable provision also applied, i.e., that a sectoral collective agreement could be deviated from only to the benefit of employees (Kahmann & Vincent, 2022: 11). In the French system, sectoral collective agreements usually contain minimum regulations, which can therefore be deviated from in favour of employees in, for example, company collective agreements.[5]

In Sweden and Italy, collective agreements contain many delegation rules that thus ensure coordination between different layers of collective bargaining (Rönnmar & Iossa, 2022: 10 ff.; Armaroli & Tomassetti, 2022: 9). The collective agreements usually contain rules on how to deal with and/or clash with collective agreements. In Spain, the law stipulates the conditions under which a sectoral collective agreement can be deviated from (Muñoz Ruiz & Ramos Martín, 2022: 3).

---

5   Other countries, for example, the Netherlands, have a similar system (Jansen & Tros, 2022: 8–11).

Another doctrine of collective law that is also an important subject of collective bargaining concerns the possibilities of derogation from legislation. Such possibilities do not exist under either Polish or Irish, while the other systems examined do have statutory derogation options for the law. In many cases, these derogations are in the form of clauses, for example, in Spain, the Netherlands, Germany, and Sweden. The possibility to deviate from the law can be seen as an important incentive for collective bargaining and makes collective bargaining attractive for employers.

In summary, in systems where sectoral collective agreements play an important role and collective agreements are negotiated at different levels, the existence of conflict rules are indispensable. It is striking that in Polish law there is little room for deviations from sectoral collective agreements and that laws and regulations cannot be deviated from by collective agreement either, and, moreover, that in Poland the sectoral collective agreement is hardly important. There seems, therefore, to be a link between the presence of conflict rules and deviation possibilities from the law and a sectoral consultation structure, but it is not clear whether the sectoral consultation is (partly) the result of the existence of conflict rules (in other words: that the presence of conflict rules positively influences the sectoral consultation) or that the presence of conflict rules is mostly a result of a sectoral consultation created by other circumstances.

Employee representation

Trade union density has been in decline in Europe in almost all countries since 1980, but rates differ significantly across countries (Chapter 7; Rönnmar et al., 2023). While successful employee representation increases with the degree of workers' organisation (Schmalz & Dörre, 2014), it is not clear how employee representation relates to (the change of) existing bargaining structures (see also Chapter 7; Rönnmar et al., 2023).

Under Dutch law, collective agreements can be concluded by employee associations with full legal capacity (trade unions). Trade unions are not subject to any further requirements in collective bargaining law regarding, for example, independence or representativeness. Dutch law thus guarantees that any trade union can enter into collective agreements. In addition, from a legal point of view, every trade union has equal opportunities to enforce consultation and strengthen negotiations. This puts every trade union in the same starting position. Whether or not trade unions succeed in achieving their objectives depends on extra-legal factors in the industrial relations arena. Works councils can negotiate on employment conditions in the Netherlands, but the results of these negotiations are not a collective agreement and are of lower legal order than the collective agreement, in the sense that a collective agreement in principle prevails in case of conflict. The possibilities to negotiate with works councils combined with the lack of a strong position of trade unions in the companies can undermine the position of trade unions when the negotiation of employment conditions shifts from sector to company. The German system is similar to this (Haipeter & Rosenbohm, 2022: 1–10).

In Poland, the works council is virtually non-existent. In Swedish law, all trade unions enjoy the same basic legal rights of freedom of association, general bargaining, collective bargaining, and collective action. Instead of establishing certain procedures or criteria for representativeness, Swedish law grants privileges to so-called established unions, i.e., unions that are currently or ordinarily bound by a collective agreement with the employer or the employer's organisation (Rönnmar & Iossa, 2022: 10). Established unions enjoy far-reaching rights to information, primary bargaining, and co-determination. The employer is obliged to negotiate primary employment conditions with the trade union before making decisions on major changes in the employer's business and operations, such as restructuring, layoffs, changes in work organisation, and appointments of new managers, or the employment conditions or employment relationship of a member of the trade union, such as transfers and changes in working hours. Such consultations take place first at the enterprise level and then at the sector level.

Italian law does not impose requirements on trade unions in the context of representativeness with regard to entering into collective agreements (Armaroli & Tomassetti: 2022: 12). Works councils can also enter into collective agreements under Italian law. This is comparable to Spanish law (Muñoz Ruiz & Ramos Martin, 2022: 6). In order to avoid undermining the position of representative trade unions, Italian law stipulates that further requirements are imposed on trade unions before a collective agreement can deviate from the law. This privilege therefore does not accrue to all trade unions, but only to the most representative trade union.

France has a system of trade union elections that determine which trade union has the authority to enter into collective agreements from time to time. If there is no trade union at the enterprise level, then negotiations can also be held at the enterprise level with an employee delegation. Depending on the size of the company's workforce, it will be determined how that employee representation and the collective agreement will be created (Kahmann & Vincent, 2022: 13).

In many European countries, collective bargaining took its dominant form in the second half of the 20th century. In that period, the degree of organisation of trade unions was generally still considerable, the number of trade unions was still manageable, and those unions were still mostly centrally controlled, and works councils were still relatively new. In most countries, this led to a consultative structure in which levels of consultation were attuned to one another and the sector collective bargaining agreement occupied an important place. The emergence of new, alternative trade unions, the decline in the membership of established trade unions, and the normalisation of the works council as a discussion partner within the company, have changed the playing field of collective bargaining. In some countries, this has led to legislation on collective bargaining and the authority to enter into collective agreements. This new legislation seems to have been motivated primarily by the goal of preserving existing structures, or at least to counteract the undermining of the position of established trade unions in the collective bargaining process. In countries where sectoral bargaining is an important pillar of employment negotiations, the decentralisation of employment negotiations has meant that established unions lose ground in collective bargaining, because in the existing structures the presence of established unions at the firm level is generally less evident.

Decentralised bargaining instruments and mechanisms

As stated in the introduction, decentralised bargaining can point to various developments in collective bargaining. For this contribution, I have distinguished three main forms. First, the decline in the importance of collective bargaining through a reduction in the scope of collective agreements or a decrease in sectoral collective agreements and an increase in bargaining at the firm level. Related to but not quite the same as this form of decentralisation is when the existing national or sectoral consultations, in the form of derogation options, create more room for the specific needs of companies (and employees working in them). This is the second main form. Finally, decentralisation can refer to the involvement of the works council (or other employee representation at the company level, other than trade unions, who are party to collective agreements) in shaping terms of employment: that is the third main form. In this section, I discuss what tools or mechanisms can be identified for each main form and how they are deployed or used to shape and streamline the decentralisation process.

Reduced scope of the collective agreement, fewer sectoral collective agreements, and more consultation at the enterprise level

In a few of the countries under discussion there has been a marked decline in the scope of collective bargaining or a decline in the number of sectoral collective agreements and simultaneous growth in the number of company collective agreements. In many of the countries surveyed, where the sectoral collective agreement is an important pillar of collective bargaining, that sectoral collective agreement seems to lead a fairly stable existence. Decreasing collective bargaining coverage is mostly limited to countries in which company level bargaining is dominant, like Ireland and Poland. The decentralisation of collective bargaining in the countries that are dominated by sector bargaining usually manifests itself in the second main form, whereby more room has been created at the sectoral level for consultation at the company level. It is worth noting that in the Netherlands and Germany there has been a decline in the coverage ratio of sectoral collective agreements, but this is not necessarily accompanied by an increase in the number of company collective agreements, while legislation does not seem to have played a role in this. In fact, new legislation in Germany, by which I mean the broadening of the possibility to declare a collective agreement binding, seems to be more in favour of the sectoral collective agreement and does not, as yet, result in an increase in the sector collective bargaining agreement coverage ratio. The result of the reduction of the sectoral collective agreement in Germany seems to be a decline in the degree of organisation on the employers' side and the introduction of the possibility for employers to be members of employers' organisations without being bound by a collective agreement. They simply leave the system of collective bargaining. Shifts in this first main form seem to be mainly the result of employer strategies. That also fits in with the existing consultations in Poland and Ireland in which employers still do not seem to feel like consulting at the sector level. As I discussed earlier, legislation seems to have only a modest effect on the genesis of the prevailing consultation structures. In particular, non-legal aspects have led to centralist consultation structures and although these structures do appear to be supported by legislation, non-legal aspects also appear to have led to the greatest changes.

Nevertheless, some mechanisms or instruments can be identified that may give rise to changes in the existing structure by making the sectoral collective agreement less attractive in a legal sense. In Spain, for example, the law was initially amended to give the company collective agreement priority over the sectoral collective agreement (see Chapter 5; Muñoz Ruis,

Ramos Martín, & Vincent, 2023). This intervened in the existing structure in Spain. After considerable criticism, particularly from trade unions, this change was reversed and the old structure seems to be maintained. In French legislation, a subdivision has been made in terms of the subjects of the employment conditions consultations that must be discussed at the sector level or company level, respectively. The shift of topics from the sector consultations to the decentralised consultations, could potentially have the effect of making the sector consultations less important. Because certain (important) subjects must still be discussed at the sector level, the effect of the legislation is rather that decentralised consultation has increased while retaining bargaining and consultation at the sector level (see Chapter 5; Muñoz Ruis, Ramos Martín, & Vincent, 2023). Finally, I would like to mention the tax legislation in Italy that stimulated consultation at the decentralised level. Because of the embedding of the sector collective agreement in the existing structure, the tax legislation has not had the effect of reducing the importance of the sector collective agreement, but rather it has increased the number of company collective agreements. The legislation has led to more intensive coordination between different levels of consultation.

More space for decentralised bargaining and works councils

In all countries with a certain sectoral bargaining structure, decentralised bargaining has been shaped mainly through the mechanism of giving more space for decentralised agreements within the structure of sectoral collective agreements. This has happened in a variety of ways.

In the first place, sectoral collective agreements have become more of a framework for further elaboration of all kinds of regulations at the decentralised level. This development is sometimes accompanied by a change in the content of consultation within the sector, as a result of a separation between subjects that are negotiated at the sector level and subjects that are left to decentralised consultation (Armaroli & Tomassetti, 2022). As already mentioned, French law even distinguishes between subjects that are negotiated at the sector level, on the one hand, and at the company level, on the other. Sometimes, the framework-setting nature of sectoral collective agreements becomes visible through the use of opening clauses in sectoral collective agreements. Such clauses entail that certain parts of the sectoral collective agreement can be deviated from (often conditionally) by company level bargaining. The use of opening clauses occurs in Germany, the Netherlands, Spain, and Italy, among other countries. Opening clauses in sectoral collective agreements allow unions at the sectoral level to maintain control over the formation of employment conditions in the sector while offering opportunities to companies to better tailor some employment conditions to the wishes and needs of companies and workers. This is also called coordinated decentralisation. This coordination often relates not only to the content of the consultation, but also to the parties to the consultation. These may be trade unions operating at the company level and often under the central direction of a trade union federation, but also, for example, works councils under the control of trade unions. If a certain control or direction of sectoral unions over employee representatives at the local level is lacking, then sectoral unions are, as a rule, less inclined to leave subjects to decentralised consultation or to include opening clauses (see Chapter 6; Rosenbohm & Tros, 2023).

More room for decentralised consultation can also be created by making it possible by law or collective agreement to deviate from collective agreements. In Spain and Italy, it has been made possible by law for decentralised consultations to deviate from sectoral collective agreements. Such deviation possibilities allow decentralisation to take place in an uncontrolled manner often at the expense of sectoral consultation. In Italy, trade unions have responded to these legal derogation possibilities by making agreements in the sectoral collective agreement on how decentralised consultation will be involved. In Spain, the change in the law was reversed due to persistent criticism from trade unions. Uncoordinated decentralised consultation can also be an issue in systems in which there are few requirements for trade unions or in which works councils can consult on employment conditions. In addition, there is a great deal of freedom for employers to enter into collective bargaining with trade unions. Decentralised consultation (possibly even with works councils or "yellow" unions) can then be used to undermine sectoral bargaining.

In conclusion

It needs to be said that it is difficult to compare systems given the peculiarities of and within countries and the changes and adjustments in different systems over time. That makes it difficult to draw broad lines from the comparisons that are also "time" and "circumstance" sensitive. Drawing conclusions in this sense is perhaps going a bit too far and so I conclude by pointing out some trends.

Firstly, the emergence of a particular bargaining structure in European countries seems to depend mainly on historical, political, and cultural factors and much less on the legal design of collective bargaining law. As a result, a fully liberal system with a lot of freedom for social partners to conclude collective agreements does not necessarily lead to the absence of a centrally (national and/or sectoral) driven consultation system and the lack of strongly embedded social partners. The legal design of collective bargaining can, however, contribute to the preservation of existing structures. In countries with a less liberal system, such as France and Sweden, the limited freedom of employers to enter into a collective agreement or not, and with which unions and at what level, does seem to have a direct influence on the emergence of certain bargaining structures. The degree to which collective bargaining is centralised (nationally or sectorally) seems to be mainly determined by non-legal factors, but the legal form of collective bargaining can help to create and maintain a certain structure.

Secondly, the possibility to make collective agreements generally binding does not seem to be decisive for the design of collective bargaining structures and the extent to which there is central control through bargaining at the national or sectoral level. After all, Polish law does provide for the possibility of declaring a collective agreement binding, but Polish collective bargaining is characterised by decentralised bargaining at the company level. Swedish law, on the other hand, does not allow for the possibility of generally binding, but Swedish collective bargaining is centrally controlled in which the sectoral collective agreement is an important pillar of collective bargaining. However, the possibility of declaring collective agreements generally binding can make an important contribution to centralised control of the negotiations.

Thirdly, in systems where the sectoral collective agreement plays an important role and collective agreements are negotiated at different levels, the existence of conflict rules are indispensable. There seems to be a certain link between the presence of conflict rules and deviation possibilities from the law and a sectoral consultation structure, but it is not clear whether the sectoral consultation is (partly) the result of the existence of conflict rules (in other words: that the presence of conflict rules positively influences the sectoral consultation) or that the presence of conflict rules is mostly a result of a sectoral consultation created by other circumstances.

Fourthly, decentralised bargaining can point to various developments in collective bargaining. In general, it is difficult to say that the importance of collective agreements in Europe has declined: significantly more collective agreements are concluded at the corporate level and the importance of the sectoral collective agreement is decreasing in some countries, but in many other countries the existing structures are quite stable, albeit the coverage ratio does seem to be declining. However, in many countries, the trend of decentralisation has led to collective agreements becoming more of a framework for further elaboration at the decentralised level. The strategy of the trade unions seems to be aimed at creating more opportunities for employers and employees to arrive at a package of employment conditions that is more in line with the wishes of the company, while retaining control at central and company level. Legislation has been used to stimulate decentralised bargaining, for example the creation of possibilities for derogation in the law, a distribution of subjects over different layers of consultation in the law and tax advantages. The effect of this legislation is often that agreements on coordination are made during bargaining. Where decentralised bargaining takes place in a coordinated manner, social partners are generally more positive about decentralisation than when uncoordinated forms of decentralisation are involved.

References

Armaroli, I. & Tomassetti, P. (2022). Decentralised bargaining in Italy: CODEBAR-project. https://aias-hsi.uva.nl/en/projects-a-z/codebar/codebar.html

Czarzasty, J. (2022). Decentralised bargaining in Poland: CODEBAR-project. https://aias-hsi.uva.nl/en/projects-a-z/codebar/codebar.html

Haipeter, T. & Rosenbohm, S. (2022). Decentralised bargaining in Germany: CODEBAR-project. https://aias-hsi.uva.nl/en/projects-a-z/codebar/codebar.html

Jansen, N, (2019). *Een juridisch onderzoek naar de representativiteit van vakbonden in het arbeidsvoorwaardenoverleg*. Kluwer.

Jansen, N. & Tros, F. (2022). Decentralised bargaining in the Netherlands: CODEBAR-project. https://aias-hsi.uva.nl/en/projects-a-z/codebar/codebar.html

Kahmann, M. & Vincent, C. (2022). Decentralised bargaining in France. https://aias-hsi.uva.nl/en/projects-a-z/codebar/codebar.html

Muñoz Ruiz, A. & Ramos Martín, N., (2022). Decentralised bargaining in Spain: CODEBAR-project. https://aias-hsi.uva.nl/en/projects-a-z/codebar/codebar.html

Muñoz Ruiz, A., Ramos Martín, N., & Vincent, C. (2023). Interplay between state and collective bargaining, comparing France and Spain. In F. Tros (Ed.), *Pathways in decentralised collective bargaining in Europe* (pp. 143–178). Amsterdam University Press.

Paolucci, V., Roche, W. K., & Gormley, T. (2022). Decentralised bargaining in Ireland: CODEBAR-project. https://aias-hsi.uva.nl/en/projects-a-z/codebar/codebar.

Rönnmar, M. & Iossa, A. (2022). Decentralised bargaining in Sweden: CODEBAR-project. https://aias-hsi.uva.nl/en/projects-a-z/codebar/codebar.html

Rönnmar, M., Kahmann, M., Iossa, A., Czarzasty, J., & Paolucci, V. (2023). Trade union participation and influence in decentralised collective bargaining. In F. Tros (Ed.), *Pathways in decentralised collective bargaining in Europe* (pp. 211–238). Amsterdam University Press.

Rosenbohm, S. & Tros, F. (2023). Does decentralisation lead to new relationships between trade unions and works councils? Germany and the Netherlands compared. In F. Tros (Ed.), *Pathways in decentralised collective bargaining in Europe* (pp. 179–209). Amsterdam University Press.

Schmalz, S. & Dorre, K. (2014), Der Machtressourcenansatz: Ein Asatz zur Analyse gewerkschaftlichen Handlungsvermogens. *Industrielle Beziehungen*, 21(3): 217–237.

Tros, F., Albeda, W., & Dercksen, W. (2006). *Arbeidsverhoudingen in Nederland* (Labour relations in the Netherlands). Kluwer.

3. Decentralisation of Collective Bargaining in the Manufacturing Sector

Thomas Haipeter, Ilaria Armaroli, Andrea Iossa, Mia Rönnmar

Abstract

Since the 1980s, there have been changes to collective bargaining structures in the manufacturing sector. The authors distinguish six pathways of decentralisation, ranging from different forms of organised decentralisation to forms of disorganised decentralisation, the latter also including collective bargaining located solely at company level. The manufacturing sector plays a trendsetting role with respect to decentralisation in Europe, to be interpreted as an element of continuity and relative strength of collective bargaining actors in the sector. In most cases, decentralisation remained within the margins of organised decentralisation, and even in cases of full decentralisation the manufacturing sector is doing better than many other sectors in terms of collective bargaining coverage and wage increases.

Keywords: collective bargaining, manufacturing sector, decentralisation, coordination, trade unions, worker representation

Introduction

The manufacturing sector has been the stronghold of collective bargaining and, more generally, of industrial relations institutions and actors in many advanced political economies for decades. The strengthening of trade unions and – mainly – sectoral collective bargaining as well as the increase of wages and the improvement of working conditions in the post-war world from the

Frank Tros (ed.). *Pathways in Decentralised Collective Bargaining in Europe.* Amsterdam: Amsterdam University Press, 2023

DOI 10.5117/9789048560233_CH03

1950s to the 1980s have their roots, to a large degree, in the manufacturing sector with its big mass-production firms, which have fuelled economic growth and became characteristic of the Fordist era of that time. Moreover, it was the manufacturing sector that set the wage norms in a process of pattern bargaining for collective bargaining in other sectors.

However, since the Fordist era the fate of the sector has changed. Its shares of total employment or GDP growth have declined, and the composition of the manufacturing workforce has shifted from blue- to white-collar employees, who, in many countries, have been much less organised by trade unions than their blue-collar counterparts. Moreover, former collective bargaining structures have changed in a process of decentralisation. As we will show in this chapter, however, this process neither led to a breakdown of trade unions and of collective bargaining in the manufacturing sector nor destroyed the sector's role as a pace-setter of norm setting through collective bargaining in advanced political economies.

That said, today, the role of the sector as a pacesetter has changed – it now shapes the process of decentralisation in its organised form (Traxler, 1995). In this way, the sector differs from many industries of the private service sector in which organised decentralisation is less developed and disorganised decentralisation plays a much bigger role (see Chapters 1 and 4 in this book). This does not mean that there is no disorganised decentralisation taking place in the manufacturing sector, but it is less radical or less severe than in the service sector and it is mitigated by the many forms in which organised decentralisation has developed.

This chapter is about these forms of decentralisation and the associated challenges for the actors involved in collective bargaining in the manufacturing sector. This refers to trade unions and the employers and their associations, whose interest in collective bargaining is dependent on the strength and the capabilities of the trade unions; that is why Franz Traxler once labelled them "secondary organisers" (Traxler, 1999). It is the trade unions that defend collective bargaining systems against erosion, and that try to control and organise decentralisation in a way that is compatible with the preservation of centralised bargaining norms, sometimes in confrontation with employers, sometimes by joining forces with them against the state. In this chapter, we will tackle the following questions: What forms of decentralisation are observed in the manufacturing sectors of the countries under scrutiny in our comparative analysis? What are the reasons for the differences in the concrete paths of decentralisation between countries? How do unions try to coordinate and organise – what we will call "articulate" – decentralisation? And, finally, what are the main challenges and problems confronting the actors in this process?

Our analysis is based on studies in eight EU countries – France, Germany, Ireland, Italy, the Netherlands, Poland, Spain, and Sweden.[1] This study contains analyses of the manufacturing sector as well as company case studies. An overview of these case studies, which are referred to throughout our analysis, is provided Table 3.1.

Table 3.1.   Case studies from the manufacturing sectors

Cases	Country	Subsector	Type of Firm	Employees (in country)
Aero	France	Aerospace	Parent Company	43000
Axis Communications AB	Sweden	IT	Parent Company	2500
DSM	Netherlands	Food, Bioscience	Parent Company	3800
Electric France	France	Energy	Parent Company	15500
Enel	Italy	Energy	Parent Company	59000
Lacroix	Poland	Electronics	Foreign Subsidiary	2000
Lights	Germany	Electronics	Parent Company	1500
Metal Forming	Germany	Metal	SME	400
Metal Industries	France	Steel	Foreign Subsidiary	250
PharmaCo.	Ireland	Pharma	Foreign Subsidiary	600
TenarisDalmine	Italy	Steel	Subsidiary	2100
VW	Poland	Automotive	Foreign Subsidiary	11000

The analysis is structured in three steps. In the first step, we give an overview of the structures of collective bargaining and its actors in the manufacturing sectors of our sample countries. Here, we also assess the role that the sector still plays in the overall national systems of industrial relations. In a second step, we identify the different pathways of decentralisation in the manufacturing sector and the commonalities and differences that can be observed between the countries of our sample. At the same time, we will identify the reasons for these commonalities and differences in terms of institutional configurations of collective bargaining systems, the resources and strategies of their actors, and the role of the state as legislator. A third

---

1   See the project website: https://aias-hsi.uva.nl/en/projects-a-z/codebar/codebar.html
The analyses in this chapter are based on the country reports in this project. In case no other
literature references are made in this text, our analysis is drawing on the findings in these
reports without referring to this.

step focuses on the activities of articulation. How do the trade unions organise and coordinate the process of decentralisation? Given that collective bargaining systems today are multi-level systems, as indeed are the trade unions, the activities of the latter increasingly relate to active articulation between these levels. The chapter ends with conclusions about comparative aspects, pathways, and the articulation of decentralised bargaining in the manufacturing sector.

The manufacturing sector: Industrial relations and collective bargaining characteristics

Characteristics of the manufacturing sector

This section introduces the main characteristics of industrial relations and collective bargaining in the manufacturing sectors of our sample countries by highlighting elements of continuity as well as elements of transformation. The manufacturing sector is multi-faceted, and industrial relations characteristics and pathways of decentralisation in this sector vary depending on industries, company sizes, social partners, and the interplay between sectoral collective bargaining, company-level collective bargaining, and legal framework.

The manufacturing sector encompasses a broad variety of industries, ranging from, among others, automotive, chemical, electric, food, and metallurgic branches. This aspect is reflected by our sample countries. The diversity of case studies encompasses companies in the chemical and pharmaceutical sectors (Ireland, the Netherlands, and Spain), the metalworking sector (France, Germany, Italy, and Poland), the tech sector (Sweden), and the electric sector (France, Germany, and Italy).

The size of manufacturing companies also varies. The manufacturing sector is composed of multinational companies with headquarters and production sites in different countries as well as medium- and small-size companies that produce mostly for the national market, but whose production operations are increasingly international. This feature is reflected by our case studies of the manufacturing sector, which include multinational companies (France, Ireland, the Netherlands, Poland, and Sweden), large-size companies mostly producing for the national market within supply chains (France), and medium-size companies, one of which has production locations abroad (Germany). In three cases (Ireland. Italy and Poland), the selected companies are subsidiaries of multinationals with main headquarters abroad.

Overall, our national and company case studies highlight the importance of the manufacturing sector in relation to the national labour markets and industrial relations systems. They also emphasise how companies in the manufacturing sector still employ a significant share of the national workforce. For instance, in France, employment in the manufacturing industry represents 10.3% of total employment in the country, while in Sweden 17.7% of the total active workforce is employed in the manufacturing industry, which has the second largest share of employees after retail (Medlingsinstitutet, 2022), and in Germany about 9% of the overall employment rate is in the metal sector. A 2019 report published by Eurofound shows that, for the year 2017, the employment share of the manufacturing sector across the countries selected in our study, ranges from slightly above 20% in Poland to slightly below 10% in the Netherlands, with Germany and Italy having a share near 20% (Eurofound, 2019). The Eurofound report also shows that, with the exceptions of France, Italy, and Sweden, all the other countries investigated here present positive trends in the average annual growth of employment in the manufacturing sector (Eurofound, 2019). At the same time, however, the Eurofound report shows negative predictions regarding the impact of the manufacturing sector on national GDP in all countries investigated (Eurofound, 2019).

From a historical perspective, the manufacturing sector has constituted the backbone of industrial relations developments across Europe in the 20th century. According to Crouch (1993: 290), the socio-economic dynamics of the sector (large-size companies, high productivity, large workforce, etc.) enabled the institutional development of organised capital and labour. However, already in the 1990s, he drew attention to the beginning of a progressive downturn of the sector in terms of downsizing production and the workforce employed, which, in his view, marked the beginning of an overall decline of industrial relations institutions in Europe. This prediction – whether or not it has come true – shows the central relevance of the manufacturing sector in analysing and understanding general developments in industrial relations.

The transformation of industrial relations and collective bargaining in the manufacturing sector also concerns the composition of the workforce. An employee in this sector is often portrayed as the "archetypical blue-collar worker," who emerged with the Fordist mode of production (Crouch & Voelzkow, 2004: 7). The French metalworking sector, for instance, is characterised by the high average age of the workforce. A similar account is found in Poland, where trade unions encounter difficulties at company level in engaging younger generations of employees in their activities (Czarzasty, 2022: 35). Despite the historical preponderance of blue-collar work in manufacturing, in some countries it is possible to identify a progressive shift towards an increasing share of white-collar employees in the sector. For instance, this is highlighted in the Swedish case, which analyses a Swedish multinational company that has delocalised most of its production abroad while maintaining its managerial headquarters and Research & Development office in Sweden. The manufacturing sector in Germany shows a similar development; here, the share of white-collar workers has outpaced the blue-collars' share since the middle of the last decade (Haipeter, 2016). One of the case studies in Italy also describes a similar shift. In this case study, focusing on a large-size electric company, the shift towards a majority of white-collar employees is explained with the introduction of new technologies and new organisational structures in the electric sector, which has then required the company to recruit different types of skills in order to match the needed tasks.

Despite those elements and overall descending trends in collective bargaining across Europe (see Waddington et al., 2019), industrial relations structures in the manufacturing sector still appear strong. Figures on trade union and employers' organisation density and collective agreement coverage rate are still relatively high and show stable patterns. For instance, trade union density in the sector is 75% in Sweden,[2] 31% in Italy, 58% in Germany, and 21% in the Netherlands; employers' density is instead 100% in France, 50% in the Netherlands, 48% in Germany, and 49% in Italy; collective agreement coverage is 100% in France, 95% in Italy, and 92% in the Netherlands.[3] Overall, it can be concluded that the scores of the manufacturing sector in terms of trade union and employers' organisation density as well as in terms of collective agreement coverage are relatively high.

The role of the manufacturing sector for industrial relations and collective bargaining

The manufacturing sector seems largely representative of the country-specific industrial relations system. In industrial relations systems characterised by trade union pluralism, such pluralism is generally also present at the company level in the manufacturing sector (see the cases in bigger enterprises in France and the case in Italy). In this regard, the Italian case

---

2   Data from 2020. The data refers to the average between blue- and white-collar employees (Medlingsinstitutet, 2022).

3   These data have been provided by national contributors in this book.

highlights how the trade union pluralism that characterises the overall industrial relations system is also present at company level where various trade unions cooperate (and disagree) within the company-level bodies for workers' representation. The Swedish manufacturing sector also reflects the overall principles of trade union organisation in the country, including the dominance of nationwide industrial unions, where blue-collar employees are organised and represented by a trade union affiliated to the *Swedish Trade Union Confederation* (LO), white-collar employees by a trade union affiliated to the *Swedish Confederation of Professional Employees* TCO), and university-graduate employees by a trade unions affiliated to the *Swedish Confederation of Professional Associations* (SACO), where the organisation in craft unions is important and various SACO-affiliated trade unions collaborate at company level within a SACO council. Close cooperation between trade unions at sectoral and company levels is a primary characteristic of Swedish industrial relations, which is reflected in the manufacturing sector (Rönnmar & Iossa, 2022; see also Rönnmar, 2019).

In industrial relations systems with a dual system of employee representation, with trade unions responsible for sectoral collective bargaining agreements and works councils, formally independent from the unions, responsible for workplace agreements, works councils play an important role in manufacturing companies – as in the case of the Dutch and German systems. In these cases, company-level industrial relations might be characterised by tensions in the coordination between employee representative actors, with well-established and well-functioning works councils that cooperate, or enter into conflict with trade unions (see also below). This is linked to the often large size of companies in the manufacturing sector, which favours formation of works councils and, at the same time, ensures a high grade of trade union density and coverage of collective agreements. In this regard, it is worth noting that, in the Netherlands, works councils are present in 88% of manufacturing companies, while in Germany, around 65% of manufacturing employees are reported to be employed in companies with works councils.

Collective bargaining in the manufacturing sector in many countries set general trends and patterns in collective bargaining at national level and for other sectors. Given its relevance, the manufacturing sector is the most influential sector for the evolution of industrial relations across the other sectors at national level and, in particular, regarding collective bargaining decentralisation trends. There is still evidence of both continuity as well as pattern setting for national-level cross-sectoral industrial relations, including the setting of pathways of decentralisation. This "pacemaker pattern" of industrial relations in the manufacturing sector is particularly evident in the Swedish context,[4] where the trends towards decentralisation have been initiated by social partners in the manufacturing sector with the signing of a separate collective agreement in 1983 between the engineering and metallurgical employers' organisation, the Association of Swedish Engineering Industries (*Teknikföretagen*, named *Sveriges Verkstadsförening* at that time) and the trade union of metallurgical workers IF Metall, the largest sectoral trade union affiliated with LO (Thörnqvist, 1999; Baccaro & Howell, 2017). Ever since, sectoral collective bargaining in the manufacturing sector has set the "standard" for an evolution towards decentralisation in other sectors. In Sweden, the relevance of the manufacturing sector (and in particular its metallurgic branch) is also strengthened by the fact that it belongs to the export sector. Negotiations on wage-setting in the manufacturing sector affect and influence wage-setting in other sectors through the mechanism of the "industry norm" (*industrimärket*). This mechanism was introduced with the 1997 Industrial Agreement as a way to ensure that salaries on the labour market would not increase at a percentage higher than the growth of the national economy. It uses the degree of international competitiveness of the Swedish economy as a way to control the inflation caused by wage increases and to keep the Swedish economy competitive. Thus, the "industry norm" has a normative effect in other sectors, as trade unions and employers' organisations adopt it as the "norm" for wage increases in collective negotiations at sectoral level (Medlingsinstitutet, 2020; Kjellberg, 2019). The industry norm anchors the wage increase of Swedish employees in various sectors of the labour market to the wage increases set by national, sectoral collective agreements in the industrial export sector, i.e., in key branches of the manufacturing sector (Rönnmar & Iossa, 2022: 13 and 43).

In the Swedish case, the influence of the manufacturing sector on the general evolution of industrial relations and collective bargaining appears stable. While this finding could have been expected for a system like the Swedish one, which is characterised by high levels of trade union and employers' association density, as well as by an articulated and coordinated system of representation and collective bargaining (Ahlberg & Bruun, 2005; Rönnmar & Iossa, 2022), this element emerges – albeit on a smaller scale – also in a country like Ireland, which is characterised by a high degree of decentralisation and a very low degree of coordination between levels (Paolucci et al., 2022). Collective bargaining at the pharmaceutical

---

4   A similar finding can be found in Italy (Armaroli & Tomassetti, 2022).

multinational company PharmaCo became a "trend setter" for collective bargaining nationwide, also beyond the manufacturing sector (Paolucci et al., 2022). PharmaCo belongs to a sector that was less affected by the 2008 economic crisis (Gunnigle et al., 2018), and is one of a number of multinational firms in the chemical and pharmaceutical sectors that continued to observe existing collective agreements and award pay increases even in the aftermath of the 2008 recession (Paolucci et al., 2022: 18). Multinational firms in these sectors introduced forms of "pattern bargaining" that set the trend in the sector as well as beyond it at a cross-sectoral level. This mechanism is described as "without precedent in Irish industrial relations" (Paolucci et al., 2022: 18). Such an evolution is described as a trade union strategy aimed at making wage negotiations in strongly unionised firms in these sectors standard-setter for general collective bargaining trends. The largest trade union in Ireland, SIPTU (Services, Industrial, Professional, and Technical Union), identified the pharmaceutical sector as strategic for influencing national collective bargaining across sectors due to the highly skilled employees and to the international competitiveness of the sector in relation with the national economy (Paolucci et al., 2022: 30; see also below).

A further common trait is the effect on industrial relations and collective bargaining in the manufacturing sector of factors like economic crises, international competition, relocation of production, and changes in technology (Müller et al., 2018). These are all aspects that have contributed to a transformation of fundamental industrial relations institutions in the manufacturing sector and to a decrease of collective agreement coverage and trade union as well as employers' organisation density in countries like Germany, and, to a lesser extent, also Italy and the Netherlands. Nevertheless, there are a number of cases in which industrial relations at company level in the manufacturing sector occurs on good terms and often with the aim of dealing in a positive manner with the effect of sectoral and company crisis. For instance, the French case studies stress the role of company-level industrial relations for the achievement of more "centralised" collective bargaining within the company groups (Kahmann & Vincent, 2022). While these cases highlight this aspect as mainly a managerial strategy to ensure uniform working and employment conditions across the different establishments of the groups and to reduce the number of negotiations and bargaining venues, it is interesting to note the interplay with the overall policy and legislative trends at national level to favour decentralisation in France. In the Swedish context, instead, the flexibility ensured to company-level industrial relations and collective bargaining within a system of "organised decentralisation," enabled social partners in the manufacturing sector to deal with the consequences of economic crisis as well as the COVID-19 pandemic by using company-level collective bargaining instruments, such as collective agreements on short-time work. The Swedish (1976:580) Co-determination Act assigns a right to primary negotiations to the trade union that is bound by a collective agreement applied in the company. The employer has an obligation to negotiate with the trade unions before making decisions regarding important alterations in the employer's activities and business, such as restructuring, redundancies, work organisation changes and appointments of new managers, or the employment conditions or employment relationship of a member of the trade union, such as transfers and working-time changes (Rönnmar & Iossa, 2022: 10).

It is interesting to notice that, also in this regard, industrial relations and collective bargaining in the manufacturing sector have influenced national developments. The first collective agreements on short-time work were concluded and implemented in the manufacturing sector to deal with the effects of the 2008 and 2009 economic crisis. The short-time work scheme was later extended to the overall Swedish labour market, and complemented by statutory regulation and state financial support, see the (2013:948) Act on Support for Short-Time Work (see Kjellberg, 2019; Glavå, 2010). A similar finding emerges from the German report. It describes how the instrument of agreements on short-time work schemes has been widely used across sectors to manage the economic consequences of the COVID-19 pandemic. Like in Sweden, the instrument had its first "boom" in the financial crisis and mainly in the manufacturing sector. Additionally, actors could make use of other instruments to reduce working times in the pandemic, among them the reduction of weekly working times to safe-guard jobs, which has been formalised since 1995 through the mechanism of "opening clauses" in collective agreements in the metallurgic sector (Haipeter & Rosenbohm, 2022). These clauses would allow for collective reductions in working time – for certain groups, departments, or whole establishments – with the aim of safeguarding employment by enabling company-level parties to agree on reductions in working hours from the collectively agreed norm of 35 hours per week down to 30 hours per week, with a proportional cut in pay. In return, the employer would commit to not introducing compulsory redundancies for up to a maximum period of 12 months (Haipeter & Rosenbohm, 2022: 31). However, in contrast to the Swedish example, these agreements have not been negotiated in the form of collective bargaining agreements but in the forms of workplace agreements between managements and works councils. This fact sheds light on the functional equivalence that might exist between the different institutions of single and dual systems. In conclusion, we see an advanced presence of organised decentralisation of collective bargaining in the manufacturing sector in Europe.

Pathways of decentralisation in the manufacturing sector

Six pathways

Decentralisation of collective bargaining is an overarching trend in the manufacturing sectors of the eight political economies under scrutiny. However, this common trend shows rather significant differences between the countries, depending very much on their institutional configurations of collective bargaining and the power and strategies of its actors, the concrete procedural norms on decentralisation in the collective regulations that have been agreed on by the collective bargaining actors and, finally, the role of the state as a legislator. Given these differences, what do the pathways of decentralisation in our eight countries look like in detail?

Today, the starting point for decentralisation of collective bargaining in most countries is the industry level. Wherever the national cross-industry level has played an important role in collective bargaining in the past – like in Sweden or Ireland – it has lost its former role and is important today only in two respects: either as the level for dealing with some general rules of collective bargaining across sectors as it has been the case for example in Italy, or as the level for defining statutory minimum wages. In Sweden and Italy there is no minimum wage regulation. Here, the minimum wage levels are defined by the sectoral collective bargaining agreements only, but based on a high coverage of collective bargaining. In the other countries, the minimum wages form a baseline for wages also in the manufacturing sector, whereas, in most – but not all – of the countries analysed here minimum standards of collective bargaining in this sector are positioned well above this baseline so that the minimum wages do not play a more exposed role.

Decentralisation of collective bargaining in the manufacturing sectors of the countries under scrutiny follows six pathways (Table 3.2.). We follow here a slightly different categorisation than in Chapter 1 with more subcategories within the pathway of institutional "layering" (Tros, 2023). Some of the pathways are more or less coordinated and agreed, or at least accepted, at the industry level, so that we can speak of pathways of organised

Table 3.2.　Pathways of decentralisation in the manufacturing sectors

	Additional Wage Bargaining on Company Level	Additional Topics of Collective Bargaining on Company level	Opening Clauses for Works Councils	Derogations on Company Level	Erosion of Collective Bargaining	Full Decentralisation
France	Firms with union presence	Introduced by the state		Legally possible but not practiced by social partners		
Germany	Only workplace agreements by works councils	Introduced by social partners (Future Agreements)	Mainly on working time flexibility and reduction	Derogations established	Decline of coverage	
Ireland						Full decentralisation with some coordination
Italy	Additional wage components	Introduced by Social Partners		Legally possible but not practiced by social partners	Application of alternative collective agreements	
Netherlands			Mainly on working time flexibility			
Poland						Full decentralisation without coordination
Spain	Big firms			Legally possible but not practiced by social partners		
Sweden	All types of firms	Introduced by social partners				

decentralisation, whereas some others are disorganised in the sense that they undermine centralised collective bargaining. The six pathways of organised decentralisation are: first, there is wage setting at the company level, in addition to the industry level, and increasing the wage levels defined there; second, additional topics of collective bargaining are negotiated at company level; third, the industry-level agreements contain opening clauses for workplace agreements at company level by works councils; and fourth, either industry collective bargaining agreements or state legislation allows derogations from collective bargaining norms at company level. This fourth type is at the interface between organised and disorganised decentralisation, depending on how far derogations have the capacity to undermine the industry norms of collective bargaining and how far and how effective they can be controlled by the collective bargaining actors with respect to their spread and their contents. The two remaining forms are disorganised without any doubt: fifth, the erosion of collective bargaining coverage in the sector; and sixth, the full decentralisation of collective bargaining in the sense that no collective bargaining takes place at the industry level any more – here, decentralisation has switched from a process to a state of affairs.

These pathways are spread unevenly among the industries across the countries with some countries combining two or more of them; in the German case, as many as five different pathways can be identified, in the case of Italy four, and in France three. In the two cases of full decentralisation, Ireland and Poland, no other forms of decentralisation can be observed, for obvious reasons. In the following, the six forms of decentralisation in the manufacturing sector will be analysed in a comparative way. How far are they shaped by actors' strategies, procedural norms of collective bargaining, and institutional structures or state regulations? The case studies can be located in different subsectors of the manufacturing sector; however, we will compare them as illustrations of the respective national manufacturing sectors as a whole.

Additional wage bargaining at company level

The first form of organised decentralisation in the manufacturing sector refers to wage increases or wage components trade unions and companies negotiate at company level. This type of additional bargaining is prominent in Italy and Sweden. Also in France and Spain, collective bargaining mainly takes place at the company level, specifically in big companies, and alongside the minimum standards set by industry or regional agreements, which are usually extended by the state. In Germany, finally, additional negotiations might also take place in big companies but, in this case, they are conducted by the works councils instead of the unions and, therefore, have the form of workplace agreements. In Italy, additional bargaining takes place in a complementary form to the sectoral agreements negotiated by the social partners. This possibility has been, most recently, formalised in a cross-sectoral agreement between the employers' association Confindustria and the three main unions in 2014: *Confederazione Generale Italiana del Lavoro* (CGIL), *Confederazione Italiana Sindacati Lavoratori* (CISL) and *Unione Italiana del Lavoro* (UIL) (Armaroli & Tomassetti, 2022). This rule leaves room for secondary bargaining at company level – and, importantly for SMEs, at regional level – to add additional wage components to the sectorally defined wage minimum. According to the data provided in Leonardi et al. (2017), secondary bargaining takes place in about 21% of the workplaces in the whole economy, with the manufacturing sector among those with a higher coverage of secondary agreements due to the above average number of bigger companies in this sector. The additional wages can take the form of either fixed components or productivity based – or in other ways variable – wages; the latter, according to a survey by the biggest employers' association, include 45% of all companies covering 80% of the workforce in the manufacturing sector. The coverage stands in a positive correlation with the company size (Federmeccanica, 2018).

In Sweden, the role of wage bargaining in national sectoral agreements has been modified by the above-mentioned 1997 Industrial Agreement (Rönnmar & Iossa, 2022: 12). Here, employers' associations and trade unions agreed that wage setting will no longer take place on the cross-sectoral level and that sectoral collective bargaining agreements would be transformed into framework agreements indicating wages for newly employed workers and setting guidelines for management regarding wage increases at the company level. In the Swedish manufacturing sector, wage setting in collective bargaining covers both more decentralised and more centralised forms within the broader trend of decentralisation, ranging from defining mandatory provisions for the wage levels to guarantee wage increases or the definition of salary pots for wage increases. The more decentralised patterns of collective bargaining agreements exist in the areas of professional, white-collar work, whereas the more centralised patterns cover the blue-collar workers in production (Rönnmar & Iossa, 2022).

France and Spain are different cases, in the sense that, here, company-level bargaining is less systematically linked to collective bargaining agreements, which, in both countries, are extended by the state. In France, for example, sectoral collective bargaining agreements define the respective minimum wages for different job demands and professions and leave room for additional wage bargaining at company level (Kahmann & Vincent, 2022). Additional bargaining takes place in all establishments with union presence; however, substantial differences to the minimum standards are mainly confined to big firms. In the manufacturing sector, the bargaining structure is rather fragmented, with a high number of territorial collective agreements, a problem that has been taken up by employers' associations and some of the trade unions, who agreed on a new national sectoral agreement to replace the former agreements at the end of 2021. At the company level, wage agreements increasingly focus on variable and individualised forms of pay, such as profit-sharing schemes. In the company case of Electric, negotiations on wages take place at the level of legal entities and are only weakly linked to sectoral agreements as they take place before the sectoral agreements are negotiated (Kahmann & Vincent, 2022). The Spanish case is similar to the French one in the sense that it is the bigger firms where additional wage increases can be achieved by the trade unions, which simultaneously fuels company strategies of outsourcing and offshoring in order to reduce costs (Muñoz Ruiz & Ramos Martin, 2022; Rodríguez et al., 2019).

In Germany, additional collective bargaining has not been established, although it was already being discussed among and within trade unions – and especially within the metalworkers' union IG Metall – in the 1970s, when a positive wage drift in the bigger companies indicated economic room for manoeuvre with respect to collective bargaining at company level. At that time, the trade unions were reluctant to act given the apparent resistance from works councils. Improving wages at the company level was an important source of legitimacy for works councils, and they did not want to transfer this advantage to the unions. Since then, wage bargaining at company level has occurred in the form of workplace agreements made by works councils, and these have increasingly been formalised in agreements on profit sharing, mainly in the bigger firms and mainly in the automotive sector. This pattern does not apply to the Netherlands where works councils do not bargain on additional wages – and, indeed, trade unions do not bargain on extra wages in the context of a sectoral agreement (Jansen & Tros, 2022). For both Germany and the Netherlands, it is the specific institutional structure of collective bargaining and the dual representation channel that explains the non-existence of additional wage bargaining in these countries.

Additional topics of collective bargaining at company level

The relevance of other collective bargaining topics at company level has increased in the manufacturing sectors under scrutiny here, too. Again, Italy, Sweden, and France are among the countries where this trend is important, with social partners in Italy and Sweden and the state in France pushing this development forwards. In Spain and Germany, the trend of additional bargaining topics is much less significant in manufacturing, although not absent, as some examples in these countries show.

In Italy, the starting point of this development was the activities of social partners at company level. According to the ADAPT database,[5] they developed new collective bargaining topics, including welfare measures such as healthcare benefits or pension schemes, which were addressed in 43% of all company agreements in 2017 – compared to a spread of only 27% in 2015. While the coverage of these measures increased rapidly, other topics, like the opportunity to convert variable pay into working times by taking it as time off in lieu of money or measures to improve work–life balance are still less common, but also growing in importance. Beyond this, digitalisation and remote working have become important topics of company bargaining, the latter fuelled by the COVID-19 pandemic. Some agreements also focus on the ecological transformation of companies in terms of defining rules for "just transitions." This trend for negotiating additional topics in company bargaining has been accompanied by participatory practices, aimed at labour–management collaboration, and the rules for this can also be negotiated in company-level agreements (Armaroli & Tomassetti, 2022). The development in Sweden shows similarities to the Italian one in the sense that new topics have developed and are negotiated at company level, too; the topics mentioned in the country report are cooperation and co-determination, working time and annual leave, or coping with redundancies (Rönnmar & Iossa, 2022).

In France, however, the process of company collective bargaining developed top down. Here, it was the state that defined additional topics for company bargaining, a process with a tradition already dating back to the 1980s, when company-level collective bargaining was made compulsory (see Chapter 5; Muñoz Ruiz et al., 2023). The last step of this process has been

---

5   See the yearly reports *La contrattazione collettiva in Italia:* https://www.adaptuniversitypress.it/

the Macron laws from 2017, which gave the company level a priority over other levels of collective bargaining for three areas: remuneration, working times, and the sharing of added value (like profit sharing); professional equality between men and women and the quality of working life; and strategic workforce planning, subcontracting, or temporary employment. Company-level bargaining has proven to be ambivalent for the trade unions, as can be shown by the example of strategic workforce planning at Electric. Here, the trade unions now get better information and are more involved, and whereas employees get more opportunities to participate in career planning, at the same time, company bargaining offers the company an opportunity to use it as an instrument of cost cutting and workforce reduction (Kahmann & Vincent, 2022). The broadening of the firm-level regulatory agenda has contributed to a loss of importance of sectoral collective bargaining in the bigger companies in France. The working conditions in large French enterprises like Electric or Aero are mainly defined by company-level agreements. Similarly, in Italy, representatives from TenarisDalmine declare that, apart from issues like disciplinary procedures and individual employment contracts, which are thought to be more genuinely discussed at the sectoral level, collective bargaining with respect to issues such as working time, wages, and skills, could be settled within the company.

Spain and Germany are far less exposed in terms of additional bargaining. In Spain, the issue of wages has traditionally dominated additional bargaining at company level; however, some new topics of additional bargaining have developed or gained importance, including health and safety, retirement, redundancy processes, and equality plans. In Germany, company bargaining on additional topics is even rarer; here, the only topic under discussion in the metalworking industry is "future collective bargaining agreements," which were added to the industry collective bargaining agreement of 2021 and which are designed to cope with long term processes of socio-ecological transformation. They were demanded by the metalworkers' union IG Metall in order to influence the process of transformation at company level. There is no list of topics defined for this except for the stipulation that they are to increase competitiveness and innovation capacities and to safeguard jobs with innovative measures, whatever the concrete topics might be. The reason for the far less developed culture of company collective bargaining on additional topics in Germany – and, even more so, in the Netherlands – is that many additional collective bargaining issues are dealt with by works councils in the form of workplace agreements.

Opening clauses for works councils

Whereas decentralisation in single-channel countries is organised via the union channel and within the collective bargaining system, in the dual systems of Germany and the Netherlands – and respectively in their manufacturing sectors – decentralisation largely takes place in the form of opening clauses in collective bargaining agreements, which delegate certain topics to works council negotiations at workplace level. This means that the treatment of these topics no longer lies in the hands of the collective bargaining actors, but in those of the works councils as workplace actors, which can simultaneously mobilise their legal rights to cope with them.

In the Netherlands, sectoral agreements have increasingly become framework agreements for decentralised bargaining, leaving broad scope for works councils to improve or shape collective bargaining norms in companies. In the 1990s, the focus was on "variable and flexible working hours and on possibilities to open for deviating regulations in maximum working hours by day, week or month" (Jansen & Tros, 2022). In the metalworking sector, trade unions were able to implement new bargaining rights at the company level within the sectoral agreements. Today, tailor-made regulations at the company level, based on consent with works councils, are widespread in the sector. It is estimated that around 70% of companies use flexibility options concerning holidays and more than 40% make agreements about on-call duties. However, there are also issues characterised by trade union bargaining or consultation rights, e.g., if a company wants to reduce the – positive – wage drift, or if a company wants to deviate from legal standards with respect to shift work or working-time schedules, or if a company wants to be excluded from sectoral agreements and negotiate its own company agreement. As the case study of DSM shows, one grey area of responsibilities between works councils and trade unions is reorganisation, with works councils having the right to be informed and consulted on these issues and the unions having the right to negotiate the terms and conditions of collective dismissals (Jansen & Tros, 2022).

Flexible working times are also at the heart of the opening clauses for works councils in the German metalworking sector. Four issues of flexible working times are addressed in the industry's collective bargaining agreements (Haipeter & Rosenbohm, 2022): flexible working hours in the form of working time accounts; provisions on workplace quotas on extending individual agreed working hours up to 40 hours a week; opening clauses allowing for collective reductions in working time down to 30 hours per week; and individual working-time reductions. Individual employees may reduce their weekly hours from 35 to 28 hours for a period of up to two years with a corresponding reduction in pay, while retaining the status of full-time workers. A second element of individual working-time reduction refers to the option to use an additional payment introduced in 2018 for eight additional free days a year. Additionally, since 2006, some of the wage agreements include deviations from pay settlements, allowing companies to postpone payment of the industry-level settlement for a couple of months or to reduce or postpone agreed lump-sum payments. Any such step must be agreed with the works councils and IG Metall.

Derogations at company level

Derogations from sectoral collective bargaining can also be regarded as an additional collective bargaining issue at company level. However, it differs significantly from the additional bargaining discussed above. Whereas additional bargaining is about norms that complement industry collective bargaining norms, derogations are about norms that substitute industry norms by undercutting them. Among the countries under scrutiny, this practice has only become widespread in the German manufacturing sector. However, the legal possibility of derogations has been introduced in three of the other countries as well.

In France, Spain and, in a different way, Italy, the state has changed labour law in order to give companies the opportunity to derogate from industry collective bargaining agreements. Whereas in Italy and Spain this initiative has been a reaction to the financial crisis and these countries' coverage by the European Stability Mechanism, in France it has been a political strategy to improve competitiveness. In Italy, the possibilities to deviate from sectoral provisions were initially envisaged in cross-sectoral collective agreements; the legal regulation allowing this came after and with some differences. However, in all the three cases, these legal changes had little practical effect. Only in Spain was it observed that wage restraint in the manufacturing sector was enhanced by the legal changes – however, largely without formal derogation from collective bargaining agreements (Rocha, 2017). The reason why derogations did not become common practice in the manufacturing sectors of these countries is that the social partners did not support the regulation. Not surprisingly, it was the trade unions that were initially unwilling to accept derogations, albeit to differing degrees. However, employers and their associations also did not insist on negotiating derogations but refrained from this option, either informally or even formally as in Italy. Here, the employers' association Confindustria and the big trade unions agreed, in a cross-sectoral agreement from 2011, not to apply the legal possibility to derogate, leaving some room to apply derogations established by social partners. The employers and their associations had manifold motives to behave this way, among them trade union resistance, the fear of sending negative signals to employees and customers, or the avoidance of wage competition. These motives played a similar role in Spain (see Muñoz Ruiz & Ramos Martín, 2022). In Italy, though, despite social partners' formal opposition, latest data report an increasing use of this legal opportunity, however, without being clear whether this is long term trend or not (Ministero del Lavoro e delle Politiche Sociali, 2023).

Given these orientations, derogations were either not practiced, as in France, or they have been practiced, but only in a small number of cases, as in Spain and, to a smaller extent, in Italy. It is these orientations towards derogations that differ from the situation in Germany (Haipeter & Rosenbohm, 2022). Indeed, Germany is the only case in our sample where derogations have become an important practice of collective bargaining in the manufacturing sector. The reason for this is a shift in the orientation and strategies of employers' associations in the 1990s. Looking at the metal industry, the umbrella employers' association, Gesamtmetall, has favoured the idea of more or less radical decentralisation of collective bargaining since the late 20th century. Undercutting of minimum standards has become an explicit part of this strategy. In 2003 and 2004, the opportunity structure for the associations improved when the federal government threatened to introduce legislation relating to opening clauses for derogations from collective bargaining agreements if the social partners in the metal industry were unable to find a solution for this. This was the background to the 2004 agreement, which formalised the practice of derogations in the metalworking industry. The agreement specified that derogation agreements are possible, provided that jobs are safeguarded or created as a result and that they improve competitiveness and the ability to innovate, as well as investment conditions.

It soon became evident, however, that the employers' associations themselves had no interest in controlling derogations in Germany. Consequently, it fell to the trade unions to exercise control. This became an urgent issue for the union as more and more cases appeared in which works council had already agreed to management's demands before the union had been asked for its opinion or taken any part in the negotiations. Consequently, *coordination guidelines* were drawn up by the trade union during 2005, including norms about transparency, about responsibilities, and about trade union members being informed about and being able to participate in decision-making. Based on the implementation of these rules, derogations became far more a quid pro quo than pure concession bargaining. The material concessions made by employees are usually matched by *counter-concessions* offered by employers, like employment protection, investment promises, the extension of co-determination rights in controlling agreements or in attending to certain measures to improve competitiveness, or profit-sharing arrangements for workers who can benefit if the situation of the firm improves – just to name three of the topics. The data available indicates that the coverage of opening clauses for derogations is between 10% and 20% among the companies bound by collective agreements (Haipeter & Rosenbohm, 2022).

Erosion of collective bargaining

Like derogations, the trend of erosion of collective bargaining coverage has taken place mainly in the German metalworking industry, but also, to a lesser degree and in different forms, in the Italian one. In Germany, this form of disorganised decentralisation was favoured by three factors. First, the lack of extension of collective bargaining agreements, an instrument that impedes erosion in France, Spain and the Netherlands and also exists in Germany, but is not used in the German metalworking industry because of a general resistance among the employer associations and also due to resistance from the trade union, which feels strong enough to hold companies to the agreements. Second, the lack of legal support for the collective bargaining of minimum standards as can be observed in Italy, where employees could demand the payment of wages according to collective agreements and where the opting out of the Italian automotive company FIAT by the employers' association remained a singular case (although it was heavily debated at that time). And third, the decline of employers' associations' organising power – and the trade unions' inability to enforce or motivate employers – especially SMEs – to join the associations. Incidentally, this marks the key difference with Sweden. However, as will be shown, it is the employers' associations and their strategies that are key to understanding the erosion of collective bargaining in the German metalworking industry.

According to membership data from the sectoral umbrella association Gesamtmetall, collective bargaining coverage – which is identical to the membership density of the associations – declined by more than 20% compared to the early 1990s, to 47% of employees in 2020. This decline is a result of decisions by individual employers to opt out of the associations or not to join them. However, disorganised decentralisation has also been actively promoted and hence legitimised by employers' associations in the sector. The instrument for this has been the establishment of "opted-out" associations, whose membership does not require involvement in or compliance with collective bargaining. By 2020, more than 13% of employees in the metalworking and electrical industry worked in companies with opted-out membership, a doubling since 2006 when the opted-out associations were admitted to Gesamtmetall, which publishes such membership data. The importance of opted-out associations is even greater when looked at from the perspective of the number of companies involved. By 2019, 15.7% of companies in the metalworking industry were members of opted-out associations, higher than the 12.9% that were members of the regular employers' associations that comply with industry agreements. The divergence between organisational density as measured in terms of companies and by employees can be explained by the high numbers of SMEs among the members of opted-out associations (Haipeter & Rosenbohm, 2022).

Signs of erosion of (representative) sectoral collective bargaining in the Italian manufacturing sector derive from the increase in collective agreements signed by non- representative trade unions and the possibility for employers to apply them in a context of no legal erga omnes efficacy of representative collective agreements. The application of alternative agreements, either signed by trade unions other than CGIL, CISL, and UIL or signed by federations of CGIL, CISL, and UIL covering different sectors (i.e., services), is an issue of increasing concern to social partners and policymakers. Despite the fact that it mainly pertains to the tertiary sector and, more generally, labour-intensive branches operating in outsourcing, Armaroli & Tomassetti (2022) also point to its diffusion in the field of plant planning, supply and application, energy efficiency services, and facility management. Employers in the industry are represented by the association Assistal, which adheres to Confindustria and signs the main national agreement for the metalworking sector along with Federmeccanica. However, as reported by *Consiglio nazionale dell'economia e del lavoro* (CNEL, 2021) there are at least ten more national collective labour agreements aiming to cover the branch, which are not signed by metalworking sectors' social partners.

Full decentralisation

Full decentralisation – i.e., the final state of the process of decentralisation – can be observed in two of our sample countries, Ireland and Poland. Here, full decentralisation became the dominant state of affairs in the manufacturing sector – as it did in other parts of their economies, with some exceptions in Ireland. However, within this general picture there are some important differences between these two countries.

In Ireland, industry collective bargaining has a weak tradition; the centralisation of bargaining that occurred from the late 1980s up to the financial crisis in 2009 took the form of cross-sectoral tripartite social dialogue, and trade unions were traditionally organised around occupations and professions, albeit weakly at the industry level. When the employers' associations collectively withdrew from the social pact in 2009, there were few institutional structures of industry collective bargaining to build on. However, the subsequent process of decentralisation was framed by a "protocol" to guide collective bargaining in private and public firms. This was followed by a phase of concession bargaining at firm level. However, coverage of collective bargaining remained robust, especially in the export-oriented manufacturing sector with its multinational firms. In this situation, the manufacturing division of SIPTU – the biggest Irish union whose main focus is the manufacturing sector – developed a new strategy to target strongly unionised firms, especially those in the chemical and pharmaceutical industries, to change the wage trends and to agree on wage increases of 2% per year, which would set the trend in the sector as a whole. This approach to implementing a new form of pattern bargaining and to replace concession bargaining in the framework of company bargaining proved to be successful in the following years, with the pay norm of a 2% wage rise widely accepted. An important precondition for this kind of coordination within decentralised bargaining has been the organisational power of the union in this sector and the fact that it developed a strategy to mobilise shop stewards and to improve the participation of members in collective bargaining, especially in the core companies of the pharmaceutical industry.

The contrast with Poland shows that the Irish manufacturing sector represents a kind of coordinated company bargaining, whereas in Poland such coordination is largely absent. Here, trade unions and collective bargaining have become marginalised with a collective bargaining coverage of about 20% in the whole economy, based on a low trade union density of about 12%. It is this low union density combined with employers' reluctance to engage in collective bargaining – also for reasons related to the complicated legal procedures involved in getting rid of those agreements – that explains the low collective bargaining coverage and the persistence of company bargaining (Czarzasty, 2019). Coordination of wage bargaining within the competing trade unions is largely absent. In the manufacturing sector, it is in the subsidiaries of multinational companies that unions have the strongest position and collective bargaining is most widespread. One of the main examples of this is the Polish subsidiary of VW, Volkswagen Poznan. However, the forms of trade union structures and collective bargaining that can be observed here are rare and concentrated on bigger firms in the Polish manufacturing sector, where fragmentation of collective bargaining and strong union competition go hand in hand (Czarzasty, 2022). This makes a re-centralisation of collective bargaining much more unlikely than in Ireland.

Articulation and the role of different actors

The issue of vertical coordination between the sector and company level

In terms of contributing to the "depth" of bargaining – originally formulated by Clegg (1976) and more recently conceptualised by Paolucci & Marginson (2020) and Müller et al. (2019) – the relationship between sectoral and local industrial relations actors is particularly important for the collective bargaining structure and, therefore, for the way decentralisation works along the different paths described above. Articulation of workplace level actors – in the sense of coordination and monitoring, on the one hand, and support and consultancy, on the other hand – at and between the different levels of bargaining and industrial relations is a crucial factor for the development of common strategies, as well as for the enhancement of resources and capabilities to influence workplace outcomes (Lévesque & Murray, 2005). It is therefore not surprising that the issue of coordination, performed by both labour and capital, has emerged, to varying degrees, in our sample countries. Table 3.3. below summarises the main findings regarding the labour side of vertical articulation.

Generally, vertical articulation performed by trade unions appears to be particularly affected by the various types of institutional channels of workplace representation. Single union channels of representation or dual channels, in which trade union bodies or delegates have a prominent role in decentralised bargaining, appear to ease the engagement of sectoral trade unions in workplaces. However, the impact of these institutional factors interacts with the organisational strength of sectoral trade unions as well as their ideas and perceptions on decentralisation, thus reinforcing the argument that coordination may partly depend upon social partners' beliefs, interpretations, and discourses (Ibsen, 2015). Interestingly, among the countries analysed, the most coordinated and structured efforts to liaise with employee representatives in workplace issues were made by sectoral trade unions in the apparently unfavourable institutional contexts of Ireland (dominated by company-level bargaining) and Germany (characterised by

Table 3.3.   Patterns of articulation in the manufacturing sectors

Country	Institutional context	Ideas on decentralisation	Vertical coordination practices
France	Two tier collective bargaining structure / Dual channel of workplace representation	Company-level bargaining interpreted very positively, as a way to invigorate workers' participation and enable union delegates to better defend and represent employees' concerns (CFDT).*	Control on the compliancy of company agreements; support mainly provided in SMEs with low union presence; coordination favoured by trade union delegates also working in sectoral structures.
Germany	Two tier collective bargaining structure / Single channel of workplace representation led by works councils	IG Metall traditionally try to play a role at the decentralised level despite the formal dual character of industrial relations.	Organising strategies aimed at the establishment of works councils; support during derogatory negotiations; works councils as targets in national or regional projects for the improvement of codetermination practices.
Ireland	One tier collective bargaining structure / Single union channel of workplace representation	The collapse of social partnership seen as a challenge for the largest trade union SIPTU. Efforts to re-engage at the workplace level. Positive assessment of decentralised bargaining in well-organised sectors.	Contribution to company-level bargaining agenda; information and practices' sharing; training for shop stewards.
Italy	Two tier collective bargaining structure / Single union channel of workplace representation	The extension of decentralised bargaining seen as a priority (FIM-CISL). Company-level bargaining should supplement sectoral provisions by improving and adapting them (FIM-CISL, FIOM-CGIL).	Sectoral trade unions as signatory parties of some decentralised agreements; coordination; support.
Netherlands	Two tier collective bargaining structure / Single channel led by works councils	Trade unions' focus on centralised levels and acceptance of the exclusive role of works councils at company level.	Coordination with works councils limited to specific issues; consultation rarely occurs.

Country	Institutional context	Ideas on decentralisation	Vertical coordination practices
Poland	One tier collective bargaining structure / Single union channel of workplace representation**	N.A.	Enterprise-level union structures but feeble sectoral union structures.
Spain	Two tier collective bargaining structure / Dual channel of workplace representation	Trade unions not against decentralisation but against the type of decentralisation imposed by government.	Coordination reported when trade unions negotiate in large enterprises.
Sweden	Two tier collective bargaining structure / Single union channel of workplace representation	Importance of creating fruitful conditions for company-level bargaining to improve and adapt sectoral regulations (IF Metall, SACO-affiliated Swedish Association of Graduate Employees).	Consultation; support; control on the quality of company-level agreements.

* Rehfeldt & Vincent, 2018
** Works councils have been introduced by Polish law in 2005, but their development is still very limited.

a dual industrial relations system). Below, we will examine these strategies and those implemented in the other considered countries in-depth.

Firstly, in countries with a single union channel of workplace representation, sectoral trade unions are found to exert a significant influence at the decentralised level, by means of information, consultation, and support for employee representatives. This is the case in Sweden, where there are frequent consultations between workers' representatives and the regional or national trade union structures, as demonstrated by analysis of the Lund site and headquarters of Axis Communications AB (Rönnmar & Iossa, 2022). This is also the case in Italy, where, despite the bargaining autonomy entrusted to the workplace labour representation structure (called RSU), local trade unionists have been known to directly sign decentralised agreements together with RSU members in certain companies. Notably, at TenarisDalmine, local representatives of the trade union federations, *Federazione Impiegati Operai Metallurgici-Confederazione Generale Italiana del Lavoro* (FIOM-CGIL), *Federazione Italiana Metalmeccanici-Confederazione Italiana Sindacati Lavoratori* (FIM-CISL), and *Unione Italiana Lavoratori Metalmeccanici-Unione Italiana del Lavoro* (UILM-UIL), are usually committed to company-level collective bargaining on macro labour topics, while RSU members autonomously participate in daily discussions with the company and negotiations over organisational and technical topics in single areas or departments. Despite the separation of their respective fields of action, the relationships between the two actors are close: they talk and coordinate with each other daily in order to build a shared path to collective negotiations; in addition, local trade unionists can intervene to support their delegates in area-specific discussions in case of conflicts with management, and the RSU members who received most employees' votes in the elections can participate in restricted meetings with the company, along with local trade unionists (Armaroli & Tomassetti, 2022).

In the decentralised context of Poland, which has no history of extended multi-employer bargaining, sectoral trade unions are depicted as feeble and this feature would seem to compromise their relationship with enterprise-level union structures (Czarzasty, 2022). By contrast, in Ireland, where the latest era of centralised social partnership lasted for 22 years, up to 2009, national trade unions are pretty strong and interpreted the end of tripartite bargaining as both a challenge to their role and an opportunity to get closer to their members. As a result, the manufacturing division of the largest trade union, SIPTU, chose to take advantage of certain favourable structural conditions within the pharmaceutical sector (i.e., high degree of internationalisation, steady demand for products, reliance on a highly qualified workforce) to decisively re-engage in workplace issues, by enhancing the decentralised bargaining skills of sector-level officials and shop stewards. This strategy is clearly illustrated by events at one particular PharmaCo site: shop stewards regularly attend the SIPTU College, where they gain a wide range of hard and soft competences in industrial relations; and a trade union official co-directs, along with a chairman elected by the workforce, the workplace representation structure (called the Committee) and provides information on the status of pay talks in other relevant companies in the sector. The coordinating strategy implemented by SIPTU in the pharmaceutical sector has been progressively formalised and become a pattern setter, initially in manufacturing and then in other industries (Paolucci et al., 2022).

France and Spain are characterised by a dual channel of workplace representation, with trade union delegates and structures privileged in bargaining processes. These countries also show a certain degree of coordination. However, in France, the intensity of sectoral trade unions' involvement in workplaces may vary according to certain organisational conditions, like the availability of resources for trade union delegates in workplaces and the role of the latter in the respective trade union organisation. Indeed, at the multinational company Electric, where trade union delegates are endowed by management with sufficient time-off, funds, and training to exert their functions, they also boast a significant deal of autonomy from trade union federations in company-level collective bargaining. By contrast, French trade unions are found to support more actively their delegates in small- and medium-sized companies with a low union presence and fewer resources. A peculiar case is that of Metal, where only the trade union CFDT operates and the trade union delegate also serves on a part-time basis as the general secretary of CFDT at the departmental level and is a member of the trade union's national executive committee. For this reason, the trade union delegate is well informed of pay trends and bargaining results in many other companies in the sector: this information and data then influences collective negotiations at Metal. Moreover, in France, there might be divergencies in the degree of involvement of different sectoral trade unions in the workplace, depending on their various types of internal organisation and democracy. Unlike CGT, CFDT has a reputation for centralism and therefore for stronger coordination by sectoral structures (Kahmann & Vincent, 2022).

Finally, in countries with workforce representation that is essentially led by works councils, the engagement of sectoral trade unions with works councils is not straightforward and depends on the perception of their respective roles and functions. For instance, in Germany, following the progressive delegation to works councils of regulatory functions – mainly on working time – as well as the introduction of opening clauses on deroga-tions in sectoral collective agreements to be negotiated between trade unions and single employers, the metalworkers' organisation IG Metall has increasingly engaged in an effort to effectively "organise decentralisation" at the workplace level. The trade union has traditionally committed itself to playing a role at the workplace and company level despite the formal dual character of German industrial relations. Moreover, the union believes that there can be no prospect of successful decentralised negotiations without or in opposition with works councils. Therefore, IG Metall currently develops "organising" strategies aimed at, among other things, the establishment of works councils in companies; the union liaises with existing works councils and ensures their support during derogatory negotiations; and it targets them in national or regional projects (i.e., Better not Cheaper, Work 2020) for the improvement of co-determination practices (Haipeter & Rosenbohm, 2022). By contrast, and despite the similar institutional setting, trade unions and works councils in the metal and electro-technical industry in the Netherlands have still not found areas of effective coordination and cooperation at the workplace level. An important explanation for this may be the fact that, traditionally, Dutch trade unions have focused on centralised levels and accepted the exclusive role of works councils at company level. As a result, not every works council member is affiliated to a trade union[6] and only a limited proportion of works councils receive advice and consultation from trade union officials.[7] Consequently, works councils have stronger ties with management rather than with trade unions (Jansen & Tros, 2022).

Overall, major problems for the labour side of vertical articulation derive from low rates of trade union density and coverage of workplace labour representation structures, especially in new business activities (e.g., information technologies, research and development) and among young, female, and highly qualified workers. Low unionisation rates are, moreover, likely to jeopardise the coordination between sectoral trade unions and works councils in dual-system countries, since it relies heavily on the fact that works council members are affiliated to trade unions (Haipeter & Rosenbohm, 2022; Jansen & Tros, 2022). In France, challenges may also arise from the evolution of the institutional setting and, more precisely, from the opportunity to perform collective bargaining in small, non-unionised companies granted to non-union representatives and even individual workers, following the 2017 Macron ordinances (Kahmann & Vincent, 2022).

As for the capital side, although there is less evidence, certain practices of vertical articulation, such as information, consultation, or assistance in decentralised negotiations, are performed by employers' associations, too, especially in some multi-tier collective bargaining systems like France and Germany (Haipeter & Rosenbohm, 2022; Kahmann & Vincent, 2022). For instance, during derogation negotiations in the German metalworking sector, the employers' association, Gesamtmetall, either directly conducts the bargaining process or provides advice to companies. Its involvement is meant, firstly, to assess whether an increase in derogations signals a need to reform the industry agreement, and secondly, to exercise control over possibly sensitive cases in which derogations might change the conditions for inter-firm competition in a market (Haipeter & Rosenbohm, 2022).

6   There is no representative research about the proportions of trade union members in works councils in the Netherlands. However, in 2015, a survey among 436 works council members counted 64% trade union membership among the respondents (Snel et al., 2016). Van den Berg et al. (2019) counted 39% membership of organised works councils.

7   A comparative study from WSI/Hans-Böckler-Stiftung about works councils in Germany and the Netherlands estimates that almost 60% of Dutch works councils never/hardly ever receives advice from trade unions, compared with 28% of works councils in Germany (Van den Berg et al., 2019).

Importantly, in the decentralised context of Ireland, the main employers' confederation, IBEC, is found to make certain coordination efforts at the company level. After the collapse of the social partnership, it agreed a protocol with the trade union confederation, ICTU, aimed at orienting collective bargaining in private and commercial state-owned companies. Moreover, although it is unusual for IBEC to directly participate in company-level bargaining, one of its representatives sits at the negotiation table of PharmaCo, given the company's role as a pattern setter in collective bargaining in the pharmaceutical sector (Paolucci et al., 2022). Generally, the involvement of employers' associations at the workplace level is structurally circumscribed by the limited coverage of decentralised bargaining across SMEs, especially in Italy, Spain, and the Netherlands (Armaroli & Tomassetti, 2022; Muñoz Ruiz & Ramos Martín, 2022; Jansen & Tros, 2022). It is no wonder, then, that, in the Netherlands, small- and medium-sized companies in the metal and electro-technical industry are covered by a specific collective agreement, whose normative standards are already differentiated according to various branches and can be subject to deviation at firm level in only a very few cases (Jansen & Tros, 2022). Similarly, in Italy, a shift backwards, from the workplace to the sector, has been reported with reference to the regulation of multi-week working times, which is no longer delegated to decentralised bargaining as it is difficult to execute, especially in small- and medium-sized metal companies (Armaroli & Tomassetti, 2022). The interests of the membership are therefore crucial in explaining the actions of employers' associations, also in the field of collective bargaining, which, in turn, are relevant for the definition, evolution, and maintenance of national collective bargaining structures. The case of Germany is exemplary in this sense, since, in an effort to counter the decline in their membership rates, many employers' associations allowed member companies to "opt out" of sectoral collective agreements, thus exacerbating the erosion of sectoral collective bargaining (Haipeter & Rosenbohm, 2022).

Firm-level coordination issues in multi-actor and multi-tier collective bargaining structures

Horizontal and vertical coordination issues, as well as problems of collective bargaining effectiveness, may arise not only between sectoral and firm levels, but also within firms. There are two factors that trigger company-level articulation problems: union pluralism and a multi-establishment corporate structure, and sometimes both factors interact with one another.

Firstly, in countries characterised by union pluralism (like France, Spain, and Italy), competition and frictions are found to affect different trade unions and/or delegates belonging to different organisations. Divergence in the ideas, values, and strategies of the various trade unions operating at company level can engender disunity on the labour side in negotiations, as shown by the cases of Electric and Aero in France. Here, CGT union delegates – who are mandated by the federations – have not always signed decentralised collective agreements along with the other representative trade unions at the workplace level (Kahmann & Vincent, 2022). Competitive relationships have also been reported in the analysis of TenarisDalmine in Italy, where the quality of interactions between trade union delegates was compromised at the turn of the 2000s–2010s by the signature of "separate" collective agreements at the sectoral level. They are so named because they were signed by the most representative trade union federations, with the exception of FIOM-CGIL, which depicted them as detrimental to workers' rights and as bowing to employers' demands (Armaroli & Tomassetti, 2022).

In addition to inter-organisational differences, problems of collective bargaining coordination and effectiveness may also arise from the presence of a plurality of orientations within a single trade union organisation. In this regard, it is worth mentioning that a certain working time arrangement established in the TenarisDalmine collective agreement, signed by all representative trade unions (FIOM-CGIL, FIM-CISL, and UILM-UIL), was not easily accepted and applied at the company's steel shop, due to the presence of a radical fringe of the trade union FIOM-CGIL, which opposed the deal (Armaroli & Tomassetti, 2022).

By contrast, more collaborative relationships and greater coordination between different workers' organisations are reported in countries such as Ireland and Sweden, where workforce representation is organised by category (e.g., blue collars, white collars, professionals and university graduates, craft workers, etc.) and there is not usually competition for members. However, divergence on collective bargaining topics can also occur between trade unions representing different workers' categories, especially if they are sat at the same negotiation table. This happens at DSM in the Netherlands, where the trade union for senior and professional staff, does not support the policy of the most representative trade union FNV regarding a levelling of wages (Jansen & Tros, 2022). Similarly, with reference to one site of FoodCo in Ireland, Paolucci et al. (2022) point to the lack of communication between SIPTU, representing the majority of employees, and Connect, which encompasses craft workers, and, subsequently, their inability to conduct joint or at least coordinated negotiations. This situation, albeit uncommon in Ireland, clearly shows that horizontal coordination on collective bargaining between different trade unions cannot be taken for granted and largely depends upon the quality of personal relationships between single trade unionists (Paolucci et al., 2022).

To further complicate this picture, it must be highlighted that firm-level collective bargaining cannot be considered as a one-tier regulation field. The geographical expansion and organisational fragmentation of corporate structures have ended up adding one or more layers to collective bargaining, taking place at group, subsidiary, establishment, and even department level in most of the analysed countries. Parallel to this, with respect to workforce representation, there is evidence of site-level employee representatives, a central coordinating structure at company or group level, as well as European or global works councils. As observed by Rönnmar & Iossa (2022), vertical articulation across different collective bargaining levels and their respective actors in multi-establishment companies can follow very different logics and pathways, depending on the specific internal practices and procedures, which are formalised to a greater or lesser degree. For instance, vertical coordination attempts are performed within TenarisDalmine in Italy, where a company-level collective agreement, signed by local trade unionists and usually renewed every three years, acts as a framework, and whose general provisions, especially in the field of work organisation, are developed in more detail and adapted in single establishments and/or departments by employee representatives. In terms of the contents of departmental agreements, they are found to be similar but not the same, depending on the specific power relations in single areas (Armaroli & Tomassetti, 2022). Similarly, at the French company Aero, there is a group-level collective agreement that sets a pay range, which every subsidiary agreement is required to stay within, whereas company-level actors boast greater autonomy from the group management with respect to other issues (Kahmann & Vincent, 2022).

With specific regard to horizontal coordination across different sites, it can be made even more complex by the presence of different trade unions. For example, the bargaining rounds at two Irish sites of FoodCo, respectively covered by SIPTU and Unite the Union (a British trade union whose representation scope overlaps that of SIPTU and that also operates in Ireland), are not synchronised and a common trade union strategy is lacking. However, this uncoordinated situation is quite exceptional in the country's decentralised bargaining landscape (Paolucci et al., 2022).

An important centralisation trend in collective bargaining has been detected in some multi-establishment firms in the Netherlands, Italy, and France, where collective regulations are increasingly agreed at group/

corporate level, with little room for manoeuvre (except on a few topics, mainly related to working time and work organisation) for workplace-level social partners. On the one hand, this trend can contribute to making labour regulations homogeneous across the different establishments, thus reducing the chances of intra-firm competition and related discontent, which is apparent, for instance, at TenarisDalmine in Italy. Indeed, some trade unionists and delegates at the company complained about the fact that, over the years, partly due to the atypical character of the area, priority has been given to collective bargaining at the steel shop, leading to wage increases that were slightly higher than in other departments and different working-time regimes (Armaroli & Tomassetti, 2022). On the other hand, centralisation in decentralised bargaining may be blamed on trade unionists who progressively widen the distance between workers, actors, and the fora of negotiations, hence compromising union legitimacy and workers' interests in applying for workplace representation roles, as proved by the experience at Electric in France. Here, according to the CGT central delegate, centralisation of company-level industrial relations would increasingly engender difficulties for trade unions in mobilising workers and persuading them to stand in professional elections for works council mandates (Kahmann & Vincent, 2022).

Finally, the quality of industrial relations processes and outcomes in multinational enterprises can depend upon coordination with foreign trade unions operating at different sites in Europe, also within the framework of European or global workforce representation structures. For instance, at the Volkswagen site in Poznań (Poland), relationships with trade unionists from the German headquarters who sit on the group's supervisory board are deemed as important for the Polish union to access relevant corporate information. Moreover, at the Lacroix plant of Kwidzyn (Poland), contacts with foreign trade unions were instrumental in the process of founding the European Works Council, which, in turn, facilitates frequent interactions between trade unions from different plants in Europe and is a valuable source of information about managerial strategies and decisions (Czarzasty, 2022).

Conclusions

The decentralisation of collective bargaining is an overarching trend in Europe's manufacturing sectors. In all the countries studied decentralisation has taken place in the one or the other way. In this chapter, we have distinguished six pathways of decentralisation, ranging from different forms of organised decentralisation to forms of disorganised decentralisation, the latter also including the state of full decentralisation with collective bargaining located solely at the company level. Given the diversity of forms, it can be stated that the manufacturing sector still plays a leading role as a trendsetter of decentralisation within the respective economies. However, we argue that this is not necessarily to be regarded a sign of the weakness of collective bargaining and its actors in this sector, but rather it is to be interpreted as an element of continuity and as an indicator of relative strength compared to other sectors, as in most of the cases decentralisation was kept within the margins of organised decentralisation. Even in the cases of full decentralisation, the manufacturing sector is doing better than many other sectors in terms of collective bargaining coverage and wage increases. In many countries, the control of decentralisation is based on a collective bargaining coverage or trade union density that exceeds the average of the economy. At the same time, the sector's leading position in decentralisation signals a shift of the role the sector plays in defining the overall pattern of collective bargaining in the economies. Whereas previously, the manufacturing sector was the core of pattern bargaining with respect to wages in many countries, today it is forming a centre of new patterns of decentralisation. Where its role as a pace setter for wages has remained, like in Italy or Sweden, it is more in the sense of guaranteeing the competitiveness of the economy. In other cases, like Germany, the former pattern has dissolved in recent decades due to low wage growth in the service sector.

However, these pathways of decentralisation can be observed in the manufacturing sectors of our sample countries to very different degrees. Some countries, like Germany and Italy, are affected by most of them, whereas manufacturing in other countries only show one or two of these pathways. Additionally, the timing of decentralisation is very different. In some cases, the financial crisis of 2008 and 2009 played an important role for – in these cases state-led – decentralisation; in other cases, decentralisation has been a trend developing over decades. There are different factors that explain these variations within the decentralisation of collective bargaining. One of them is the institutional differences between the countries of our sample in terms of the channels of representation. In countries with single channels formed by only trade unions, or in dual channel systems with trade unions as actors in local bargaining, organised decentralisation mainly takes the form of additional collective bargaining either on wages or on new topics, which are located at the company level. In systems with single channels led by works councils, the topics for the company level are usually dealt with by works councils in terms of workplace agreements, either as a part of their usual business or based on opening clauses in the sectoral collective agreements if these topics refer to issues dealt with in these agreements.

A second factor is the role of the state as a legislator framing the legal context of collective bargaining. In many of our cases, the state has played an active role in decentralisation. In the financial crisis, in Italy and Spain the state created a legal frame for derogations; in France, the state developed this possibility later; and in Germany, it put pressure on the collective bargaining actors in the manufacturing sector to define an opening clause in the collective agreements for this purpose. In Ireland, the state has not maintained the practice of national social pacts in the financial crisis. Finally, in Poland, the state has created complicated legal regulations for the after-effects of collective bargaining agreements when they have expired, which leads companies to refrain from collective bargaining.

A third important factor for the variations in decentralisation in the manufacturing sector is the strategies, resources, and capabilities of the collective bargaining actors – the trade unions, on the one hand, and the employers' associations or single employers, on the other hand. In most of our countries, it is the employers' camp that is the driving force of decentralisation. Striving for decentralisation, employers demand either collective bargaining regulations that are more tailored to what they consider to be the needs of their companies and establishments, or they opt for less and weaker regulations that allow them to reduce labour costs. However, looking at the employers' associations of the manufacturing sectors in the sample countries, it can be stated that there are some fundamental national differences regarding employers' orientations. On the one hand, in countries like Spain, the Netherlands, and Italy, most SMEs are covered by sectoral bargaining but are not willing to perform decentralised bargaining, mainly due to high transaction costs and the reluctance to involve trade unions in their work settings. In the Italian metalworking sector, there has even been a regulatory shift backwards, from the workplace to the sector, with respect to the regulation of multi-week working times, which is no longer delegated to decentralised bargaining as this is difficult to be execute in certain SMEs. On the other hand, in Germany, Ireland, and Poland and, to a lesser extent in Italy, employers are keen to avoid either sectoral regulations or collective bargaining at all. In Germany, the employers' association of the sector has successfully enforced both derogations to fall short of sectoral wage norms and allowed associations to "opt-out," of and thus break with the obligation to implement sectoral bargaining norms. In Ireland, the employers left the tripartite social dialogue in the financial crisis and, by doing so, dissolved national and sectoral collective bargaining. In Poland, many companies reject collective bargaining with trade unions in the first place. In Italy, employers in labour-intensive and outsourcing branches may be attracted by the application of "cheaper," non-representative sectoral collective agreements to remain competitive. However, in most of the countries, the employers largely refrained from the strategies of disorganised decentralisation, even when, like in France, Italy, and Spain, the state has created legislative opening clauses for derogations. Whereas in Spain and, to a lesser extent, in Italy this was used only in a small number of cases, in France it is virtually absent. In the German manufacturing sector, with its widespread use of derogations, it was only thanks to the coordination efforts of the trade union that it was possible to reconcile the practice of derogations with sectoral collective bargaining.

However, decentralisation has proven to be in favour of the trade unions too, for two reasons. On the one hand, it might bring negotiations closer to the employees, so that the motivation to take part in labour actions might increase and the legitimacy of the trade unions improves. In this way, it allows to combine collective action and organising efforts of the unions at the workplace. On the other hand, decentral regulations might increase the autonomy of workers for instance in terms of the options of working time flexibility they can make use of, which might increase their satisfaction with their labour representatives.

However, our analysis also shows the importance of articulation between the different levels of trade union interest representation – or workers representation by works councils – practiced by the trade unions as a precondition for organised decentralisation. It is trade union articulation in the sense of coordination and monitoring, on the one hand, and support and consultancy for the local level, on the other hand, which has proven to be a core precondition for the practice of organised decentralisation. Trade unions have to coordinate and control local bargaining in a way that minimum standards, defined at sectoral level, are adhered to at company level. At the same time, they should also control local parties in those cases where company bargaining takes place outside the scope of sectoral bargaining. Moreover, they have to ensure that the local actors have resources and skills at their disposal to be able to negotiate collective agreements effectively. Skills can be enhanced by training programmes or consultancy given by the unions. Among the most advanced practices in this area are the campaigns of the German IG Metall to activate works councils to cope more effectively with new topics like digitalisation, which is a step beyond reactive consultancy. The collective bargaining practises adopted by Swedish social partners in the manufacturing sector to deal with the impact of the COVID-19 pandemic on employment can also be classified as an example of functioning coordination between levels of negotiations. The quick response and the high number of collective agreements on short-term work signed in the sector show the high degree of coordination and the possibility for local level to respond to expertise and experience from national sectoral levels. However, in many countries, trade union articulation in the manufacturing sectors is far from being all-encompassing or sufficient, either because of a lack of resources at the unions' headquarters or because of a lack of trade union – or works councils – presence at the level of companies or establishments. Indeed, this seems to be the Achilles' heels of organised decentralisation in the manufacturing sectors in most European countries.

References

Ahlberg K. & Bruun N. (2005). Sweden: Transition through collective bargaining. In Blank T. & Rose E. (Eds.), *Collective bargaining and wages in comparative perspective: Germany, France, the Netherlands, Sweden and the United Kingdom* (pp. 117–143). Kluwer Law International.

Armaroli, I. & Tomassetti, P. (2022). Decentralised bargaining in Italy: CODEBAR-project. https://aias-hsi.uva.nl/en/projects-a-z/codebar/codebar.html

Baccaro, L. & Howell, C. (2017). *Trajectories of neoliberal transformation: European industrial relations since the 1970s.* Cambridge University Press.

Clegg, I. A. (1976). *Trade unionism under collective bargaining: A theory based on comparisons of six countries.* B. Blackwell.

CNEL (2021). 14° Report periodico dei Contratti Collettivi Nazionali di Lavoro vigenti depositati nell'Archivio CNEL. https://www.cnel.it/Portals/0/CNEL/Reports/CCN-L/14%C2%B0_report_CCNL_vigenti_31_12_2021.pdf?ver=2022-01-26-150458-350

Crouch, C. & Voelzkow, H. (2004). Introduction. In Crouch C. et al. *Changing governance of local economies: Responses of European local production systems* (pp. 1–10). Oxford University Press.

Crouch, C. (1993). *Industrial relations and European state traditions.* Clarendon Press.

Czarzasty, J. (2022). Decentralised bargaining in Poland. CODEBAR-project. https:// aias-hsi.uva.nl/en/projects-a-z/codebar/codebar.html

Czarzasty, J. (2019). Collective bargaining in Poland: A near-death experience. In: Müller, T., Vandaele, K., & Waddington, J. (Eds.), *Collective bargaining in Europe. Towards an endgame* (pp. 465–481). ETUI.

Eurofound (2019). *The future of manufacturing in Europe, Publications Office of the European Union.*

Federmeccanica (2018). Indagine sul lavoro nell'industria metalmeccanica. https://www.federmeccanica.it/centro-studi/indagine-sul-lavoro-nell-industria-metalmeccanica.html.

Glavå M. (2010). Kunskapssamhället, facket och den svenska modellen: Reflektioner kring ett lönesänkningsavtal. In Ahlberg K. (Ed.), *Vänbok till Ronnie Eklund* (pp. 245–253). Iustus.

Gunnigle, P., Lavelle, J., & Monaghan, S. (2018). Multinational companies and human resource management in Ireland during the recession: A retrospective from a highly globalized economy. *Thunderbird International Business Review*, 1(9): 481-489.

Haipeter, T. (2016). The interests of white-collar workers and their representation in the German manufacturing sector: New initiatives, opportunity structures, framing and resources. *Industrial Relations Journal* 47 (4): 304–321

Haipeter, T. & Rosenbohm, S. (2022). Decentralised bargaining in Germany CODEBAR-project. https://aias-hsi.uva.nl/en/projects-a-z/codebar/codebar.html

Ibsen, C. L. (2015). Three approaches to coordinated bargaining: A case for power-er-based explanations. *European Journal of Industrial Relations*. 21(1): 39–56.

Jansen, N., Tros, F. (2022). Decentralised bargaining in the Netherlands. CODEBAR-project. https://aias-hsi.uva.nl/en/projects-a-z/codebar/codebar.html

Kahmann, M. & Vincent, C. (2022). Decentralised bargaining in France. CODEBAR-project. https://aias-hsi.uva.nl/en/projects-a-z/codebar/codebar.html

Kjellberg, A. (2019). Sweden: Collective bargaining under the industry norm. In Müller, T., Vandaele, K., & Waddington, J. (Eds.) *Collective bargaining in Europe: Towards an endgame*. (pp. 583–603). ETUI.

Leonardi, S., Ambra, M. C., & Ciarini, A. (2017). Italian collective bargaining at a turning point. WP CSDLE 'Massimo D'Antona'.INT – 139/2017. https://csdle.lex.unict.it/working-papers/wp-csdle-m-dantona-int/italian-collective-bargaining-turning-point

Lévesque, C. & Murray, G. (2005). Union involvement in workplace change. *British Journal of Industrial Relations*, 43(3): 489–514.

Medlingsinstitutet (2020). *Avtalsrörelsen och lönebildningen 2019. Medlingsinstitutets årsrapport.* Medlingsinstitutet.

Medlingsinstitutet (2022). *Avtalsrörelsen och lönebildningen 2021. Medlingsinstitutets årsrapport.* Medlingsinstitutet.

Ministero del lavoro e delle politiche sociali (2023). *Report deposito contratti ex art. 14 d.lgs. 151/2015.*

Müller, T., Dølvik, J., Ibsen C., & Schulten, T. (2018). The manufacturing sector: Still an anchor for pattern bargaining within and across countries? *European Journal of Industrial Relations*, 24(4): 357–372.

Müeller, T. Vandaele, K., & Waddington, J (2019). *Collective bargaining in Europe: Towards an endgame.* ETUI.

Muñoz Ruiz, A. & Ramos Martín, N., (2022). Decentralised bargaining in Spain. CODEBAR project. https://aias-hsi.uva.nl/en/projects-a-z/codebar/codebar.html

Paolucci, V. & Marginson, P. (2020). Collective bargaining towards mutual flexibility and security goals in large internationalised companies: Why do institutions (still) matter? *Industrial Relations Journal*, 51(4): 329–350

Paolucci, V. Roche, W.K., & Gormley, T. (2022). Decentralised bargaining in Ireland. CODEBAR-project. https://aias-hsi.uva.nl/en/projects-a-z/codebar/codebar.html

Pedersini, R. (2019). Italy: Institutionalisation and resilience in a changing economic and political environment. In: Müller, T., Vandaele, K., & Waddington, J. (Eds.), *Collective bargaining in Europe: Towards an Endgame* (pp. 337–359). ETUI.

Rehfeldt, U. & Vincent, C. (2018). The decentralisation of collective bargaining in France: an escalating process. In Leonardi, S. & Pedersini, R. (Eds.). *Multi-employer bargaining under pressure: Decentralisation trends in five European countries* (pp 151–184). ETUI.

Rocha, F. (2018). Strengthening the decentralisation of collective bargaining in Spain: Between legal changes and real developments. In: Leonardi, S. & Pedersni, R. (Eds.), *Multi employer bargaining under pressure: Decentralisation in five European countries* (pp. 225–261). ETUI.

Rodríguez, C. J. F., Rojo, R. I., & Lucio, M. M. (2019). Spain: Challenges to legitimacy and representation in a context of fragmentation and neoliberal reform. In: Müller, T., Vandaele, K., & Waddington, J. (Eds.), *Collective bargaining in Europe. Towards an endgame* (pp. 563–581). ETUI.

Rönnmar, M. & Iossa, A. (2022). Decentralised bargaining in Sweden. CODEBAR-project. https://aias-hsi.uva.nl/en/projects-a-z/codebar/codebar.html

Rönnmar, M. (2019). Autonomous collective bargaining in Sweden under pressure. In López J. (Ed.), *Collective bargaining and collective action: Labour agency and governance in the 21st century?* (pp. 189–212). Hart Publishing.

Thörnqvist, C. (1999). The decentralisation of industrial relations: The Swedish case in comparative perspective. *European Journal of Industrial Relations*, 5(1): 71–87.

Traxler, F. (1995). Farewell to labour market associations? Organized versus disorganised decentralisation as a map for industrial relations. In: Crouch, C. & Traxler, F. (Eds.), *Organized industrial relations in Europe: What future?* (pp. 3–20). Avebury.

Traxler, F. (1999). Gewerkschaften und Arbeitgeberverbände: Probleme der Verbandsbildung und Interessenvreinheitlichung. In: Müller-Jentsch, W. (Ed.), Konfliktpartnerschaft. Akteure und Institutionen der industriellen Beziehungen, 3rd edn, (pp–78). Hampp.

Waddington J., Müller, T., & Vandaele, K. (2019). Setting the scene: Collective bargaining under neoliberalism. In Müller, T., Vandaele, K., & Waddington, J. (Eds.), *Collective bargaining in Europe: Towards an endgame* (pp. 1–32). ETUI.

4. Decentralisation of Collective Bargaining in the Retail Sector

Valentina Paolucci, Jan Czarzasty,[1] Ana Belén Muñoz Ruiz,[2] Nuria Ramos Martín

Abstract

This chapter shows that traditional industrial relations classifications, based on national institutional features, have become sector-specific. Company case studies indicate that in retailing, which is characterised by generally poor working conditions, market structures and company characteristics tend to condition unions' capacity to engage in collective bargaining. Only in Sweden, where the institutional framework continues to provide a significant degree of procedural security through coordinating mechanisms, have unions been able to retain control over the decentralisation process and to play an important role at the company level. Nevertheless, in large, often internationalised companies, unions that are proactive and willing to mobilise their organisational resources, as demonstrated by Irish and German cases, are still able to make a positive difference for workers.

Keywords: retailing, trade union strategies, institutions, markets, collective bargaining decentralisation

Introduction

Following the increasing decentralisation of collective bargaining across all EU countries, recent research suggests that greater attention should be paid

1   The Polish contribution to this chapter is based on work published as part of an international research project co-financed by the Ministry of Science and Higher Education in Poland, under the "PNW" scheme in 2020–2022, under agreement no 5159/GRANT KE/2020/2.

2   Ana Belén Muñoz Ruiz has conducted the qualitative research related to the case study on Spain. The data extracted from the interviews have been managed according to the rules and protocols applicable at the UCIII-Madrid.

Frank Tros (ed.). *Pathways in Decentralised Collective Bargaining in Europe.* Amsterdam: Amsterdam University Press, 2023

DOI 10.5117/9789048560233_CH04

to the role of sectoral/structural conditions in order to understand the kind of industrial relations (IR) that may affect a company (Bechter et al., 2011; Keune and Pedaci, 2020). Hence, this chapter explores the responses of trade unions to the decentralisation of collective bargaining in the retail sector across varying countries characterised by different institutions (Visser, 2009). The focus on the retail sector is interesting for two reasons. Firstly, volatile market conditions have made retailing a particularly hostile context for trade unions to represent workers and engage in collective bargaining. Secondly, in contrast to manufacturing, there is little empirical evidence to date on the strategies of trade unions in retailing following the decentralisation of collective bargaining. Our distinctive comparative focus, in which sectors are compared within their national contexts and companies within their sectoral contexts, expands our understanding of the institutional and non-institutional factors that shape the strategies, processes, and outcomes of collective bargaining. In line with Thelen's (2014) work, we find that all countries have been affected by decentralisation in the process of bargaining, reducing differences amongst them and, consequently, there is a need for revising existing theoretical lenses that classify countries according to a static notion of industrial relations institutions . Moreover, in a retail context, where industrial relations institutions are deteriorating, market structures are found to play the most significant role in explaining unions' positions and their capacity to participate in the regulation of working conditions at the sector level. Finally, a key finding is that the weakness of both institutional and structural conditions can sometimes revitalise unions at the company level and encourage them to embrace new opportunities and resources to organise workers.

A multi-level comparison of decentralised bargaining across six countries

Streeck and Thelen (2005) have contributed to the field of comparative institutional analysis by formulating the notion of geographical specificity and suggesting that there is a link between the mechanisms that shape institutions and the specific structures of the society within which they emerge (Streeck, 1992; Crouch, 2005; Streeck & Thelen, 2005). Furthermore, these scholars have applied the idea of embeddedness to the study of capitalist diversity, arguing that the different impact that similar developments have in different countries can be explained through an analysis of the alternative institutional arrangements found in the various nation states (Locke

& Thelen, 1995; Crouch & Streeck, 1997; Streeck & Thelen, 2005). Finally, these authors have underscored the role of power relations and conflict and, at the same time, attempted to reconcile the structuring capacity of institutions with a space for individual agency and "conflictual encounters" (Djelic, 2010:25). It is in their particular interpretation of institutions that this chapter finds its theoretical underpinning, as it helps to observe six countries – Sweden, Germany, Spain, Italy, Ireland, and Poland – in relation to the institutional frameworks in which they are embedded. Consistent with Streeck and Thelen's approach, we contextualise the cross-national comparison at the sector and firm levels. We explore how an important trend, such as collective bargaining decentralisation, is mediated by sector-specific and companies' institutional arrangements, and subsequently translated into actors' strategies in a way that accounts for both similarity and diversity of outcomes across cases (Thelen, 2010).

Crucially, when exploring differences and similarities, we assume that, not only do institutional rules matter but so do the identities, interests, and resources of actors involved in them (Crouch, 2005; Streeck & Thelen, 2005; Thelen, 2010). Actors may be socialised by institutions or deliberately conform to them. In addition, they may also stray from or re-interpret institutions in a way that alter their foundations (Locke & Thelen, 1996; Crouch 2005; Campbell, 2009). This theoretical perspective allows a focus on *institutionalisation as a dynamic and actor-centred social process* (Hirsch, 1997; Jackson, 2009:67) as well as acknowledging that actors and institutions may change over time in a recursive and dialectical fashion (Streeck, 2009; Thelen, 2010). We go beyond an ideal-typical interpretation of case studies, which treats boundaries as impenetrable and systems as closed. Instead, we proceed at two levels simultaneously: the level of systems – macro-social level – and within the systems themselves. Specifically, our cross-national comparison involves countries with different institutional systems. Moreover, while the focus is on a single sector of economic activity, the retail sector, we explore collective bargaining developments at the company level. Thus, our research design reflects the multi-level nature of this study in which sectors are compared within their national contexts and companies within their sectoral contexts.

Classification of countries and the sector-focus approach

Visser (2009) systematises the existent countries' classifications around three emerging themes: employment regimes (Gallie, 2007; Esping-Andersen, 1990; Amable, 2000); industrial relations regimes (Crouch, 2005; Schmidt, 2006;

Molina & Rhodes, 2007); and production regimes (Hall & Soskice, 2001). Consistent with previous attempts, his classification captures the interaction between public policies, collective bargaining, and social dialogue in relation to different state traditions, institutions, and practices. In addition, Visser's clusters, namely, North, Centre-West, South, West, and Centre-East (see Table 4.1.), offer a more nuanced comparative lens whereby diversity can be approached from different perspectives. For example, these clusters help formulate series of expectations not only on the relationship between international trends – such as collective bargaining decentralisation – and institutions of industrial relations, but also of economic and social coordination. They are based on the assumption that dealing with policymakers does not necessarily mean that research needs to be concerned only with formal rules or the restraint of economic actors (Crouch 2005:44). Indeed, Visser's clusters acknowledge that institutions can also be interpreted as open boundaries, and not only as constraining factors. The main advantage of this analytical approach is that it takes into account different forms of institutionalisation (Bechter et al., 2012; Prosser, 2015) and that it reflects important factors of labour market governance (Esping-Andersen, 1990). These are all expected to interplay with actors' strategies and contextual issues, producing cross-national similarities (and/or within countries differences), which this chapter aims to explain. A summary of Visser's classification is provided further in Table 4.1.

In order to explore collective bargaining decentralisation across countries, we apply a sector-focus approach and assume that employers and employees belonging to the same industry experience similar technology challenges and market environments, and therefore also similar postures on collective bargaining decentralisation (Marginson & Sisson, 2006). The selected countries are Sweden, Germany, Italy, Spain, Ireland, and Poland, each embodying one of the Visser's country clusters (2009), namely, North, Centre-West, South, West, Centre-East, respectively, while the selected sector is retailing, which is often described as a hostile context for trade unions to engage in negotiations (Mrozowicki et al., 2013). This is a low wage and low-skill sector, which, due to its tenuous workers' structural resources, has been characterised by a strong deterioration of working conditions and employment relations (Geppert et al., 2014).

A comparative analysis across these countries, and sector, makes a series of theoretical contributions. First, it sheds light on the role of national- and sector-level actors and institutions in shaping varying models of decentralised bargaining. Second, it elucidates whether the existence of a national framework that steers local bargaining is a pre-condition for collective

Table 4.1.   Visser's classification of countries in Europe

	North	Centre-west	South	West	Centre-east
Production regime	Coordinated market economy		Statist market economy	Liberal market economy	Statist or liberal?
Welfare regime	Universalistic	Segmented (status-oriented, corporatist)		Residual	Segmented or residual?
Employment regime	Inclusive	Dualistic		Liberal	
Industrial relations regime	Organised corporatism	Social partnership	Polarised/state-centred	Liberal pluralism	Fragmented/state-centred
Power balance	Labour-oriented	Balanced	Alternating	Employer oriented	
Principal level of bargaining	Sector		Variable/unstable	Company	
Bargaining style	Integrating		Conflict-oriented		Acquiescent
Role of social partners in public policy	Institutionalised		Irregular/politicised	Rare/event-driven	Irregular/politicised
Role of the state in industrial relations	Limited (mediator)	"Shadow of hierarchy"	Frequent intervention	Non-intervention	Organiser of transition
Employee representation	Union based/high coverage	Dual system/high coverage	Variable (*)	Union based/small coverage	
Countries	Denmark Finland Norway Sweden	Belgium Germany (Ireland) Luxembourg Netherlands Austria Slovenia (Finland)	Greece Spain France Italy (Hungary) Portugal	Ireland Malta Cyprus UK	Bulgaria Czech Republic Estonia Latvia Lithuania Hungary Poland Romania Slovakia

Source: J. Visser, extended on the basis of Ebbinghaus & Visser (1997), Crouch (1993, 1996), Esping-Andersen (1990), Schmidt (2002, 2006) and Platzer & Kohl (2007).
(*) In France, employee representation in firms incorporates both principles, in Spain and Portugal it is dualist, in Italy and Greece it is merged with the unions but based on statutory rights.

bargaining to take place at the company level. Third, it reveals whether and how company-level actors engage with the competences they have been assigned by higher institutional levels, and helps in assessing the outcomes of their interactions. Finally, in contexts where multi-employer bargaining is not in place, it sheds light on the actors' capability to develop their own strategies in response to their embedded interpersonal network. It also provides information on the meaning that these particular issues possess for their identities.

Varieties of collective bargaining decentralisation

In her work on varieties of liberalisation, Thelen (2014) argues that political-economic institutions – collective bargaining included – have followed three trajectories of change: (1) deregulatory liberalisation; (2) dualising liberalisation; and (3) embedded flexibilisation.

It is through these theoretical lenses that we observe current developments in collective bargaining decentralisation across Ireland, Poland, Germany, Italy/Spain, and Sweden. We argue that, despite belonging to different country clusters, these countries have all undergone one of the following liberalisation processes. By reshaping their IR landscape, such change processes have either reduced or widened the institutional variation across them.

Deregulatory liberalisation: This approach to bargaining decentralisation involves the active dismantling by the state (or employers' associations) of the coordinating capacities of bargaining institutions and actors, as well as the reduction of bargaining coverage. Deregulation is characterised by change through "displacement" because mechanisms aimed at regulating collective bargaining are "set aside in favour of arrangements that re-impose the discipline of the market" (Thelen, 2014:13). Such positions towards collective institutions and regulations can be found in countries including Ireland and Poland. In both contexts, employers do not possess stable coordinating capacities and have thus been successful in weakening unions as well.

Dualising liberalisation: This approach to bargaining decentralisation involves continued institutional coordination but in a context of the number of firms and workers covered by collective bargaining narrowing. Dualisation does not involve a clear attempt at dismantling bargaining arrangements. In fact, while such arrangements display a varying degree of resiliency – depending on the country and the sector (Paolucci & Marginson, 2020) – the system allows for unregulated and unorganised sub-systems that are characterised by inferior status and protections for workers outside the national or sectoral coordinating framework. Dualisation can be the result of increasing cooperation between unions and employers' associations in certain sectors, such as the chemical and pharmaceuticals sectors in Italy (Paolucci & Galetto, 2019), or between organised workers and management in large firms, such as in Germany (Thelen & Kume, 2006). Dualisation is characterised by change through "drift," whereby collective bargaining institutions remain in place, but they "fail to take hold outside the industrial core" (Thelen, 2014: 14). This is the case in countries such as Germany, Italy, and Spain where membership of unions and employers' associations is, indeed, concentrated in traditional industries (i.e., manufacturing, see Chapter 3; Haipeter et al., 2023) and collective bargaining coverage does not reach sectors such as retail.

Embedded flexibilisation: This approach to bargaining decentralisation involves the flexibilisation of collective regulations but "within the context of a continued strong and inclusive framework that collectivises risks" (Thelen, 2014:14). More specifically, collective bargaining institutions are aimed at making workers more flexible and mobile, while simultaneously protecting them from external risks. This form of decentralisation is offered through the "functional conversion" of collective bargaining to new goals and to the reconfiguration of relationships between all the actors involved. Embedded flexibilisation promotes equality, but not deliberately to it is not premised on protect workers from market forces. Rather, it makes sure that they adapt their skills and capacities to changing market conditions.

Accounting for the role of both institutions and actors in facilitating and constraining the decentralisation of collective bargaining

The features of collective bargaining systems are important in facilitating (and constraining) company-level negotiations (Marginson & Galetto, 2016; Pulignano & Keune, 2015). So long as they are encompassing in their workforce coverage, the possibility of individual employers exiting in favour of unilateral management regulation is minimised (Traxler 2003). The resulting procedural security is of particular salience for trade unions and their propensity to accept an expansion of competences in local-level negotiations. Decentralisation within such arrangements offers the promise of combining the advantages of common standards on major substantive issues, such as pay scales and the duration of working time, with scope for local variation in implementation and detail (Marginson & Sisson 2006).

There are, however, some key cross-national differences between collective bargaining arrangements that may affect actors' capacity to facilitate the conclusion of company-level collective agreements. We assume that the most relevant difference is the depth of bargaining, originally defined by Clegg (1976:8–9) as the "involvement of local union officers and shop-stewards in the administration of [sector-level] agreements." Indeed, as collective bargaining systems underwent a process of decentralisation, whereby the competences of company-level actors have significantly expanded, unions have gained a greater role in administering and applying the terms and conditions set forth by higher level agreements and, within their own remit, negotiate further provisions. In this context, collective bargaining systems have been redefined as deep when the main social actors, and the outcomes of their interaction, are coherent "from the central level and right down to the company level" (Madsen et al., 2001:12). More specifically, depth of bargaining has begun to indicate the way in which the bargaining process, which is controlled by the articulating mechanisms provided at the sector-level, first reaches local actors and then unfolds at the workplace (Muller et al., 2019:25). Thus, while in Clegg's work (1976) the emphasis was on depth at the sector-level – with centralised bargaining being the rule rather than the exception – in this chapter, we look at depth from a company's perspective. Here, there are two dimensions that can capture this important institutional feature: one is the capacity of trade unions to access employees within firms; and another is their participation in the negotiation of company-level agreements. The assumption is that, in companies where employees are not consistently represented by trade unions, it is unlikely that shop stewards will guarantee the negotiation of any meaningful collective agreements. The reason is that high depth of bargaining gives confidence to unions to both provide (at the sector level) and accept (at the company level) further delegation of bargaining competences, and avoids representation problems so that employers can expect shop stewards to take the lead in negotiating agreements (Paolucci & Marginson, 2020).

The power resource theory suggests that there are two further factors that may account for the capacity of social partners to engage with their competences at the company level. In particular, these are, firstly, the commitment of organised (and individual) employers to maintain and respect a shared framework for wage bargaining and, secondly, the strength and organisational capacity of the trade unions (Thelen, 2014). The contribution of this chapter is therefore to explore the interplay between institutional features and the strategies of the actors involved with them in order to explain the impact that different paths to decentralisation may have had on the role, scope, and outcomes of collective bargaining within the retail sector. In the next section, we review the institutional and legal framework for collective bargaining in the selected countries, namely, Poland, Ireland, Italy, Germany, Spain, and Sweden.

The changing contours of collective bargaining

With the exception of Italy and Spain, both belonging to the South cluster (Visser 2009), all the selected countries feature a different legal and institutional framework for collective bargaining. We suggest that, as a result of collective bargaining decentralisation, differences across them have become less pronounced and, consequently, new IR classifications of country clusters are required.

The case of Ireland and Poland

Ireland and Poland have ratified ILO Convention 98, so the mentioned states are obliged to support collective bargaining. Article 4 of ILO Convention 98 establishes that: "Measures appropriate to national conditions shall be taken, where necessary, to encourage and promote the full development and utilisation of machinery for voluntary negotiation between employers or employers' organisations and workers' organisations, with a view to the regulation of terms and conditions of employment by means of collective agreements". Moreover, the states are obliged to promote collective bargaining because of the European Social Charter, which is also binding for both. However, in practice, their national legal framework does not facilitate the promotion of the right to negotiate collective agreements.

On the one hand, the institutional framework for collective bargaining in Ireland is underpinned by the principle of voluntarism. Ireland's 1937 Constitution provides that workers have a right to form and join trade unions, but the law courts have stated that this does not imply that an employer is required to bargain with them. A 1995 case in the Ireland's High Court offered a clear statement of this legal principle, which had been established in earlier cases: "I do not consider that there is any obligation imposed by ordinary law or the Constitution on any employer to consult with or negotiate with any organisation representing his employees or some of them, when the conditions of employment are to be settled or reviewed" (Justice O'Hanlon in Association of General Practitioners and Others v Minister for Health, 1995).

Regarding the Irish case, under the 1990 law, trade unions might face legal action by employers if they organised industrial action without following a strict set of rules regarding ballots, ratification, and notice. Since unions engaged in recognition disputes were often unable to demonstrate that they had followed these rules, and since they faced growing resistance to gaining recognition, calls for a "right to bargain" re-emerged as an industrial relations and political issue. Laws were enacted to secure such a right. The so-called right to bargain procedure was of limited impact and was effectively nullified by the Supreme Court's judgement in 2007 in the Ryanair case (D'Art & Turner, 2006; Roche, 2007a). The result of this case law is that employers cannot be forced by law to bargain with trade unions if they do not wish to do so, an interpretation that means that employees have no fundamental right to bargain. Employers and trade unions voluntarily engage in collective bargaining, and their agreed terms and conditions of employment are not legally binding. Workers have the right to form and join a trade union. However, unions cannot force employers to enter collective bargaining, meaning that there is no legal right to collective bargaining in Ireland. Following the collapse of the national social partnership in 2009, collective bargaining, where it exists, occurs solely at the company level.

In the case of Poland, it is not possible to identify any action of the national legislator aiming to promote collective bargaining, apart from establishing the Labour Law Codification Committee in 2016 with a view to consensually drafting a new, two-piece labour act (collective and individual), which, however, proved to be an unsuccessful initiative. There are even examples of actions taken by the state that could be seen as obstructive to collective bargaining. For example, an amendment to the Act on Higher Education, which explicitly excluded the state minister responsible for educational affairs as a potential party to a multi-enterprise collective agreement covering university employees, triggered a protest by the sectoral trade unions (specifically, the National Education Section of NSZZ "Solidarność"). In its reply, the ministry claimed that furnishing the Minister of Science and Higher Education with the right to conclude collective labour agreements could be considered a restriction of the right to negotiate. Moreover, if a minister acted as a party in a multi-enterprise collective labour agreement it would be contrary to the principle of the limited role of the state in collective labour relations (Czarzasty & Surdykowska, 2020). In Poland, collective bargaining is regulated by the Chapter 11 of the Labour Code of 1974. Yet, there is no explicit definition of collective agreement in the Labour Code. For that reason, the definition of that right is based on the jurisprudence. Following the ruling by the Constitutional Court of 20 January 1988, collective agreements should not be seen as normative acts adopted by state bodies, but rather as special sources of labour law. Regarding collective agreements, the law follows two major principles. One is "freedom of contract," with the exception of provisions jeopardising the rights of third parties. The other is "favourability," by virtue of which collective agreements cannot introduce provisions less favourable for employees than those envisaged by law (Czarzasty, 2019).

Despite the existing differences between these two countries (the trade union power in Ireland is centralised and in Poland is decentralised), weak positions of trade unions and hostility of employers towards collective bargaining are noticeable in both countries. In particular, in the Irish case, under the 2015 Industrial Relations Act, if an individual employer does not want to recognise a union for collective bargaining purposes, the union must demonstrate that it is substantially representative of the workers in the company to activate a bargaining process. This involves the intervention of the Labour Court and the possibility that pay will be fixed by law when groups of workers are shown to be out of line with comparable groups performing similar work. In practice, it has been difficult to meet the representativeness requirement required to activate the intervention of the Labour Court. As a result, most employers do not recognise trade unions for collective bargaining purposes.

Under these circumstances, following the collapse of the social partnership, the Irish Congress of Trade Unions and the main employers' confederation, the Irish Business and Employers' Confederation (IBEC), agreed a "protocol" in 2010, to guide collective bargaining in private and commercial state-owned firms that prioritised job retention, competitiveness, and orderly dispute resolution. The ICTU–IBEC protocol framed the orderly decentralisation of collective bargaining to the firm level across most of the private sector and state-owned commercial firms (Roche & Gormley, 2017, 2018). Sectoral collective bargaining continued to prevail in low-paid, low-union-density industries, in construction and allied sectors, and in public services. Yet, negotiations mainly take place at the company level.

In Poland, the roots of decentralisation within the union movement can be traced back to the pre-1989 era of authoritarian state socialism. Workplace-centred union movement emerged in the period of the 1st Solidarity (1980–81). Even after Solidarity was banned, the new "official" trade unions would be shaped as a loosely coupled confederation. *Ogólnopolskie Porozumienie Związków Zawodowych* (OPZZ) was built in a bottom-up manner, albeit one administered from above by the government. Company-level organisations were organised and sectoral unions (autonomous organisations and federations) were set up, and, finally, a national-level association was called into existence (Gardawski, Mrozowicki, & Czarzasty, 2012).

The case of Germany, Italy, and Spain

In the selected group of countries (Germany, Italy, and Spain), the policy-makers promote the right to negotiate following the international duties undertaken due to the ratification of ILO Convention 98. In Spain, the right to collective bargaining and the binding character of collective agreements is enshrined in the Spanish Constitution (Article 37.1). The system of collective bargaining is thoroughly regulated in Title III of the Workers' Statute (WS). In particular, Article 82.3 establishes the legally binding character of collective agreements negotiated in conformity with the rules of the Workers' Statute.

In the same sense, in Germany the provisions of the collective agreement have the character of mandatory legal norms.[3] In the case of collective bargaining, the basic legislation is the Collective Bargaining Act (Tarifvertragsgesetz), which was passed in 1949 at the time of the founding of the Federal Republic, the constitution of which (the Basic Law) also provides for freedom of association. According to the Collective Bargaining Act, the negotiating parties – trade unions and employers' associations or individual employers – set employment conditions that have legally binding effect without external influence by the state. Hence, in Germany, the collective bargaining system is also referred to as "collective bargaining autonomy" or "free collective bargaining" (Haipeter & Rosenbohm, 2022).

The legal systems examined are characterised by complexity, due to the alternative channels for workplace representation; moreover, disparities in the distribution of functions are quite different among the various systems. In Spain, both trade unions and works councils have the capacity to negotiate collective agreements at enterprise level. At sectoral level, the right to negotiate is attributed only to trade unions. However, in Germany, trade unions relieve works councils of the burden of having to negotiate on contentious issues, such as pay increases or the length of working hours, for which they are ill-equipped, given that they lack the right to strike.

The promotion of the collective bargaining decentralisation is observed in times of crisis, and the setting of some restrictions to sector-level collective bargaining during economic recovery processes have been noticed. For example, in Italy, there were attempts to boost second-level collective bargaining through governmental economic incentives (especially after the onset of the 2009 economic crisis). In line with the overall concept of responsive regulation, since the onset of the 2009 economic crisis, cross-industry collective agreements opened-up to a process of organised

3   The analysis on Germany is based on Haipeter & Rosenbohm (2022).

decentralisation: opening clauses entitle decentralised bargaining to deviate from standards set by the national agreements, provided that the derogatory agreement is approved by sectoral trade unions (Armaroli & Tomassetti, 2022). Usually drawn up at sectoral level or based on statutory provisions, opening clauses provide the space for company-level bargaining to derogate from standards set under sectoral agreements, in order to adapt them to the circumstances of individual companies, while preserving multi-employer bargaining (Keune, 2011).

In Spain, the strong impact of the 2009 economic crisis, the problems affecting the labour market (in particular the high unemployment level, with youth unemployment at maximum rates), and the lack of effective mechanisms for wage bargaining and internal flexibility, operated as grounds to transform the system of collective bargaining and impose a trend towards decentralisation. The 2012 reform attempted to decentralise collective bargaining and to grant more power to employers in the bargaining process. The goal of decentralising collective bargaining is clear in the 2012 labour reform. However, its practical results are mixed and the number of employees covered by firm-level agreements has not visibly risen (see Chapter 5; Muñoz Ruiz, Ramos Martín, & Vincent, 2023). The decline in collective bargaining coverage due to companies leaving or staying away from employers' associations is the main driving force behind wild or uncontrolled decentralisation (Bispinck, 2004) in the German retail sector. As a result, some sectors, the most organised being on the employers' side (i.e., manufacturing) remain covered by collective bargaining, while others have been left outside of its remit (Haipeter & Rosenbohm, 2022). A similar development can be seen in Spain. Relevant to this chapter, the weakness of the business associations at state level is pointed out as a main concern in the retail sector. Consequently, there are sector-level collective agreements that regulate the working conditions of only 50 employees. One of the main problems is that the structure of the retail sector is focused on the provincial level. In fact, collective agreements at provincial level have been negotiated without clear guidelines.

The case of Sweden[4]

The Swedish labour law and industrial relations system is based on self-regulation through autonomous collective bargaining, social partnership, and the strong legal rights and industrial relations practices of employee

---

4   The analysis on Sweden is based on Rönnmar & Iossa (2022).

representation and information, consultation, and co-determination (Rönn-mar & Iossa, 2022).

Collective bargaining is regulated by the Co-determination Act (MBL) (Government Bill prop. 1975/76:105, Bil. 1). The Codetermination Act (Med-bestämmandelagen, MBL, 1976:580) regulates employee consultation and participation in working life. The MBL is the main law for the system of collective regulations. It is a framework law that must be implemented through collective agreements. A collective agreement is statutorily defined as "an agreement in writing between an organisation of employers or an employer and an organisation of employees about conditions of employment or otherwise about the relationship between employers and employees" (Section 23 MBL). Within its area of application, a collective agreement is legally binding, not only for the contracting parties to the agreement, but also for their members (Section 26 MBL). In addition, an employer bound by a collective agreement is obliged to apply this agreement to all employees, irrespective of trade union membership.

Employee participation is carried out within a single-channel trade union system, where trade unions both negotiate and conclude collective agreements, and take part in information, consultation, and co-deter-mination at workplace level. Sweden has a tradition of high trade union density rates, but the share of Swedish workers who are members of a trade union has dropped in the last decade from 80% to 70%. This rate seems high in comparative terms, but Sweden is also one of the countries where unionisation is declining most rapidly (Eurofound, 2015). Trade union density was 65.2% in 2019 (OECD, 2022). Nevertheless, a strong position of trade unions in the retail sector has been noticed (60% union density). Also, the trade union organisation rate in the retail sector is around 60% on average (the trade union organisation rate is 52% for blue-collar employees, and 67% for white collar employees) (Medlingsinstitutet, 2022).

Several practical factors impact on the promotion, negotiation, and conclusion of local collective agreements in Sweden. The representatives of employers and trade unions at cross-sectoral, sectoral, and local level highlight the importance of good and cooperative relations between local employers and trade union representatives. The mentioned guide has positive effects on the decentralisation of collective bargaining. Thanks to those guidelines, decentralisation has occurred within a steady and coordinated system for collective bargaining. A series of articulation mech-anisms are in place to provide clear competences to different bargaining levels: sectoral, company, and workplace levels (see further Rönnmar & Iossa, 2022).

Characteristics of the retail sector

Comparative research suggests that employment relations are sector-specific (Bechter et al., 2012). Thus, in order to understand the responses of unions to the decentralisation of collective bargaining, this chapter solely focuses on the retail sector. Several studies points to retailing as an interesting context in which to explore developments in collective bargaining as it is characterised by a series of market conditions that have made it possible for employers to sidestep employment relations institutions – and explore so-called exit options (Doellgast et al., 2018). Unlike manufacturing, retailing is a low-wage and low-skilled industry where unsociable working hours and part-time are the norm, employment contracts are notoriously precarious, and the share of female employment is significant (Geppert et al, 2014; Mrozowicki et al., 2013). Moreover, the sector is dominated by small businesses, on the one hand, and a few large, often international companies, on the other. Here cost-cutting strategies prevail and the level of employee turnover is high (Carré et al., 2010). Against this backdrop of workers' vulnerability, our expectation is that unions struggle to resist collective bargaining decentralisation and, at the same time, to negotiate company-level agreements. Table 4.2. summarises the most relevant labour market indicators across all the countries investigated.

Table 4.2.   Labour market indicators in the retail sector

	All employed	Part-time	Temporary workers	Young workers	Female	Wage Female	Wage Man
Germany	5,195.7	1,489.4	504.1	224.4	2,685.4	14.24	18.3
Ireland	295.4	66.4	29.3	32.2	141.8	15.75	18.73
Spain	2,951.6	348.7	450.2	88.2	1,469.9	8.77	10.64
Italy	3,087.4	532.0	343.3	109.7	1,340.4		
Poland	2,209.6	94.2	372.7	31.9	1,253.9	4.67	6.23
Sweden	519.6	89.5	68.1	51.6	218.4		

Source: Eurostat (https://ec.europa.eu/eurostat/web/labour-market/overview)

Carré et al., (2010:5) defines the retail sector as a "laboratory for changes in labour market institutions." The generally precarious conditions of workers, coupled with the increasing need of employers for flexible work arrangements to meet changing customers' demands, have exerted greater pressure on bargaining arrangements in retail than in other industries, and facilitated an extreme relaxation of collective regulation. In the past, centralised and coordinated national- and sectoral-level institutions, when present, were capable of sheltering the retail sector from market pressures. However, as a result of bargaining decentralisation, social parties in retail have now been left to their own devices. In fact, except for Sweden, where the industrial relations landscape has remained relatively stable over time (Rönnmar & Iossa, 2022), the picture we have in all the other countries, in which sector level institutions are still the main locus of negotiation (Germany, Italy, and Spain), is far more complex. In Italy, retailing features a strong fragmentation both in workers' and employers' representation, which has resulted in the proliferation of industry-wide agreements. Over 75 such agreements were mapped by *Consiglio nazionale dell'economia e del lavoro* (CNEL) only in 2020 (Armaroli & Tomassetti, 2022). However, the majority of workers is still covered by collective agreements signed by the most representative trade unions. While the scope of company-level bargaining has progressively increased to encompass items such as working time, work organisation, job classification, temporary contracts, work-life balance, equal opportunities, training, health and safety, and welfare benefits, the capacity of management and shop stewards to engage with these competences remains limited. Given the huge presence of small companies with less than 50 employees (99% of all the enterprises in retail), unions have struggled to enter the workplace. Union density is, in fact, one of the lowest compared to other industries and it stands at around 17% (Carrieri & Feltrin, 2016 in Armaroli & Tomassetti, 2022). It follows that decentralised bargaining in retailing is confined primarily to few large retailers.

The situation is similar in Spain, where most companies lack the necessary employee, or union representation to initiate the formal process of decentralised bargaining. In addition, here, the sector is characterised by strong fragmentation of bargaining units both at provincial and national level and, unlike in Italy, the sectoral business association is weak. All these conditions have made it particularly difficult for Spanish unions to sign industry-wide collective agreements. Currently, there is one sector-level agreement in force in retail, covering about 50 employees. Most bargaining activity takes place at provincial level and in large retailers (Muñoz Ruiz & Ramos Martín, 2022).

In Germany, less than half of all retail workers are covered by a collective agreement and between 80% and 90% of workplaces are outside the scope of collective bargaining (Haipeter & Rosenbohm, 2022). This significant reduction in workers' protections in retail, resulting from an extreme deterioration of bargaining institutions, was due to large retailers withdrawing from collective bargaining in recent years. In particular, the discontinuation of extension provisions in the sector and the possibility for employers to join the business association, while opting out of collective bargaining, have produced a sharp decline in bargaining coverage and triggered a process of wild and uncontrolled decentralisation (Bispinck, 2004 in Haipeter & Rosenbohm, 2022). The weakness of unions at the workplace level has further impinged on the stability of the system and limited bargaining activity.

In Ireland and Poland, the retail sector does not have multi-employer bargaining arrangements in place and negotiations only occur at the company and workplace level.

Hence, the first questions that this chapter answers is whether and, if so, how trade unions have responded to the decentralisation of collective bargaining in the retail sector.

Table 4.3.   Institutional context for collective bargaining in retail

	Collective Bargaining system	Dominant bargaining level	Collective bargaining coverage	Establishment covered by company level bargaining	Union density
Germany	Multi-employer	Sector	25%	4%	Not Available
Ireland	Single-employer	Company	Not Available	Not available	Not Available
Spain	Multi-employer	Provincial			
Italy	Multi-employer	Sector	80%	Not Available	17% *
Poland	Single-employer	Company			
Sweden	Multi-employer	Sector	85% **		60%

* Trade Sector, data not available for retail only (Carrieri & Feltrin, 2016).
** Aggregate figure for private sector (Rönnmar & Iossa, 2022).
Source: Haipeter & Rosenbohm, 2022; Armaroli & Tomassetti, 2022; Paolucci et al., 2022; Muñoz Ruiz & Ramos Martín, 2022; Rönnmar & Iossa, 2022; Czarzasty, 2022.

The companies selected for this study are all large retailers where trade unions are present and where there is some degree of collective bargaining activity. While these may not necessarily be representative of the retail sector, which is heavily dominated by small- and medium-sized enterprises lacking employee representation, they are still interesting contexts in which to explore union responses to the decentralisation of collective bargaining, for two reasons. Firstly, we have limited empirical evidence to date on the strategies that unions have devised, in these contexts, to take advantage of the opportunities offered by bargaining decentralisation and to negotiate company-level agreements. Secondly, the evidence we have is not conclusive.

Some scholars highlight that, in large retailers, unions can only play a marginal role (Armaroli & Tomassetti 2022). Thin margins for profits, the high incidence of labour costs, and constant changes in customers' demands push employers to squeeze labour costs, which, in turn, reduce the opportunity for unions to make gains through collective negotiations (Nespoli, 2021). For example, in Italy, dynamics of outsourcing in the retail value chain have exacerbated social dumping and led to fraudulent practices, such as undeclared work and the application of so-called *pirate contracts*[5] (Armaroli & Tomassetti, 2022). Under these conditions, the most representative unions find it difficult to sign meaningful collective agreements. By contrast, other comparative studies indicate that unions in large retailers across Ireland, Spain, and Poland benefit from some benevolent conditions (i.e., market share, size of establishments, number of employees, integrated human resource practices), which facilitate cooperation with management and strengthen their capacity to enter into negotiation with them (Geppert et al., 2013). In order to clarify this inconsistency, this chapter explores the role and strategies of trade unions in large retail companies across Sweden, Italy, Germany, Spain, Ireland, and Poland. Hence, the second question that this chapter addresses is whether and, if so, how trade unions have responded to the decentralisation of collective bargaining at the company level.

Union strategies in coordinating collective bargaining across countries and companies

In this section, we will first seek to answer to the question how trade unions have responded to the decentralisation of collective bargaining in retail at the sector level. Secondly, we will ponder the issue of how unions have responded to the decentralisation of collective bargaining at the company level. Finally, we discuss the institutional and non-institutional factors affecting union strategies towards bargaining decentralisation. In other words, we investigate how unions' strategies are linked to the institutional and structural context in which they operate.

In line with Visser's proposal, the countries in our sample represent the union strategies of all clusters towards bargaining decentralisation. In other words: how are unions' strategies distinguished in, in particular, North (Sweden), South (Italy and Spain), West (Ireland), Centre-West (Germany), and Centre-East (Poland). As a consequence, there is a spectrum of all types of collective bargaining in terms of principal level covered. In North and Centre West, sectoral level prevails, contrasting with West and Centre-East, where company level dominates. In the South, the leading pattern is

---

5   Collective agreements that are not signed by the most representative trade unions.

branded as "variable" (Visser, 2009). There are also different trends towards decentralisation in each of them – as theorised by Thelen. In particular, we argue that, in our country sample, we are witnessing dualising liberalisation (Italy and Germany, to some degree also Spain), embedded flexibilisation (Sweden), and deregulatory liberalisation (Ireland and Poland).

As for the first question, it is important to stress that there is no such challenge in the countries belonging to the clusters where collective bargaining is at the company level (Ireland and Poland). Decentralisation is a state, not a process, hence the deregulatory liberalisation label. More specifically, in Poland, unions could not respond to decentralisation at the sector level due to the fact that the structure of collective bargaining has been decentralised for many years. Furthermore, the main challenge confronting the unions is not the type of bargaining in terms of levels, but the collapse of bargaining in general. In the retail sector, there is no multi-employer agreement and no tripartite body responsible for the sector. By contrast, in Ireland, despite the lack of a sectoral-level framework, the collective bargaining system, while being confined to company level, has remained relatively viable. The collapse of the social partnership system in the aftermath of 2008 crisis left a mark on the entire system of industrial relations in the country, but the Irish Congress of Trade Unions and the Irish Business and Employers' Confederation reached a bipartite agreement on a "protocol" to guide collective bargaining in private and commercial state-owned firms that prioritised job retention, competitiveness, and orderly dispute resolution (Paolucci et al., 2022). In other words, despite sharing a pluralist IR tradition and a similar institutional setting (based on single employer bargaining), social actors in Ireland and Poland have made different strategic choices. In particular, in Ireland as opposed to Poland, some employers have showed a greater willingness to continue engaging in collective bargaining.

In the remaining countries that we focus on in this chapter, decentralisation of collective bargaining at the sector level is, indeed, a problem for trade unions, albeit its weight varies, depending on the national context. Italy, Germany, and Spain all fit into the type of process that is called dualising liberalisation. In fact, tenuous market characteristics have made it possible for individual employers to sidestep the national collective bargaining system, which, despite formally remaining in place, is no longer able to secure a high level of inclusion.

In Italy, there is a serious challenge in the form of a spontaneous/disorganised decentralisation advancing through so-called *pirate contracts*. This phenomenon can be described as: "smaller unions (without real representation) and compliant business associations sign alternative sectoral collective agreements in order to cut labour standards and costs" (Armaroli & Tomassetti, 2022:9). While such agreements can be considered nothing more than legal window-dressing, they apparently obstruct collective bargaining. Retail is one of the sectors especially prone to contamination from such regulations as, due to low added value and profit margins, employers seeking to reduce labour costs are tempted to resort to such practices. Legitimate trade unions recognise *pirate contracts* to be a serious problem that "has reached such dimensions in many sectors that appears to be more threatening for the functioning of the whole industrial relations system in Italy and the subsequent maintenance of sustainable labour standards, than the possibility for decentralised bargaining to derogate from certain national terms and conditions of employment" (Leonardi, 2017). Nevertheless, they are struggling to address it effectively. Moreover, while the sectoral framework has remained largely unaltered and continues to establish clear mechanisms of delegation of bargaining competences across levels, a reduced depth of bargaining in Italy and a limited presence of shop stewards at company level have made it quite difficult for retail companies to be covered by collective agreements. Due to the hostility of employers, unions are able to engage with decentralised bargaining and secure the enforcement of sectoral agreements only in companies where they can effectively represent workers. It follows that there are substantial within-country differences with respect to the capacity of unions to protect workers. Dualisation is evident in the fact that the bargaining system remains well-articulated in the most strongly organised sectors (both on the side of unions and employers), such as manufacturing; whereas in others, where representation is more fragmented, such as in retail, the opportunities for actors to negotiate company-level agreements are limited.

The German retail sector has been a scene of "wild," that is to say, disorganised, decentralisation. The decline in collective bargaining coverage due to companies leaving or staying away from employers' associations is the main driving force of wild or uncontrolled decentralisation (Bispinck, 2004, in Haipeter & Rosenbohm, 2022: 27). This has had important implications from an institutional perspective. While some workers are still covered by the sectoral framework (which has remained relatively stable over time), others, such as those in retail, cannot avail themselves of the same level of protection. Thus, similarly to Italy – albeit for different reasons – the IR system in Germany is increasingly dualised. However, derogations are not a significant factor for decentralisation in the retail sector. Unions recognise the need for modernisation of collective bargaining, as they notice it is outdated in many respects (for example, pay structure), yet they are aware of the risks any future changes might bring with regard to their main constituency (specific job groups). There is a gap between the strategic approaches of unions in service sector (Ver.di) and metalworking (IG Metall). While in the metal sector unions are quite open to derogations, those in the service sector are more reserved. "Overall, ver.di has been quite reluctant to accept derogations or deviations from the standards stipulated in regional industry-level agreements" (Haipeter & Rosenbohm, 2022).

In Spain, the sector (mainly provincial-level) agreements continue to predominate, reinforced by a recent legislative change (2021). In the retail sector, a strong fragmentation of the bargaining units at state as well as provincial level is observed. This fragmentation is explained by the difficulties of negotiating a sectoral collective agreement at state level. The weakness of the business association at state level is the main concern in the retail sector (Muñoz Ruiz & Ramos Martín, 2022). As the root of the problem is on the employers' side, the unions are in a difficult position to produce a consistent strategy on how to address it.

In Sweden, there is no trend towards increased "disorganised" or disruptive decentralisation, so the phenomenon is not seen as a threat (Rönnmar & Iossa, 2022). The system has adapted to the need for increasing flexibility by providing clear articulation mechanisms coordinating the relationship between bargaining levels. Company-level agreements – like in the case of a retail chain being subject to the national case study – cannot deviate from upper-level agreements (favourability principle), thus the two levels of bargaining are regarded as complementary. Moreover, union density remains relatively high in the sector, meaning that unions can retain control of the bargaining process at the local level. No major tensions are reported regarding the link between upper and lower bargaining levels. Within this context, trade unions are not overwhelmingly concerned about decentralisation.

As for the second question, that is, the trade unions' dealings with decentralisation at company level, the issue is more complex, especially due to the nature of the companies selected (large retailers), where unions, despite a variation across cases, tend to retain a relevant role. In Poland, the lack of any formal regulation (no collective agreement), as exemplified by the company Megastore (a subsidiary to a Dutch-domiciled multinational chain), seems to be the main challenge. The company's adversarial stance towards trade unions suggests that the chances of striking any formal bipartite agreement are slim. This is to some degree compensated by micro-bargaining on issues such as pay rises or occupational welfare. The union (there is only one in the company) has no bargaining power strong enough to push their agenda more effectively. Considering the pluralist and highly fragmented shape of unionism in the country, any intervention from the upper levels of union structures, either sectoral or central, are unlikely. It is hard to discuss bargaining outcomes in an environment without a formal agreement, however, the above-mentioned micro-bargaining has produced some tangible effects, including the establishment of a company social benefits fund[6] (Czarzasty, 2022).

In Germany, there has been at least one innovative practice of successful union organising via works councils in the retail sector. The retail network in focus, Fashion, had initially not been covered by a collective agreement and it also did not have a works council. Nevertheless, in a bottom-up move, a works council was established, with the support of ver.di, which was followed by an increase in union density. Finally, the company agreed to sign a "recognition agreement," under which the company will adhere to the standards stipulated in the branch-level agreement after a transition period (Haipeter & Rosenbohm, 2022: 68).

A Spanish case provides for an interesting finding pertaining to decentralisation. Precisely speaking, in one of the cases, the decentralisation of collective bargaining in which independent trade unions were involved brought improvements to working conditions and pay in the retail networks (Lidl and Mercadona), while in the chains where so-called instrumental (presumably, "yellow") unions were present (such as Decathlon) there have been problems with pay, resulting in the wages of Decathlon employees being lower than those hired by Lidl and Mercadona (Muñoz Ruiz & Ramos Martín, 2022: 27).

In Ireland, in the RetailCo case, the prerequisite is that, unlike other major retailers in Ireland, RetailCo recognises unions (Paolucci et al., 2022: 47). This creates a basis for negotiations, resulting in what is described as a de facto closed-shop agreement in place in the company, which secures 100% union representation (Paolucci et al., 2022: 47). Despite those better-than-average circumstances, the unions still had to make an enormous effort to mobilise workers in a sector that, due to its structural conditions (low pay, high labour turnover, or competition between employers) is an extremely difficult field to operate in. What they did (not only in the retail sector) was utilise their own organisational resources to empower shop stewards and revitalise their company-level structures. There is one accomplishment that seems to be of particular value for the ultimate success of collective bargaining

---

6   Major, company-level type of occupational welfare scheme in Poland.

in the company. In the institutional context, where a central coordination mechanism is virtually absent, unions have developed mechanisms of vertical coordination through the establishment of formal workplace representation structures, elected by the members and linked to the sector level via highly trained full-time sectoral union officials (that is, shop stewards) (Paolucci et al., 2022).

In Italy, the main challenge in the company under scrutiny appears to be a lack of harmonisation in the different terms and conditions of employment of all workers hired from three different cooperatives to work for Coop Alleanza 3.0, following its establishment in 2016. This is the result of there being no comprehensive collective agreement signed (Armaroli & Tomassetti 2022: 42). In other words, the three collective agreements concluded in the companies that would eventually form the Coop Alleanza 3.0 prior to the merger are still referred to in the day-to-day practise of labour relations, and unions have been making efforts to keep those agreements alive, also by means of collaboration. At the same time, no new collective agreement embracing all employees in the newly founded company has been signed. This appears to be a Catch-22 situation and the trade unions are yet to devise a strategy on how to deal with it.

In Sweden, with no observed tensions between various levels of bargaining, the strategy of trade unions at company level is not defensive. The case of the chain covered shows that such agreements are regarded as complementary to the upper-level agreements. This is evident in the capacity of the social partners to negotiate a cross-sectoral agreement in 2020–2021, covering issues such as security, employee transition and life long-learning, and employment protection, all of which have significant implications in the workplace. This type of agreement, especially in the private sector, was perceived as a successful initiative by autonomous industrial relations actors, who are still able to operate within a well-functioning, multi-employer bargaining system. Nevertheless, it is notable that the employers' association and some trade unions in the public sector were excluded from the negotiation of this agreement. This perception is likely to be exacerbated by the signing of a cross-sectoral, social-partner agreement on security, transition, and employment protection for 2020 and 2021 (Rönnmar & Iossa, 2022).

Another example worthy of attention is the case of Lidl and Mercadona in Spain (with a negative frame of reference provided by Decathlon), where the dedication of trade unions to negotiating the collective agreement resulted in better pay conditions in the former companies than at Decathlon, where the unions reportedly did not commit themselves overly to the process. In Germany, a deliberate choice by IG Metall to "jump on the decentralisation wagon" created an institutional basis for the effective overseeing and enforcement of collective agreement by the works council (in close collaboration with the unions), following the employer's pledge to observe the branch-level agreement. Even in Poland, in the context of adversarial industrial relations and the absence of collective agreement (with little chance to conclude one in the foreseeable future), informal micro-bargaining has produced some tangible benefits to employees. Thus, the lesson learnt is that the resilience of trade unions pays off, even though it may not be enough to stop or reverse decentralisation, wherever trade unions see it as undesirable phenomenon.

Conclusion

This chapter explored the responses of trade unions to the decentralisation of collective bargaining in the retail sector across countries characterised by different industrial relations systems. Its multi-level focus makes a series of contributions to extant research. In the empirical part of the chapter, we concentrated on large retail companies where trade unions are present, and at least some degree of collective bargaining activity is observed. While that could be considered a limitation of the study – given the retail sector in general is dominated by small- and medium-sized enterprises – it still widens our knowledge on the strategies that unions formulated after the decentralisation of collective bargaining in several countries.

Firstly, we find that, in the face of recent decentralisation pressures, traditional classifications, which are based on national industrial relations arrangements (Visser, 2009), are no longer able to fully capture similarities and differences across countries. On the contrary, our findings suggest that these classifications have become sector- (rather than country-) specific. We showed that two different countries, such as Ireland and Poland, prominent examples of the West and the Centre-East clusters, respectively, have both experienced a sudden collapse of multi-employer bargaining affecting all industries alike, thereby becoming an increasingly similar context where trade unions and individual employers negotiate. By the same token, Germany, on the one hand, and Italy and Spain, on the other, have been treated, from an institutional perspective, as instances of different industrial relation regimes (Visser, 2009). Nevertheless, a greater delegation of bargaining competences, from the sectoral to the company level in all three countries, has progressively reduced the degree of institutional variation between them. In particular, decentralisation has meant that while formally, bargaining institutions have remained in place at the national level, a reduced presence of unions at the workplace level (depth of bargaining) in Italy and Spain, and the unwillingness of employers to uphold the multi-employer bargaining system in Germany, have de facto limited the enactment of these institutions to traditionally unionised sectors, such as manufacturing, and left outside many others, most notably retail. This explains why, in manufacturing, the effects of collective bargaining decentralisation mirrors differences across countries – and are broadly in line with existing industrial relations classifications (see Chapter 3; Haipeter et al., 2023), while in retailing this is not the case. In fact, the Italian and German cases show that if de jure coordinating mechanisms (i.e., delegation) may still exist in both sectors, in retailing these mechanisms have ceased to effectively exert their function. Here, (weak) social partners are unable to derive power from such institutions to negotiate company level agreements. This finding suggests that as bargaining decentralisation increases, institutional mechanisms of coordination become subject to sectoral contingencies, for instance, the presence (or not) of strong trade unions and employers' associations that are capable of, and/or willing, to use them. Hence, national institutions alone are no longer sufficient to secure even coverage of collective bargaining across sectors and companies, also in countries where these arrangements are still in place. Finally, consistent with the Nordic model, Sweden remains a case of stable industrial relations, where collective bargaining continues to play an important role in the regulation of the labour market. Here, the procedural security offered by clear articulation mechanisms and a widespread presence of unions across companies (depth of bargaining), have given to local negotiators the flexibility they require to engage (or not) with their bargaining competence.

Secondly, a close up of the retail sector demonstrates that decentralisation has taken different shapes across the selected countries. Ireland and Poland are cases of "deregulatory liberalisation" where trade unions can avail themselves of very limited institutional resources, collective bargaining takes place only at the company level and increasing hostility of employers has dramatically reduced collective bargaining coverage. Germany, Italy, and Spain have experienced "dualising liberalisation," meaning that while multi-employer arrangements continue to remain in place in all sectors, in sectors where market conditions are unfavourable to workers, such as in retailing, employers have been able to circumvent them. It follows that there are significant within-country variations in the capacity of trade unions to protect workers as well as to secure the enforcement of sector- and company-level agreements. Depending on sectoral characteristics, trade unions may or may not be able to control decentralisation. The Swedish case depicts a different scenario. Coordination between bargaining level is strong despite increasing decentralisation. The link between sector- and company-level social partners has created an incentive for enacting their bargaining competences and, by making institutions relevant and functional, they also legitimate their role in the labour market. Institutional change in Sweden has followed the trajectory of "embedded flexibilisation." This is evident in the fact that decentralisation has been assimilated – rather than resisted – by existent institutional arrangements. Through this process of interaction, industrial relations actors and institutions in Sweden have remained active and representative at all levels.

Thirdly, the analysis of our company cases suggests that wherever trade unions can retain/gain any degree of control over the process of decentralisation, regardless of the country and the path the process takes (i.e., deregulatory liberalisation, dualising liberalisation, and embedded flexibilisation), the outcomes of collective bargaining are more or less positive for employees. This is not to say that institutions are not relevant. On the contrary, in a stable institutional context such as the Swedish one, unions are found to be in a stronger bargaining position and able to protect even workers in retailing, where market conditions are not favourable to them. In a shaky institutional environment (as in the case of Italy or Spain), the outcomes may vary, and their quality is not only determined by the structure of the bargaining system, but also by the interplay of other factors including attitudes of stakeholders, market pressures, technological advances, and inherent characteristics of the retail sector, such as low profit margin, translating into low pay. The wide spectrum of possible outcomes of bargaining as illustrated by our cases studies contains, success stories such as the Irish Retail.Co, where the leading union (Mandate) is reportedly satisfied with the outcomes of decentralised bargaining, and in spite of the financial difficulties the company, and the hostile institutional context it operates in, the union maintains collaborative relations with management. Equally fascinating is the German case, which demonstrates that, sometimes, it is the deterioration of institutions itself that can trigger a union's responses to liberalising pressures and provide them with an opportunity to (re)organise vulnerable workers.

In sum, our company cases show that, independent of the country, in a context such as retailing, which is characterised by generally poor working conditions, market structures and company characteristics tend to condition unions' capacity to engage in collective bargaining. Only in Sweden, where the institutional framework continues to provide a significant degree of procedural security through coordinating mechanisms, have unions been able to retain control over the decentralisation process and to play an important role at the company level. Nevertheless, in large, often internationalised companies, such as those investigated, unions that are proactive and willing to mobilise their own organisational resources, as demonstrated by the Irish and the German cases, are still able to make a positive difference for workers.

References

Amable, B. (2000). Institutional complementarity and diversity of social systems of innovation and production. *Review of International Political Economy*, 7(4): 645–687.

Armaroli, I. & Tomassetti, P. (2022). Decentralised bargaining in Italy. CODEBAR-project. https://aias-hsi.uva.nl/en/projects-a-z/codebar/codebar.html

Bechter, B., Brandl, B., & Meardi, G. (2012). Sectors or countries? Typologies and levels of analysis in comparative industrial relations. *European Journal of Industrial Relations*, 18 (3): 185–202.

Bispinck, R., (2004). Kontrollierte Dezentralisierung der Tarifpolitik-Eine schwierige Balance. *WSI Mitteilungen* 5, 237–245.

Campbell, J. (2009). Institutional reproduction and change. In Morgan, G., Campbell, J., Crouch, C., Pedersen, O.K, & Whitley, R. (Eds.), *The Oxford handbook of comparative institutional analysis*. Oxford University Press.

Carré, F., Tilly, C., Van Klaveren, M., & Voss-Dahm, D. (2010). Retail jobs in comparative perspective. In Gautié, J. & Schmitt, J. (Eds.), Low-wage work in the wealthy world (pp. 211–268). Russell Sage Foundation.

Carrieri, M. & Feltrin, P. (2016). *Al bivio: Lavoro, sindacato e rappresentanza nell'Italia d'oggi*. Donzelli.

Clegg, H. A. (1976). *Trade unionism under collective bargaining: A theory based on comparisons of six countries*. B. Blackwell.

Crouch, C. (2005). *Capitalist diversity and change: Recombinant governance and institutional entrepreneurs*. Oxford University Press.

Crouch, C. & Streeck, W. (Eds.) (1997). *Political economy of modern capitalism: Mapping convergence and diversity*. Sage.

Czarzasty, J. (2022). Decentralised bargaining in Poland. CODEBAR-project. https://aias-hsi.uva.nl/en/projects-a-z/codebar/codebar.html

Czarzasty, J. (2019). Collective bargaining in Poland: A near-death experience. In Müller, T., Vandaele, K., & Waddington, J. (Eds.), *Collective bargaining in Europe: Towards an endgame* (pp. 465–481). ETUI.

Czarzasty, J., Adamczyk, S., & Surdykowska, B. (2020). Looking for European solutions. Trade unions in Central and Eastern Europe striving for cross-border solidarity. *Transfer: European Review of Labour and Research*, 26 (3): 307–323.

Czarzasty, J. & Surdykowska, B. (2020). Legal conditions and practice of social dialogue in the local government sector in Poland. In Czarzasty, J. (Ed.), *Local government and trade unions: The conditions, potential and perspectives of social dialogue*. https://www.miasta.pl/zalaczniki/5553

D'Art, D. & Turner, T. (2006). Union organising, union recognition and employer opposition: Case studies of Irish experience. *Irish Journal of Management*, 26 (2): 165–183.

Doellgast, V., Lillie, N., & Pulignano, V. (2018). *Reconstructing solidarity: Labour unions, precarious work, and the politics of institutional change in Europe*. Oxford University Press.

Djelic, M.L. (2010). Institutional perspective: Working towards coherence or irreconcilable diversity? In Morgan, G., Campbell, J., Crouch, C., Pedersen, O.K., & Whitley, R. (Eds.), *The Oxford handbook of comparative institutional analysis*. Oxford University Press.

Esping-Anderson, G. (1990). *Three worlds of welfare capitalism*. Princeton University Press.

Gallie, D. (2007). Production regimes, employment regimes, and the quality of work. In Gallie, D. (Ed.), *Employment regimes and the quality of work*. Oxford University Press.

Gardawski, J., Mrozowicki, A., & Czarzasty, J. (2012). *Trade unions in Poland*. ETUI.

Geppert, M., Williams, K., Wortmann, M., Czarzasty, J., Kağnicioğlu, D., Köhler, D-D., Royle, T., et al. (2013). Industrial relations in European hypermarkets: Home and host country influences. *European Journal of Industrial Relations*, 20 (3): 255–271.

Keune, M. (2011). Decentralizing wage setting in times of crisis? The regulation and use of wage-related derogation clauses in seven European countries. *European Labour Law Journal*, 2(1): 86–95.

Keune, M. & Pedaci, M. (2020). Trade union strategies against precarious work: Common trends and sectoral divergence in the EU. *European Journal of Industrial Relations*, 26 (2): 139–155.

Hall, P. & Soskice, D. (2001). *Varieties of capitalism: The institutional foundations of comparative advantage*. Oxford University Press.

Haipeter, T. & Rosenbohm, S. (2022). Decentralised bargaining in Germany. CODEBAR-project. https://aias-hsi.uva.nl/en/projects-a-z/codebar/codebar.html

Haipeter, T. & Bromberg, T. (2015). *Country report: Wage setting and wage inequality in Germany*. Manuscript.

Hirsch, P. (1997). Sociology without social structure: Neoinstitutional theory meets brave new world. *American Journal of Sociology*, 102 (6): 1702.

Jackson, G. (2009). Actors and institutions. In Morgan, G., Campbell, J., Crouch, C., Pedersen, O.K., & Whitley, R. (Eds.), *The Oxford handbook of comparative institutional analysis*. Oxford University Press.

Justice O'Hanlon (1995). Association of General Practitioners Ltd. and Others versus Minister for Health. High Court.

Leonardi, S. (2017). Il salario minimo, fra legge e contrattazione. Una comparazione europea. In Birindelli, L., Leonardi, S., & Raitano, M. *Salari minimi contrattuali e bassi salari nelle imprese del terziario private* (pp. 89–124). Ediesse.

Locke, R. & Thelen, K. (1995). Apples and oranges revisited: Contextualized comparisons and the study of comparative labor politics. *Politics and Society*, 23: 337–368.

Madsen, J., Andersen, S., & Due, J. (2001). From centralised decentralisation towards multilevel regulation. Paper at IIRA's 6th European regional congress. Oslo 2001.

Marginson, P. & Galetto, M. (2015). Engaging with flexibility and security: Rediscovering the role of collective bargaining. *Economic and Industrial Democracy*, 37, (1): 95-117.

Marginson, P. & Sisson, K. (2006). *European integration and industrial relations: Multi-level governance in the making*. Palgrave Macmillan.

Medlingsinstitutet (2022). *Avtalsrörelsen och lönebildningen 2021. Medlingsinstitutets årsrapport*. Medlingsinstitutet.

Molina, O. & Rhodes, M. (2007). The political economy of adjustment in mixed market economies: A study of Spain and Italy. In Hancké, B., Rhodes, M., & Thatcher, M. (Eds.), *Beyond varieties of capitalism: Conflict, contradictions and complementarities in the European economy* (pp. 223–252). Oxford University Press.

Mrozowicki A., Roosalu T., & Senčar T.B. (2013) Precarious work in the retail sector in Estonia, Poland, and Slovenia: Trade union responses in a time of economic crisis. *Transfer: European Review of Labour and Research*, 19(2): 267–278.

Müller, T., Vandaele, K., & Waddington, J. (2019). *Collective bargaining in Europe: Towards an endgame. Volume I–IV*. European Trade Union Institute.

Muñoz Ruiz, A.B. & Ramos Martín, N. (2022). Decentralised bargaining in Spain. CODEBAR project. https://aias-hsi.uva.nl/en/projects-a-z/codebar/codebar.html

OECD (2022), Trade union Dataset. https://stats.oecd.org/Index.aspx?DataSetCode=TUD

Paolucci, V., Roche, W., & Gormley, T. (2022). Decentralised bargaining in Ireland. CODEBAR-project. https://aias-hsi.uva.nl/en/projects-a-z/codebar/codebar.html

Paolucci, V. & Galetto, M. (2020). The collective bargaining of flexicurity: A case for sector-level analysis? The Italian chemical and metalworking sectors compared. *Human Resource Management Journal*, 30 (2): 165–179.

Paolucci, V. & Marginson, P. (2020). Collective bargaining towards mutual flexibility and security goals in large internationalised companies: Why do institutions (still) matter? *Industrial Relations Journal*, 51(4): 329–350.

Prosser, T. (2015). Accounting for national and sectoral variance in the implementation of European social partner "soft" law: The cases of the implementation of the telework and work-related stress agreements. *British Journal of Industrial Relations*, 53: 254–277.

Pulignano, V. & Keune, M. (2015). Understanding varieties of flexibility and security in multinationals: Product markets, institutions variation and local bargaining. *European Journal of Industrial Relations*, 21 (1): 5–21.

Roche, W. (2007a). Developments in industrial relations and human resource management in Ireland. *Quarterly Economic Commentary*, edition? 62–77.

Roche, W. & Gormley, T. (2017). The durability of coordinated bargaining: Crisis, recovery and pay fixing in Ireland. *Economic and Industrial Democracy*, 41(2): 481–505.

Rönnmar, M. & Iossa, A. (2022). Decentralised bargaining in Sweden. CODEBAR-project. https://aias-hsi.uva.nl/en/projects-a-z/codebar/codebar.html

Schmidt, V. (2006). *Democracy in Europe: The EU and national polities.* Oxford University Press.

Streeck, W. (1992). *Social institutions and economic performance: Studies of industrial relations in advanced capitalist economies.* Sage Publications.

Streeck, W. (2009). *Re-forming capitalism: Institutional change in the German political economy.* Oxford University Press on Demand.

Streeck, W. & Thelen, K. (2005). Institutional change in advanced political economies. In Streeck, W. & Thelen, K. (Eds.) *Beyond continuity: Institutional change in advanced political economies.* Oxford University Press.

Thelen, K. (2010). Beyond comparative statics: Historical institutional approaches to stability and change in the political economy of labor. In Morgan, G., Campbell, J., Crouch, C., Pedersen, O.K., & Whitley R. (Eds.). *The Oxford handbook of comparative institutional analysis.* Oxford University Press.Thelen, K., (2014). *Varieties of liberalization and the new politics of social solidarity.* Cambridge University Press.

Thelen, K. & Kume, I. (2006). Coordination as a political problem in coordinated market economies. *Governance*, 19 (1): 11–42.

Traxler, F. (2003). Bargaining (de) centralization, macroeconomic performance and control over the employment relationship. *British Journal of Industrial Relations*, 41(1): 1–27.

Visser, J. (2009). *Industrial relations in Europe 2008.* European Commission.

5. Interplay between State and Collective Bargaining, Comparing France and Spain

Ana Belén Muñoz Ruiz, Nuria Ramos Martín, Catherine Vincent

Abstract

The authors examine Spain and France, where the state intervened to reform collective bargaining systems through legal regulation. French and Spanish policymakers used the same rhetoric to justify the reforms: the alleged rigidity of their labour markets and collective bargaining systems. Nevertheless, several differences are noticed, especially regarding the strategies of social partners. The idea of decentralisation as a unidirectional and comprehensive process is challenged when examining both countries. In France, the concept of articulation over that of determination is preferred when referring to the collective bargaining decentralisation process. In Spain, the effect of the reforms has been the creation of a new pattern of fragmentation in industrial relations rather than a clearly decentralised collective bargaining system.

Keywords: decentralisation of collective bargaining, state intervention

Introduction

It is now commonplace to assert that the industrial relations systems of most European countries have been reshaped in recent decades in order to enhance economic efficiency, and that the decentralisation of collective bargaining has been the preferred instrument to achieve this objective (Marginson, 2015; Leonardi & Pedersini, 2018; Müller et al., 2019). This

Frank Tros (ed.). *Pathways in Decentralised Collective Bargaining in Europe.* Amsterdam: Amsterdam University Press, 2023

DOI 10.5117/9789048560233_CH05

finding resonates in this book, which shows that collective bargaining systems are under pressure. With the stated intention of achieving greater labour flexibility and improving competitiveness, most governments and employers' organisations have attempted to limit the scope of collective bargaining, viewed as sources of rigidity, and industry-level bargaining in particular. The outcomes are a dominant pattern of decentralisation in collective bargaining.

Nonetheless, the European countries under review reveal the impressive diversity of institutional forms and paths of evolution in industrial relations. Beyond each national tradition and history, these different trajectories of change came primarily from the ways that the parties in collective bargaining – employers, trade unions, and the state – have adjusted their strategies to meet new circumstances. In some countries, the social partners have themselves taken charge of reshaping the bargaining system, while in others the changes have taken place through more or less concerted government intervention. This observation is not new, either. The national industrial relations institutions and collective labour law emerged through the interplay or negotiation between social partners and the state. The Fordist compromise of the glorious thirties was founded on the fact that governments, employers' organisations, and top trade unions reached an accommodation that was the establishment of sectoral collective bargaining (Crouch, 1993). The motivation of the parties to sector-level collective bargaining was similar despite differences among countries. In addition to removing competition from wages and ensuring social peace, employers benefited from sectoral bargaining insofar as it restricted the power of unions at the workplace, thus, protecting the exercise of managerial prerogative (Sisson, 1987). For trade unions, sectoral collective bargaining had implications for their power relations and a protective function for workers, enabling them to develop solidaristic wage policies. Lastly, for the state, the institutionalisation of sector-level bargaining systems, in the absence of industrial conflict, achieved stability and provided a platform for economic growth.

In recent decades, the assumptions underpinning the utility of sectoral collective bargaining have been called into question. The financialisation of corporate governance, the globalisation of exchange, and the shift towards greater labour market flexibilisation have destabilised the mode of growth of advanced capitalisms (Streeck & Thelen, 2005). To confront this permanent uncertainty, and in a context of weakened organised labour, employers' organisations have become less likely to support long-standing collective bargaining institutions. In this new power balance, employer-led decentralisation has been supported by governments, directly or in a more concerted way. The transformation of collective bargaining systems has become a political issue, moving in the direction of greater employer discretion within the company.

In Western European countries, the decentralisation of bargaining primarily resulted from the actions of employers who have striven for decentralised bargaining arrangements or from the state, which has supported employer-led decentralisation. It also resulted from the limited capacity of trade unions to sustain sectoral bargaining. This tendency could lead to some breakdown in collective bargaining structures or to "incremental corrosion" (Marginson, 2015). Depending on the country, different mechanisms have been used to achieve this decentralisation: deregulation; derogation; circumvention of institutions by the actors (see Tros, 2022), but in most countries, it took the form of "organised decentralisation" (Traxler, 1995). National trajectories have been adapted to the identities and strategies of the actors. Baccaro and Howell assume that "the *trajectory* of institutional performance across countries is convergent, but not the *form* of institution" (Baccaro & Howell, 2017: 16). We can add that the role played by the different actors in these convergent evolutions has not been the same in the various countries. In some countries, the social partners influence the shaping of the collective bargaining system. In Sweden, for instance, in line with the tradition of autonomous collective bargaining, an organised decentralisation was established through cross-sectoral agreements. In Germany, too, an organised decentralisation has been implemented by trade unions and employers' organisations through the possibility of opting out of sectoral agreements. However, a form of disorganised decentralisation is developing on the initiative of German employers' organisations, giving companies the possibility of joining without being obliged to apply sectoral agreements. The result is an erosion of bargaining coverage, without the government intervening in the extension procedures.

Italy is a good example of a joint intervention by the state and the social partners. Decentralisation of collective bargaining has been promoted since the 1990s and moved decisively after the 2008 economic and financial crisis. In 2010, the Italian government legislated a fiscal incentive linked to local- or company-level bargaining on performance-related pay and new opportunities for derogation from sectoral agreements (in 2011). In parallel, the social partners opened up a process of organised decentralisation based on derogations approved by sectoral trade unions.

In other countries, the state showed a more active role, intervening directly in the legal regulation of collective bargaining. That was the case in France and Spain. This chapter focuses on a comparison of legislative shaping of collective bargaining in these two countries and on the influence of trade unions and employers' organisations. We will go into depth about the reforms in the two countries and will analyse the interplay between the state and the social partners in these. After having described the institutional framework designed by these reforms and analysed their actual effects on actors' strategies, we will come to comparative conclusions on the interplay between state and collective bargaining in France and Spain.

An overhaul of the French and Spanish collective bargaining systems imposed by the state

Institutional framework of collective bargaining in France

In France, collective bargaining has been built on a statutory basis since 1936 but did not become the normal mode of social relations until recently (see for more elaborations Kahmann & Vincent, 2022: 5–20).[1] During the "Glorious Thirties," sector-level bargaining emerged as the pillar of French industrial relations. Despite one of the lowest rates of union density, the French bargaining coverage rate is among the highest in OECD countries: 96% in the private sector. The high coverage level results from two factors. First, collective agreements apply to all employees of a company covered by them, regardless whether or not they are trade union members. Second, and above all, bargaining coverage has been broadened by the general use of administrative extension of industrial agreements. The state has compensated for employers' hostility to bargaining using two other tools. First, in order to level social inequalities and to compensate for a deficient bargaining process, a statutory national minimum wage was implemented, by a 1950 law, and revised in 1970. The government set its rate annually, according to strictly established rules. Linkages between the minimum wage and wage bargaining are rather complex, but the minimum wage

---

1   The first law establishing a collective bargaining system dated back to 1919. Because of the outbreak of the Second World War, but also of the hostility of employers toward unionism, the 1936 law was not implemented. The 1950 law consolidated the 1936 terms.

increase more or less set the pace for sectoral wage agreements (Delahaie & Vincent, 2021). Second, until the late 1990s, representative unions had a monopoly in collective bargaining at all levels. More recently, new rules for union representativeness and the validity of agreements have also sought to support the security of bargaining.

Nevertheless, since the mid-1980s in the French case, the driving force of sectoral collective bargaining has been eroded by an early development towards the decentralisation of collective bargaining to the company level. Successive governments have favoured or even prioritised company bargaining. Two devices have facilitated this. Firstly, in 1982, the so-called Auroux laws made it mandatory for any establishment counting one or more union representative to negotiate annually on wages, working time, and work organisation (without obligation to reach an agreement). Since then, the catalogue of compulsory bargaining items at firm level has continuously evolved. The Auroux laws also strengthened the prerogatives of union delegates and the elected workplace representation bodies. Compulsory firm-level bargaining marked a departure from the state's and the unions' long-standing preference for (national) sectoral and (national) multi-sectoral bargaining.

Secondly, in the 1990s, successive legislative reforms, enacted by conservative governments, introduced derogations from the Labour Code – mainly on statutory working time – through sectoral or company agreements. A step forward was taken in 2004 when the Fillon law allowed for company-level derogation from sectoral agreements, except for minimum wages, job classifications, supplementary social protection, and vocational training. However, sector-level negotiators could "lock up" other topics and exclude them from company-level derogations.

Even if the changing pattern of collective bargaining has gradually delineated the coupling between the central and company levels, the system remained coordinated by law and the favourability principle (Vincent, 2019).

All the above-mentioned reforms were preceded by consultation with social partners. Whereas employers' associations were generally satisfied with these changes, national union confederations were divided over them. However, that tradition of consultation was broken by the labour market/collective bargaining system reforms introduced by the socialist Hollande government, whose labour law reform in 2016 conferred more autonomy on company bargaining (Rehfeldt & Vincent, 2017). A year later, the 2017 Macron Ordinances replaced this legislation with a compulsory division of topics between bargaining levels.

Table 5.1.   Principal characteristics of collective bargaining in France, before and after 2016/2017

Key features	Before 2016	2016/2017
Actors entitled to collective bargaining	At national level: representativeness based on workplace election criteria (8% at industry and national levels). Five representative unions. Three employers' organisations fulfil representativeness criteria based on membership. In enterprises: for unions, representativeness based on workplace election criteria (10% at least). without a union, possibilities to bargain with elected representatives or mandated employees (10% at enterprise level;	At national level: No change

In enterprises without a union, drastic extension of the possibilities to bargain with elected representatives or mandated employees |
Importance of bargaining levels	– erosion of industry level but still the reference, particularly in SMEs	– increase of company agreements, less coordination between bargaining levels
Favourability principle / possibilities to derogate from sectoral agreements	– strict favourability principle among levels – possibilities to derogate from labour code or sectoral level mainly on working time	– compulsory division of certain topics among levels – for other topics, priority to workplace level
Collective bargaining coverage (%)	96%	96%

Source: Kahmann & Vincent (2022); OECD/AIAS ICTWSS database, 2021.

In the last two decades, the above-mentioned legal reforms have significantly modified industrial relations and the labour market. In their wake, the 2017 ordinances have profoundly disrupted the previous system by weakening the individual and collective protections provided by the Labour Code: increased decentralisation of collective bargaining; overhaul of workplace representation; and a further step towards deregulating the labour market, notably by easing economic dismissal procedures and introducing a compensation cap in the event of legal action. The employers' organisations have clearly supported the ordinances, which meet many of their demands, while all the unions are strongly opposed.

Institutional framework of collective bargaining in Spain

In the last decade, there have been several legal reforms aimed to flexibilise and decentralise the system of collective bargaining in Spain (see for more elaborations Muñoz Ruiz & Ramos Martín, 2022: 2–17). They were a response to the severe economic crisis that affected Spain between 2009 and 2016, and to the trends in some (mostly economic) circles that advised subsequent governments in Spain. These trends supported the idea of higher economic efficiency through the decentralisation of collective bargaining, in particular regarding wage negotiation and swift adjustment of salaries to the economic cycle. Most of these legal reforms have been heavily criticised, both by trade unions and legal scholars, due to the fact that they clearly weaken collective labour rights.

A major reform of the Labour market legislation took place with the introduction of Law 35/2010 on 17 September 2010. Although this law was not directly aimed at reforming collective bargaining, several of the modifications implemented had an impact on the system of collective bargaining, mainly through the possibilities for opting out of sectoral-level collective agreement provisions regarding wages via a company agreement. In relation to collective bargaining, the law expanded the possibilities for internal functional flexibility in companies, as well as salary flexibility, and it made it easier to use wage opt-out clauses to deviate from wages and other working conditions (such as working time) set at the sectoral level.

In 2010, Article 82.3 of the Workers' Statute was amended establishing that, following a consultation procedure, a company agreement between the employer and the employee representatives might depart from the wages fixed by a collective agreement negotiated at a higher level. This might happen when, as a result of the application of those wages, the economic situation and prospects of the company could be damaged and the level of employment could be affected. This system of wage opt-out was later reformed in 2011 and 2012, because it did not reach the aimed goal of making decentralised bargaining on wages easier for companies. The strict regulation of the opt-out clause made it complex and difficult to be applied in practice. Thus, some legal scholars argued that the stringent requirements of the wage opt-out clauses played against the whole aim of more flexibility at company level in case of economic difficulties (Pose Vidal, 2009).

In 2011, the system of collective bargaining was reformed again by Law 7/2011 of 10 June, this time with respect to urgent measures for the reform of collective bargaining. This reform was adopted without prior consensus with the social partners, due to the impossibility of reaching a tripartite agreement addressing the problems affecting the collective bargaining system. The main objective of this reform was to restructure collective bargaining by eliminating excessive extensions in relation to collective agreements and by facilitating internal flexibility at company level[2] and swift negotiation of wages. The reform adapted the rules of legitimation of collective bargaining to the new business realities and the role of unions in companies. A Labour Relations and Collective Bargaining Council was also set up, with the aim of strengthening the competent public institutions in collective bargaining. The main rule affecting collective bargaining priority rules was a provision in this Law 7/2011 establishing that the content of company agreements prevailed over what was agreed in collective agreements at higher level, giving rise to an increase in the possibilities of decentralised collective bargaining.

A major reform of the labour market in Spain, and the change most criticised by the trade unions, was adopted in 2012 through Royal Decree-Law 3/2012 of 10 February 2012 for urgent measures for labour market reform. It built upon the labour market reform of 2010, as the Spanish economic and labour market (unemployment rate) situation worsened. This reform introduced new rules on dismissal, more flexibility for employers to adjust working time, work shifts, employees' functions, and salaries. The reform also established new incentives for permanent hiring and changed the rules applicable to collective dismissals in public administrations and companies, among other measures. The new legislation also reformed the rules regarding collective bargaining (see summary of the main changes in Table 5.2.). The reform introduced the possibility of employers to opt-out from the provisions of the statutory collective agreement if they had substantial economic, technological, organisational or productivity reasons to adapt the company to the financial situation of the undertaking. The law modified the rules applied to the prevalence of collective bargaining at a higher level, favouring decentralisation and giving priority to company-level agreements (Del Rey, 2012).

The 2012 labour market reform clearly lowered the employment protection of workers in Spain. Some of the main changes introduced by the reform aimed at promoting internal flexibility in companies (powers of employers to modify working conditions such as wage or working time), both in relation to working conditions agreed in collective agreements and collective dismissal

2   In Spain, in the literature, legal scholars often use the terminology "internal flexibility measures" to refer to the expanded possibilities to use company agreements to deviate from the working conditions standards set at collective agreements of a higher level.

procedures. In addition, the level of compensation in case of unfair dismissal was lowered and the administrative authorisation requirement in the case of collective redundancies (ERE) was eliminated.

Table 5.2.   Main issues and aims of the Labour Law Reform 2012 in Spain

Issues	Aim of the Reform	New regulation
Duration of collective agreements	To update collective agreements	Limit the period of duration
Collective agreements at company level	Decentralisation	Priority of collective agreement at company level over the sectoral agreement
Opt-out	To increase the internal flexibility	More flexible causes of opt-out and a simple procedure

Source: Muñoz Ruiz & Ramos Martín, 2022.

In an attempt to counteract some of the effects of the 2012 reform, the Spanish left-wing coalition government approved the Royal Decree-Law 32/2021, on 28 December 2021. This new legislation is based on an agreement reached between the government, trade unions, and employers' organisations in order to structurally reform the Spanish labour market. One of the most relevant changes introduced by the 2021 labour law reform is the reinstalment of the so-called ultra-activity of collective bargaining agreements (the automatic continuation of collective agreements beyond their expiry date until there is a new collective agreement signed). This is an important legal development, which counteracts the attempt of the 2012 labour law reform to provide more power to employers at the bargaining table. Already in 2014, a controversial decision by the Supreme Court had established that employees should continue to enjoy the same employment conditions while a new collective agreement was being negotiated. Another important amendment is that the prevalence of the sectoral agreements over the company agreements concerning wages is restored by the reform.

There are two main reasons why this reform was passed. Firstly, a number of artificial bargaining units were created in order to apply the priority of company collective agreements. For example, in cases where a collective agreement was signed by the company and a single representative of the workers (often not joined to any trade unions). Secondly, some company agreements were negotiated with the sole purpose of avoiding the applicability of the sectoral collective agreement, in particular the higher wages set at the sectoral level (Mercader Uguina, 2021).

Drivers of the reforms: Increasing labour market flexibility and facilitating decentralised collective bargaining

The 2010–2012 reforms in Spain and the 2016 and 2017 reforms in France were largely driven by national responses to European Commission's recommendations that member states should adopt ambitious "structural labour market reforms" and follow the flexibilisation trends predominant in the EU's agenda at the time. The ideological neoliberal background of the reforms was the need to reform inflexible and strongly regulated labour markets (both countries' labour legislations were indicated as such at the time). The main policy approach informing the structural reforms in both countries was the lifting of regulations that, it had been argued, produced rigidities in the labour market (Knegt & Ramos Martín, 2016) This narrative was grounded on the economic arguments supporting the enhanced efficiency of decentralised collective bargaining, and the need to quickly counteract the negative effects of the economic recession, which started in 2008, by facilitating the development of bargaining parties at company level.

Decentralisation of the negotiations on terms and conditions of employment (in particular concerning wages), was seen as the ultimate solution to the perceived problems regarding slow or inflexible bargaining systems. It was considered as a suitable means of adjusting to adverse economic circumstances and an efficient response to the economic downturn. Both countries were facing explicit EC recommendations to adopt structural measures at the beginning of the 2010s. The stagnation of the rates of economic growth and the persistent relatively high unemployment rates were seen as growing concerns.

The pressure in the Spanish case was stronger, in the sense that even when the country has not been officially bailed out, it did receive substantial financial aid from the EU (specifically for restructuring the banking sector).

The impact of EU recommendations in the French case is much more ambiguous (Pernot, 2017). Most of the recommendations relate to fiscal measures designed to reduce the public debt and to ease mobility on the labour market. Recommendations on wages mainly concerned the legal minimum wage policy, which is considered too high and too dynamic: "The minimum wage in France is such that it allows beneficiaries to enjoy a purchasing power among the highest in the European Union. It is therefore appropriate the minimum wage should continue to evolve in a manner conducive to competitiveness and job creation."[3] There was no recommendation

---

3   European Commission, COM (2014) 411 final, p 6.

concerning the form and content of collective bargaining. Clearly, the level of decentralisation in collective bargaining in France, i.e., significant corporate collective bargaining empowerment and a wide area for waivers, falls within the scope of the forms of industrial relations generally promoted by the EU's Council and Commission. Moreover, from the start of the crisis, the French government anticipated European demands by creating a new type of agreement in 2008, so-called competitiveness-employment agreements, which are a French version of concession bargaining. In these agreements, unions exchange guarantees on employment against the lowering of social standards laid down in past company agreements. The conclusion of this type of agreement by companies in economic difficulty has been facilitated by an interprofessional national agreement signed by the social partners in 2013.[4]

The main argument behind the reforms of labour and social regulation in both countries was that policymakers have identified employment protection legislation as a major cause of the high unemployment rates. Even when no direct commands from the EU institutions were imposed on these two countries, governments closely followed the recommendations issued by the EU institutions, aiming to develop a "flexicurity" approach when dealing with amendments of legislation in the social field. Consequently, we can talk of "monitored structural reforms" by the EU in these cases (Knegt & Ramos Martin, 2016)

The processes of labour law reform in Spain and France, which have pursued further decentralisation of collective bargaining systems, are similar in terms of the crucial role of the state in the decentralisation process and in the ideological argumentations supporting those reforms. The main differences are that the process in France started much earlier and it has been more progressive and long-standing, which could explain the later opposition to those reforms (from 2016) of the trade unions than in the Spanish case. In Spain, the strategy of the unions was clearly to resist the changes in the collective bargaining system, to lobby for a counter-reform, and to bargain with employers against the spirit of that law. The derogation by the 2021 labour market reform of the most controversial provisions of the previous 2012 reform can be seen as a victory by their camp concerning this issue.

---

4   The 11 January 2013 agreement introduced a new type of derogatory agreements, namely, the *Accords de maintien dans l'emploi*, AME (job retention agreements), allowing employers to stand outside higher-level agreements for a time; based on the model of company-level agreements signed in Germany during the 2008–2010 crisis.

Role of the various actors in the reforms

State intervention and different reform paths

The broader industrial relations context in France is heavily shaped by the strong and interventionist role of the state, which, at different points in time, has served different purposes (see for more elaboration: Kahmann & Vincent, 2022: 5–20). For example, by the turn of the twentieth century, the purpose was to offset the organisational weaknesses of both unions and employers. Then, after the Second World War, the state wanted to incorporate trade unions and employers' organisations in the formulation of social and welfare issues by treating them as partners, albeit often only in an advisory capacity. As a result, a very detailed and broad Labour Code was established, granting individual rights and benefits directly to employees but undermining the unions' role in collective bargaining development.

This Fordist compromise collapsed in the late 1980s as a result of the shift away from industry to the service sector and the rise of unemployment and precarious forms of employment. Meanwhile, as a third kind of state intervention, neoliberal policies have gradually been implemented, although a number of welfare safety nets have been retained. These changes have gone hand in hand with a decline of trade union structural power (Pernot, 2017). Since then, decentralisation of collective bargaining has been a central theme of industrial relations reforms. As we have seen, in the last two decades, several laws have significantly modified industrial relations and the labour market.

All these reforms were preceded by consultation with social partners. Continuing this tradition, President François Hollande and his government sought to involve unions and employers' organisations in major decisions on public policy in the social field, or to consult them, at least. These tripartite summits, however, were placed under threat of legislative action and framed by government "roadmaps," the features which were often very close to the employers' demands. Lastly, these negotiations frequently revealed deep disagreements among the trade unions. The 2013 national interprofessional agreement – entitled "For a new economic and social model in the service of business competitiveness, job security and career paths" – is derived from the agenda and roadmaps that the government had submitted to the social partners at the start of the 2012 social conference. It was signed by three of the five unions authorised to bargain (CFDT, CFTC, CFE-CGC)[5]; it

---

5   CFDT: the French Democratic Confederation of Labour (*Confédération Française Démocratique du Travail*; CFTC: the French Confederation of Christian Workers (*Confédération Française des*

was strongly rejected by the other two (CGT, FO)[6]. Transformed into a bill, the government asked Parliament to enact, without substantive changes, the project it had submitted and pledged to abide by the spirit – and often the letter – of the agreement.

From 2015, Hollande geared his government towards a clear supply-side policy to promote growth, imposing lower labour costs and firm-friendly public support on investments. Dissatisfied with the pace of structural reforms, the socialist government ended up imposing an overhaul of collective bargaining without consultation (Rehfeldt & Vincent, 2017). Prime Minister Manuel Valls assembled a commission of experts in April 2015, to make "bold" proposals to "go further" than the previous reforms. The commission was supposed to draw on the experience of other countries and also take into account recent reports by think tanks on the same subject, most of them in favour of the prioritisation of company agreements by introducing a general derogation principle. The commission's report (Combrexelle, 2015), presented in September 2015, advocates reversal of the hierarchy of norms, giving priority to company agreements in order to ensure "proximity regulation." The 2016 bill on the reform of collective bargaining was based on this report. It was unanimously rejected by all representative trade union organisations, prompting the Minister of Labour to negotiate some changes with the CFDT union. Despite this, it triggered numerous strikes and mass demonstrations over a period of four months, which were organised by student unions and a trade union coalition between CGT and FO. The core of the 2016 Labour law regarding collective bargaining was to make the company the decisive bargaining level, limited in a first step to working time and overtime pay, paid holidays, and weekly rest.

During the presidential elections of 2017, candidate Emmanuel Macron announced that he would speed up the labour law reforms. Once elected, in order to avoid long debates in the parliament and possible demonstrations, a *loi d'habilitation* (framework law) was passed in the Parliament by a majority of the new presidential party, authorising the government to execute its reform project through *ordonnances* (government decrees). These were issued in September 2017, after one-to-one formal consultations with unions and employers 'organisations.

Travailleurs Chrétiens); CFE-CGC : the French Confederation of Supervisors-General Confederation of Clerical and Managerial Staff (*Confédération Française de l'Encadrement-Confédération Générale des Cadres*).

6   CGT : the General Confederation of Labour (*Confédération Générale du Travail*) ; FO : Worker Force (*Force Ouvrière*, officially CGT-FO).

Finally, the role of the state remains one of the most peculiar features of the French collective bargaining system, whose strength and spread have never relied on the existence of strong and encompassing bargaining parties, but on support from the state, particularly in the form of extension procedures and the statutory minimum wage. Political intervention both reflects and maintains the loose links between the social partners.

In the last decade, Spain has seen several legislative attempts to transform the system of collective bargaining and impose a trend to decentralisation (see for more elaboration: Ramos Martín & Muñoz Ruiz, 2022: 2–16). The unilateral reform of the collective bargaining system in June 2011 by the then socialist government was a substantial compromise between the position of social partners and the "Troika" demands on labour market structural reforms. A changed political constellation in November 2011 urged social partners to reach a social pact; however, it was ignored by the new conservative government, which unilaterally adopted a Decree in 2012 with further changes in labour law. This caused a general strike in March 2012 and a collapse of tripartite social dialogue for a few years (Knegt & Ramos, 2016; Mercader Uguina et al., 2016a).

Until the last collectively negotiated reform in December 2021, most labour market reforms in Spain had been passed without the support of the trade unions, due to the reduction of labour rights introduced by them. While the socialist government attached more importance to social dialogue in the 2010 reform, the conservative government in office from 2012 until 2018 in Spain paid little attention to it. While the 2010 and 2011 labour market reforms were preceded by negotiations between the social partners and the government, no form of social dialogue took place for the 2012 reform passed by the then conservative government. Furthermore, the conservative government in office completely ignored the agreement reached by the social partners some weeks before the adoption of the 2012 major labour law reform. A very "aggressive reform," including profound changes in labour law, was approved instead, with the clear opposition of the main trade union confederations (Knegt & Ramos, 2016; Mercader Uguina et al., 2016a).

Role of the social partners and reactions to the various reforms

Role of the social partners and reactions to the reforms in France
Within the employers' camp, the political line towards decentralisation initially fluctuated in the 1970s (Amable 2016). Employers have long preferred to negotiate at sectoral level, where they felt stronger, or cross-industry

where they can rely on governments that were often sensitive to their concerns. Therefore, the main employers' association MEDEF[7] (former CNPF) met the Auroux laws with hostility, fearing the strengthening of radical unions at workplace level. Yet, slow growth and mass unemployment stifled labour radicalism and employers soon came to realise the advantages of company bargaining. Finally, MEDEF reconsidered its position on collective bargaining by the late 1990s and had chosen to privilege company-level bargaining to weaken the constraints imposed by legislation or by sectoral bargaining.

MEDEF aspired to safeguard industrial democracy from such state interventionism and to foster the emergence of "credible, representative and modern trade unions." Underlining the decidedly political ambitions of its project, it also called for the recognition of the right to bargain collectively in the Constitution and an affirmation of the normative authority of social partners.

As mentioned above, employers' associations were generally satisfied with the series of legislative measures to reform industrial relations that were passed by conservative governments in the 2000s. Later labour law reforms adopted unilaterally by the Hollande and Macron governments in 2016 and 2017 have been welcomed by the employers' organisations.

The French trade union movement has traditionally been marked by pluralism, rivalry between union confederations and a lack of financial and organisational resources. Trade union membership statistics have always exhibited lower rates in France than in other European countries, barely reaching 20% even in the late 1960s. The oil shocks and recession of the 1970s further narrowed the base and trade union membership has been constantly low since then, at a mere 10%: roughly 8% in the private sector and 20% in the public sector in 2019 (Dares et al., 2021). Despite these weaknesses, unions have achieved a high level of employee participation in elections for company representatives and are able to mobilise workers with great success.

Until the 1970s, collective bargaining hardly existed without conflicts and collective agreements were often signed after strikes. The promotion of contractual policy, traditionally worn by the CFTC, CGC, and CGT-FO, also became the spearhead of the CFDT in the 1980s. The conversion of the CGT to bargaining was more gradual but was achieved at the dawn of the 1990s. All the confederations favoured reaching agreement at industry level. When the Auroux laws were adopted, unions welcomed them. They viewed them

7   MEDEF : Movement of French Enterprises (*Mouvement Des Enterprises De France*).

as a way of invigorating worker participation and enabling union delegates to better defend and represent worker concerns. This seemed all the more desirable as the coordination among different levels was legally governed by the favourability principle. Trade unions have always been opposed to company bargaining being *in pejus*, except when the company's economic survival is at stake.

The priority given to company bargaining by the 2016–2017 laws meant that they have been rejected by all the representative trade unions. However, not all of them called for mobilisation. The Labour Law bill of 2016 led to numerous strikes and mass demonstrations organised by a coalition of CGT, FO and some autonomous and student unions over a period of four months. These mobilisations, often violently repressed, did not prevent the adoption of the law. The rejection of the 2017 ordinances was also strong, but as they came just after the presidential elections, the unions gave up mobilising.

Role of the social partners and reactions to the reforms in Spain
In Spain, during the decades of the eighties and the nineties, the actors leading the design of the institutional setting governing the collective bargaining process were the unions. This situation is explained by the national political context in which the constitutional right to collective bargaining was established. An incipient context of democratisation, in which collective rights and freedoms were new and where trade unions could play a major role. Besides, in the so-called transition period to democracy, trade union organisations had an important social and political influence. However, over the years, the unions' power and influence in political decision-making has been declining in Spain. From the mid-1990s, reforms of the collective bargaining system were meant to adapt it to the economic context and to the demands of the EU for more ambitious labour market reforms. All these factors influenced the changes of collective bargaining regulation in Spain, which have been implemented by successive reforms throughout the 2000s and culminating in the 2012 reform.

In the Spanish case, one of the strategic responses of the trade unions to the failure of tripartite social dialogue before the state-driven 2012 major labour law reform, was to strengthen and develop bipartite social dialogue at sector level. Unions tended to consider the 2012 reform as ideologically rather than economically motivated and opposed it by keeping the traditional trend to sign sector collective agreements. However, at company level, agreements on reduction of working hours and pay in exchange for restrictions on layoffs were not uncommon during the years following the 2012 reform. In the end, the unilaterally imposed reforms of the collective bargaining system have had little effect on the dynamics of collective bargaining, as unions started a judicial battle against them and continued bargaining on working conditions and wages in collective agreements preferably at the sector level (Knegt & Ramos Martín, 2016; Mercader Uguina et al., 2016a).

In contrast, bipartite dialogue has been reinforced between unions and business associations since the adoption of the 2012 labour market reform. In fact, a main strategic response of the social partners to the failure of tripartite social dialogue has been to stimulate bipartite social dialogue at all levels: sectoral and enterprise. Social partners have signed relevant agreements regarding the maximum period of collective agreements and wage moderation, among other issues. The 2012, 2014, 2016, and 2018 In-ter-confederal Agreement on Employment and Collective Bargaining (AENC) clearly represented these trends. In particular, these agreements seem to have produced some positive effects on collective bargaining coverage since it have encouraged social partners to renegotiate collective agreements. At company level, though, serious doubts have risen regarding the freedom of unions or work councils to negotiate the working conditions, as agreements (for example, on a reduction of wages) have sometimes been signed merely to avoid more dramatic consequences such as layoffs (Knegt & Ramos Martín, 2016)

The opposition of the unions to the imposed labour law reforms, espe-cially to the legislation adopted in 2012, led to increased judicialisation of the labour conflict (with growing litigation and collective disputes) and the organisation of general strikes. Despite the increase in the number of strikes during the period that followed the adoption of the 2012 reform, the economic impact was not particularly high in comparison with previous years. In 2012, the number of participants in collective actions increased but strikes had shorter duration (Mercader Uguina et al., 2016b). The 2012 reform made a clear commitment to the reduction of judicial control over redundancies, and unlawful dismissal and redundancy costs were reduced. Two general strikes followed the 2012 labour market reform. These measures not only heightened tensions and hindered collective bargaining, but also led to an imbalance in labour relations and bargaining power. By making it easier to carry out redundancies, worker representatives were frequently compelled to accept the internal flexibility measures proposed by the employer to avoid them (Knegt & Ramos Martín, 2016).

The 2012 reform attempted to decentralise collective bargaining and to grant more power to employers at the bargaining process. From the perspective of unions, this reform has undermined their position. The reform enhanced the role of the company agreements, while the unions' strength has traditionally lied at the sectoral level of collective bargaining (Knegt & Ramos Martín, 2016).

The purpose of decentralisation of the 2012 reform has been achieved only to a certain extent. Decentralisation has proven to be difficult in a country with an extremely high density of small- and medium-sized undertakings, most of which lack the necessary employee or union representatives to initiate a formal process of collective bargaining. Indeed, strongly increasing flexibility in company-level wage bargaining is seen as undesirable in the Spanish context, where 82.8% of companies have two employees or less. Due to the large number of SMEs operating in Spain, this could undermine the stability of the industrial relations and collective bargaining system (Ramos Martín, 2016).

Apart from the reluctancy of trade unions to negotiate wages and working conditions at company level, according to Casas Baamonde (2018), there are other reasons that explain why companies and employees' representatives do not often negotiate specific company agreements. This includes the lack of negotiating knowledge/experience on the part of both the employers and the employees' representatives, the absence of employees' representatives in the company, and the refusal of the employers to bargain at lower levels, mainly due to the fact that the collective agreements at sector level suit businesses/companies' needs (Casas Baamonde, 2018).

There is a trend of large companies with several establishments located in Spain including all those establishments under the scope of the agreement negotiated at company level[8] (Muñoz Ruiz, 2014; Fernández Villazón, 2018).

Regarding those companies where there are no employees' representatives (trade unions or works council), the employees may directly bargain with the employer and be bound collectively, but when they do, the agreement can only be qualified as non-statutory collective agreement lacking binding force *erga omnes* (not negotiated in conformity with the Workers' Statutes rules and non-legally binding for all falling under its scope).[9] Such an agreement has limited effectiveness, since it only affects those who sign it or those who are formally represented by those who sign it (Muñoz Ruiz, 2014).

8   See case law: SAN de 16 de septiembre de 2013, Procedimiento núm. 314/2013 and SAN de 11 de septiembre de 2013, Procedimiento núm. 0000219/2013.
9   See case law: SSTSJ de Andalucía, Sevilla, de 7 de diciembre de 1999 (R° 3719/1999) y 23 de mayo de 2000 (R. 2999/1999).

Finally, the labour reform of 2021 has been praised by legal experts as sensible, reasonable, and balanced. Especially relevant here is the fact it has been the result of a long and complex tripartite negotiation process in which the social partners have had the merit of reaching the necessary agreements with the government in the sinuous field of labour market reforms (Mercader Uguina & de la Puebla Pinilla, 2021). The Government, and the most representative trade unions (UGT, CCOO) and the main employers' associations (CEOE and CEPYME) have achieved a deliberate balance when addressing controversial issues regarding the system of collective bargaining where they traditionally had opposing points of view.

Role of the social partners and reactions to the reforms: Comparative perspectives
When looking at the employers' agenda in both countries under consideration, there is a clear similarity in terms of the goals of the employers' organisations to support a trend to deregulation of the labour market and to ease bargaining at the company level. In the employers' camp, the 2016 and 2017 reforms in France and the 2012 reform in Spain (which facilitated flexibility in wages, working hours, skills, mobility in companies, etc. and reduced dismissal costs) were most welcome.

However, in the Spanish case, the employers' representatives recognise that sectoral-level collective bargaining suits employers' interests, especially for setting minimum wage levels, due to the business industrial structure (with many small- and medium-sized undertakings) but they have strongly opposed the ultra-activity (automatic continuation) of collective agreements after their period of termination originally signed. However, they finally accepted the legal reestablishment of that continuation rule in the compromised tripartite reform adopted in December 2021. On the contrary, the employers in France have not accepted a new compromise to revise the 2017 Macron reforms.

The trade unions responses to the latest reforms in both countries under consideration have been quite similar. Unions have been defending central structures, organising strikes, and lobbying for a derogation of the most aggressive parts of the reforms, including controversial issues facilitating negotiations of company agreements when the representativeness of the employees was not optimal. That has also been accompanied in both countries with using the available opportunities to reach agreements in multi-level involvements and engage in company bargaining when the conditions were suitable and, also, when it was necessary to accept adjustments in the working conditions to avoid redundancies.

Organised decentralisation: Incremental "layering"

From derogation and compulsory bargaining to a division of competences among bargaining topics (France)

In France, until 2017, the movement of decentralisation of collective bargaining initiated by the state was done according to two modalities. The first one was the introduction of derogations from statutory working time. Initially only possible at the level of sectoral agreements, these derogations have spread to the company level and have been extended to all aspects of the organisation of working time. The other modality consisted in the introduction of mandatory negotiations. Since the Auroux law of 1982, annual bargaining on wages and working time has been compulsory in any company hosting one or more unions; even so, no settlement is required. In the last two decades, state interventionism in collective bargaining goes so far as to define a part of its agenda, both at sectoral and company level. Successive legislations have introduced the obligation to negotiate at sector level on various topics. At the present time, in each bargaining sector, every four years the employer and union negotiators are obliged to open discussions on a certain number of topics: pay; work-life balance; working conditions; strategic workforce planning; exposure to occupational risks. Every five years, the sectoral social partners must examine whether the job classification scheme of the collective agreement is still up to date. They may also conclude an agreement that changes the rhythm and redefines the topics of sectoral bargaining. Importantly, there is no obligation to reach an agreement between the social partners, only to open discussion. However, in practice, almost all bargaining sectors regularly conclude agreements on these topics.

In 1982, the law also introduced compulsory bargaining at the company level, which is specific to France. In companies with at least one trade union delegate, the employer must enter into negotiations on a number of topics, while at sectoral level, there is no obligation to conclude an agreement. Negotiations can take place at corporate group or company level, or if there is no union presence, at establishment level. The topics for compulsory negotiation at the company level have increased over time. Since 2015, they have been grouped into three areas:

(i)   Remuneration, working time, and the sharing of added value in the company (profit-sharing, incentive schemes, and employee savings); these topics must be negotiated annually.

(ii) Professional equality between women and men and quality of working life (employment of disabled workers, right to disconnect, reconciliation of work and family life, home-work mobility, etc.); this topic must also be negotiated every year.

(iii) Strategic workforce planning (GPEC, *Gestion prévisionnelle des emplois et des compétences*), training, subcontracting, temporary employment, career of trade union delegates, etc. GPEC is a potentially innovative collective bargaining item. It is a genuinely French HR concept (Gilbert, 2006). Originally developed in the 1990s, its aim is to anticipate organisational restructuring and to cushion its potential effects on employment by collectively putting into place measures that promote training as well as the internal and external mobility of workers. Since 2005, companies with at least 300 workers are legally obliged to negotiate a GPEC agreement every three years.[10]

The assessment of the impact of these obligations on company bargaining is not unequivocal and has been the subject of much research.

Regarding collective bargaining at company level, it is the trade union delegates from the representative unions who negotiate with the employer. Workplace agreements take effect once the signing unions represent 50% or more of the votes in the works council elections. Since the early 2000s, to offset the fact that non-unionised firms, mainly SMEs, could not bargain because of a lack of union delegates, the social partners advocated non-union negotiators. For trade unions, this could have been an opportunity for new settlements. Since the early 2000s, successive legislation has extended the possibilities for non-union representatives to negotiate in non-unionised workplaces (with employees specifically mandated by unions, or with elected employee representatives, such as works council members or employee delegates). The Macron ordinances have drastically extended the scope of the device. Three different regimes have been introduced, depending on the size of the non-unionised workplace.

As far as collective bargaining is concerned, in line with the 2016 Labour Law, the 2017 Ordinance replaced the articulation between sectoral and company level with a compulsory division of topics among levels. In the new collective bargaining architecture, coordination between levels is no longer based on the "favourability principle," but rather on the complementarities of bargained topics. Regarding competencies in standard setting, the division is as follows:

(i) Formally, the role of sectoral level agreements is reinforced since there are now 13 topics on which derogation is forbidden. This reinforcement

---

10   The legislation on strategic workforce planning is symptomatic of both the tendency of public policy to manage employment *via* company bargaining as well as the difficulties of the sectoral level to find its place on employment matters (Tallard & Vincent, 2014).

has taken place at the expense of the law, however, and not at the expense of company agreements.

(ii) The sectoral-level "lock up" faculty, unlimited under the 2004 Law, has now been reduced to four areas, which mainly concern issues of occupational safety and disabled workers. The weakening of sectoral level bargaining is evident here.

(iii) The primacy of company agreements concerns everything that does not fall into the two previous blocks, a considerable quantity. Regarding wages for example, all remuneration rules are now solely governed by the company agreement, with the exception of agreed minimum wages, classifications, and overtime premium.

Spanish case: Derogations from sector level agreements and priority rules for collective agreements

The Spanish model of collective bargaining is complex due to the dual channel system. It means that trade unions as well as works councils have the capacity to negotiate collective agreements at enterprise level. At sectoral level, the right to negotiate is given only to trade unions.

The right to collective bargaining and the binding character of collective agreements is enshrined in the Spanish Constitution (Article 37.1). The system of collective bargaining is thoroughly regulated in Title III of the Workers' Statute (WS). In particular, Article 82.3 establishes the legally binding character of collective agreements negotiated in conformity with the rules of the Workers' Statute. The main provision dealing with decentralisation of collective bargaining in Spain is current Article 84.3 WS, which stipulates that company agreements may deviate from several working conditions set by a statutory collective agreement negotiated at a higher level, providing certain requirements are fulfilled.

Although at the sectoral and company level the most representative unions have the legitimacy to negotiate, at the company level there is a duplication of actors. This is because both unions and work councils can negotiate. In the case that both parties want to start the negotiation, the union party has preference. The Workers' Statute establishes that the intervention in the negotiation will correspond to the union sections when they so agree, provided that they have the majority of the members of the works council or among the personnel delegates.[11]

11   See Article 87 of Workers' Statute.

The Workers' Statute establishes a theoretical priority/prevalence of the company agreement (except for wage setting *in peius*, according to the last labour law reform in 2021). Nevertheless, collective bargaining traditionally takes place mainly at sectoral level. Sectoral agreements are signed at the national level (for example, in the construction, banking, and chemical sectors) or in certain sectors at the provincial level (for example, in the commerce, transport of goods and passengers, and bakery sectors). Company agreements are much less common and concern mainly large companies (in sectors like gas, oil, car manufacturing, air transport, research and development) and the public sector (Pérez Infante, 2003).

Comparing legal techniques to achieve the same goal: Complex dualisation of bargaining levels

In both countries, the right to collective bargaining and the binding character of collective agreements is established in the labour law legislation. In the Spanish case, the system of collective bargaining is thoroughly regulated in the Workers' Statute, and in France, in the Labour Code. So, there has been a clear interventionist role of the state in the regulation of the collective bargaining system. Both case studies are similar in the sense that, with low trade union density, they show high levels of employees covered by collective agreements.[12] In both countries, in the last decade, there have been series of legal amendments leading to an overhaul of collective bargaining imposed by the State. All those reforms (with the exception of the Spanish labour market reform in 2021) were adopted without prior negotiation with the social partners.

Moreover, both legal systems are characterised by the complexity of bargaining levels and outcomes due to the alternative channels for workplace representation. Whilst differences in the distribution of functions and competences are noticed when comparing the two systems. In Spain, trade unions as well as works councils have the capacity to negotiate collective agreements at company level. On behalf of the workers, the works council, the staff delegates, or the union sections, (if any), which make up the majority of committee members, could negotiate at company level. As mentioned above, in France, state intervention in the regulation of collective bargaining has gone as far as to define part of its agenda, both at sectoral and company level. The latest legal reforms have introduced the obligation to negotiate at sector level on various topics and have established a compulsory articulated

---

12   That is partly due to the quasi-automatic "extension procedure" applicable in both countries.

division of topics among the different bargaining levels. That set of rules is topped up with a primacy of company agreements regarding every bargaining topic that does not fall into the legally predetermined blocks of competences per level. So, the French system is clearly pre-structured by a complex division of bargaining competences between the various levels.

A clear similarity in both countries is the persistent trend towards decentralisation to the company level by widening the scope for derogations from the sector level agreements and by expanding the possibilities for non-union company bargaining. However, these state-led decentralisation processes are not unidirectional and, in both countries, multi-sectoral bargaining has regained importance in the last years.

Effects of the reforms: Real impact versus intended impact

Real impact of the reform in France

From a quantitative point of view, company bargaining has developed considerably in the last decade. The number of agreements signed in bargaining units[13] increased substantially between the 1980s and the 2010s, from 3,900 in 1984 to 34,000 in 2011. Since then, the number of agreements concluded each year continued to increase, despite a slight decline in 2013–2014 (see Figure 5.1.).

It is worth noting that, in 2019, almost half of these agreements were concluded in enterprises with less than 50 employees, up by 10% compared to 2018. This change is due, on the one hand, to the establishment of new employee representation bodies, but, on the other, to the widening opportunities to negotiate without union presence.

Regarding all the enterprise agreements, including those signed by employee representatives and those adopted by referendum, 41% relate to profit sharing and participation, 22% to wages, 17% to working time and 13% to trade union rights and the functioning of works councils (+1 point compared to 2018). This last theme weighed 9% in 2017, before the implementation of the Macron Ordinances.

In 2018, collective bargaining took place in only 16.7% of bargaining units with more than 10 employees; yet, they were employing 63% of the workforce. More than 82% of these negotiations resulted in an agreement.

---

13   Negotiations can take place at company level in the strict sense, at group level, or at a more decentralised level (in one or more establishments of the company).

Figure 5.1. Numbers of agreements signed annually in bargaining units, 2000–2019, France

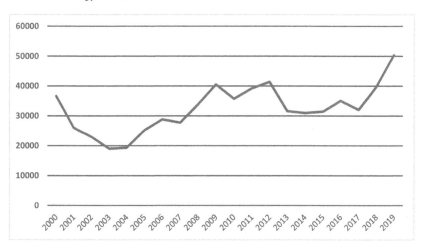

Note: Including agreements signed by union delegates and employees mandated by trade unions.
Source: *Bilan annuel de la négociation collective* from 2000 to 2019, Ministère du travail.

Agreements were signed in 11.7% of all bargaining units and in 68.6% of those with union representation.

Bargaining at company level has developed considerably in the last two decades, but decentralisation does not necessarily mean derogation (agreement *in pejus*). In practice, the use of derogations has remained limited (SECAFI, 2020). Three reasons may explain the lack of success of derogations at company level. First, because otherwise unions would have refused to sign them. Second, the standards imposed at sectoral level are already the result of minimal compromises and leave little room for less favourable agreements. Finally, derogation agreements are not relevant tools for management. In large companies, if economic survival is not at stake, opening negotiations on derogation clauses sends a very negative message both to unions and employees. SMEs are less likely to sign their own agreements, whether or not they include derogations, because maintaining the reference to sectoral-level agreements seems less time-consuming and risky.

Despite this quantitative success, French scholars have emphasised the inconsistencies and ambiguities of the state-led decentralisation process in terms of bargaining results. The quality of company agreements has generally fallen short of public policymakers' expectations. Formalism and the tendency to stick to minimal agreements are widely recognised as a problematic feature in France, even if this tends to vary regarding the issues that are negotiated (Mias et al., 2016). For example, compulsory agreements on strategic workforce planning tend to be richer in content than those on senior workers.

In their study on company social dialogue, Béthoux and Mias (2019: 13) point to the restrictiveness of the legal framework as a potential source for the impoverishment of company bargaining whereby legal compliance takes precedence over other goals and benefits. There is also evidence that the devolution of an increasing number of bargaining topics challenges the capacities of firm-level actors. As a rule, management has been better equipped to cope with this challenge. In larger companies, France has seen the emergence of a distinct human resource management function that is almost exclusively dedicated to the pursuit of collective bargaining. Trade union delegates, on the other hand, can barely cope with the consequences of decentralisation, due to a lack of time, skills, or activist resources. To meet deadlines, they may content themselves with pasting and copying legal requirements into agreements or embracing "good practices" defined by the law itself. Such behaviour entails a strong standardising effect on company bargaining.

Nevertheless, Béthoux and Mias (2019) observe some variation in bargaining content and outcome between company cases.[14] Other than factors such as company size, workforce composition, or industry, they attribute this variation to differences in the "place given to law and the way it is used" by company actors. Differences in the actors' "legal consciousness" explain the type of industrial relations actors develop in the company (Béthoux & Mias, 2019: 11). In their sample, they identify four such types of, which they term "proactive," "a-legalistic," "formalistic," and "locally focused." Accordingly, bargaining may either be an "empty shell" and "lose any substance" or it may break free of "traditional forms of negotiation, bringing a deliberative component" and potentially innovative issues into the picture. Béthoux and Mias underline that the latter ("best case") scenario typically coincides with certain – rather rare – conditions: the existence of networks of long-established institutions in the workplace, or the strong commitment from worker representatives who manage to effectively "orchestrate" the representative structures in the company.

The shift in the level of bargaining has changed the link between sectoral and company levels, but only in very large firms where trade unions are encouraged by company management to participate in anticipating economic changes and their impact on employment as expected. Even though

14   Other recent studies combining quantitative and qualitative approaches confirm the variety of French workplace industrial relations (e.g., Giraud & Signoretto, 2021).

managing employment, an intrinsic element of human resource management within companies, has been admitted to bargaining, it remains a managerial initiative, in the form of "managerial social dialogue" (Groux, 2010). In accordance with the same logic, large companies, major car manufacturers in particular, have signed so-called competitiveness-employment agreements, which are a French version of concession bargaining. In these agreements, unions exchange guarantees on employment against the lowering of social standards laid down in past company agreements.

In many small companies, the rare agreements signed offer little benefit to employees and sectoral agreements remain the reference. However, regarding recent and upcoming legal changes, in particular the introduction of ballots, the balance of power risks becoming less favourable to trade unions in enterprises.

Real impact of the reform in Spain

According to the OECD, the 2012 reform had the potential to boost the productivity growth and competitiveness of the labour market in the long term (OECD, 2013: 1–5), but at the cost of the worsening of labour conditions and reduction of wages for employees.

The goal of the 2012 Labour Law reform was clearly to decentralise collective bargaining. However, due to several factors, such as the prevalence of cultural patterns, path dependency trends, lack of resources of the social partners and/or willingness to bargaining at lower levels, it has not led to a high increase in the number of collective agreements at company level (see Figure 5.2.). In 2011, while 929,000 employees were covered by firm level collective agreements, 9,733,800 were covered by sectoral collective agreements. In 2014, the number of employees covered by firm-level agreements was 932,700, while the number of those covered by sectoral agreements was 9,332,700 (Mercader Uguina et al., 2016a).

Average salaries have decreased in the last decade. They began to decrease in 2008. However, the so-called internal devaluation is not solely the result of the 2012 labour reforms. A better explanation is the appalling conditions on the Spanish labour market over the last decade, especially for the less skilled and in the worst paid occupations (Mercader Uguina et al., 2016a).

When it comes to opt-out agreements at firm level, the statistics also show that they have not caused a big impact on the structure of collective bargaining. In 2013, which is the year with the highest number of opt-out agreements, there were 2,512 firm-level agreements opting out of some kind of working conditions (wages, for the most part) established by sectoral

Figure 5.2.   Numbers of collective agreements at company and sectoral level, 2011–2020, Spain

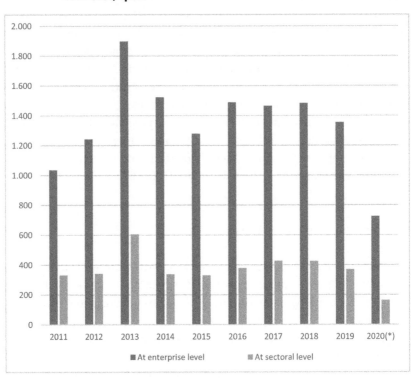

Source: CCOO, Balance de la Negociación Colectiva, September 2021.

agreements. These firm-level agreements covered only 159,550 employees (Mercader Uguina et al., 2016a).

The labour market liberal reform of 2012 responded to decentralisation trends and discourses raised due to the global financial crisis. The justification was that the dramatic situation of the Spanish economy required a modernisation of the collective bargaining institutional framework in favour of decentralisation to the company level. This reform clearly benefited employers' interests and the main criticism is that the shift in collective bargaining power resulting from this latest reform has had a detrimental effect on working conditions and has increased employment precariousness. In general terms, the main trade unions refused to negotiate worst working conditions at company level. However, in some cases, and mainly due to economic pressures, in the years immediately after the 2012 reform, some employees' representatives at the company level indeed negotiated lower salaries, greater function flexibility, and longer working hours, in order to avoid dismissals. This was a exchange of security of employment for flexibility in working conditions and lower salaries. For many scholars (such as Valero Otero, 2019), this reform has been an involution in workers' rights, especially at the collective level, as it has limited the prerogative of the social partners to deviate from that priority rule of the company agreement by collective agreements at a higher level (by an interprofessional agreement) (Fernández Villazón, 2018).

In sum, the effects of the 2012 labour market reform have been mixed and not very substantial in terms of renewal and flexibilisation of collective bargaining.

Firstly, a growth in the number of collective agreements at enterprise level was observed in the initial years the reform was applicable. However, the number of employees covered by company-level agreements has not really increased. The possibility of an opt-out has been used in several firm-level agreements but these covered only 1.5% of workers. However, the percentage of workers not covered by a collective agreement has risen by three points to 12% (Lahera Forteza, 2022).

Secondly, there are cases where some bargaining units were explicitly created to apply the priority of company agreements and avoid compliance with the higher wages set by sectoral collective agreements (Mercader Uguina, 2021) These cases, where the bargaining power of the employees' representative is lacking and there was an unilateral imposition of the working conditions by the employer, suggest the existence of dubious collective agreements. Some of them have been declared invalid by the Labour Courts (Muñoz Ruiz, 2015).

Finally, the 2012 reform did not change the traditional pattern of the social partners of negotiating mainly at provincial sector level. The Spanish system is characterised by the solid power of trade unions at sector level (state, regions, and provinces) and the proliferation of this type of agreement is exemplary of this. In some sectors, such as the retail sector, provincial collective agreements remain predominant.[15] In that sector, some large companies (for example, Mercadona, Lidl, and Decathlon) have negotiated their own company agreements at national level but these are a minority of cases.

Summing up, decentralisation of collective bargaining in Spain has proved difficult because there are many small companies without shop-level worker representation. The reform was imposed from above and lacked any social support, which clearly explains the opposition it has met from the trade unions (Mercader Uguina et al., 2016).

---

15   See the analysis of collective agreements of retail sector at provincial level in Muñoz Ruiz & Ramos Martín (2022: 25–38).

Comparative conclusions

In France as well as in Spain, the goal of promoting collective bargaining decentralisation has been pursued by most governments, albeit earlier in France, and with greater emphasis in Spain during times when economic crisis affects the labour market. In both countries, new regulatory frameworks inspired by employers' demands have been put in place. They were aimed to transform and flexibilise the system of collective bargaining and to grant more bargaining power to employers.

In practice, however, the effects have been dubious and the number of employees covered by firm-level agreements has not risen significantly after the 2012 Spanish reform and the 2016/2017 French reforms. It should be noted, however, that the scope of company bargaining is not the same in the two countries. The Spanish case is characterised by a strong fragmentation of the bargaining units. This fragmentation is explained by the difficulties bargaining parties experience in negotiating sectoral collective agreements at state level. In the French case, there is a weaker tradition of autonomous cross-industry bargaining than in Spain (for example, there is no equivalent of the national framework agreements, AENC); however, sectoral bargaining is more centralised at sectoral level, leading to a "coordinated decentralisation" with a clear division of competences between the different bargaining levels.

When assessing the reforms, it becomes clear that there are divergent evaluations of their impacts by trade unions and employers. The changes and mixed impacts of the 2012 labour market reform in Spain have been welcomed by the employers' representatives while the trade unions considered that the quality of employment has deteriorated and labour precariousness increased, accompanied by of that reform have been corrected by new legislation, adopted in December 2021. In France, an evaluation of the effects of the ordinances was conducted by a tripartite committee (administration, trade unions, and employers' organisations). Regarding collective bargaining, the committee concludes that "the quantitative and qualitative elements do not reflect major changes in social dialogue practices, but rather a continuation of previous trends" (France Stratégie, 2021: 14). Indeed, the reform has not helped to reverse the previous trend of a weakening of unions' bargaining power.

In general terms, the reaction of the trade unions has been to oppose the reforms and to continue following the traditional patterns of collective bargaining. The union's strategy of expressing their disagreement with the labour market reforms is more explicit in the Spanish case, where the main trade union confederations have been actively bargaining against the spirit of the 2012 labour market reform. By contrast, in France, the trade unions confederations appeared divided and have exhibited a scattered response.

Looking at possible future scenarios, there are new challenges for the implementation of the latest reforms in a difficult economic context (expected recession, current energy crisis, growing inflation rates in the EU) where the social partners have opposing interests and views. For trade unions, the key priority is recovering the purchasing power of wages lost during 2021/22. In contrast, employers aim at maintaining wage moderation to avoid a negative impact on economic recovery (Eurofound, 2022a, 2022b).

Bachalach and Lawler argue that "power in collective bargaining stems from multiple legal, economic, social and structural sources" (Leap & Grigsby, 1986). With this in mind, it is interesting to establish a comparison about how some of these factors have determined the bargaining power dynamics in both countries. Legal and economic factors were similar in both the French and Spanish context (with a higher prevalence of the economic drivers in the latter case due to the severity of the crisis in Spain). From a legal point of view, both countries share similar legislative traditions of wide-ranging state intervention in the regulation of employment law and in the adoption of guidelines on the functioning of the industrial relations institutional setting. While some labour market factors might be similar (i.e., growing unemployment rates in the period examined), we can also underline differences in the economic structures in both countries, such as a greater weight of SMEs in Spain and, above all, a greater presence of subsidiaries of large foreign groups.

French and Spanish policymakers used the same rhetoric to justify the reform, i.e., the alleged rigidity of their labour markets/collective bargaining systems. The same argument has been made that "no other feasible orientation of labour market regulation was possible due to the competition pressures in a globalised flexible market economy," which shows a comparable pattern. Nevertheless, some of the dissimilarities in the changes in collective bargaining in the two countries may lie in the different strategies of the social partners. We have already pointed out this difference with regard to the trade unions. Unlike the Spanish employers, French employers, particularly those of the large multinationals, have long made company negotiations their own priority. The main employers' organisation is more centralised and has strong links with political staff and high-level civil servants. The 2017 reform strengthened the bargaining power of employers, which was already in place.

Finally, the idea of decentralisation as a unidirectional and comprehensive process can be challenged when examining the French and Spanish cases (see Hege et al., 2015 for research on company-level bargaining). In France, sociologists have been critical of the idea of centralisation/decentralisation, thus questioning the impact of the "hierarchy of norms" that prevailed in labour law until the Macron Ordinances. In opposition to the idea of a predominant centralised and unified system with legal norms, from which derogation is possible only if it is more favourable to the worker, and with national agreements stronger than sectoral agreements, themselves superior to company agreements, scholars have emphasised the relative autonomy of bargaining levels (Jobert et al., 1993). A central feature, common to both countries under study, is that each level of bargaining has its specific actors and a "certain degree of autonomy and therefore evolves according to its own rhythm and internal dynamics...the coordination of the system is guaranteed, also because each actor has its own institutions of coordination" (Jobert et al., 1993). More specifically, scholars insisted on the relative autonomy of the firm from the sectoral level, building on the observation that the actors at this level adapt, define, transgress, or, indeed, impulse the typically general rules contained in the sectoral agreements in line with their own priorities and rules (Sellier, 1993). Against this background, French researchers have preferred the concept of articulation over that of determination (see further Kahmann & Vincent, 2022: 5–20).

In the Spanish case, it is also difficult to see a clear decentralisation pattern. The collective bargaining system in Spain is neither completely decentralised nor entirely centralised. It is a "mixed system" (Bentolila & Jimeno, 2002). This mixed structure of Spanish collective bargaining has persisted after the series of legislative reforms/state regulatory interventions of the last decade. A worrying impact of those reforms is that, instead of a clear decentralised collective bargaining system, they created "a new pattern of fragmentation and decentralisation within industrial relations" (Fernández Rodríguez et al., 2014). A main aim of the last labour law reform passed in December 2021 is to correct that undesirable effect.

References

Amable, B. (2016). The political economy of the neoliberal transformation of French industrial relations. *ILR Review*, 69 (3): 523–5.50.

Baccaro, L. & Howell, C. (2017). *Trajectories of neoliberalism transformation. European industrial relations since the 1970s.* Cambridge University Press.

Bentolila, S. & Jimeno, J. (2002). La reforma de la negociación colectiva en España. ftp://ftp.cemfi.es/pdf/papers/sb/benjimeno.pdf

Béthoux, E. & Mias, A. (2019). How does state-led decentralization affect workplace employment relations? The French case in a comparative perspective. *European Journal of Industrial Relations*, 27 (1): 5–21.

Casas Baamonde, M. (2018). Los equívocos de la representatividad para negociar convenios colectivos sectoriales estatales ante la descentralización de la negociación colectiva Derecho de las relaciones laborales, ISSN 2387-1113, Nº. 5, (2018): 469–486.

Combrexelle, J.-D. (2015). *La négociation collective, le travail et l'emploi. Rapport au Premier Ministre.* France Stratégie.

Crouch, C. (1993). *Industrial relations and European state traditions.* Clarendon Press.

Dares, (2021). *Données, La syndicalisation* https://dares.travail-emploi.gouv.fr/donnees/la-syndicalisation

Delahaie, N. & Fretel, A. (2021). *Vers un basculement de la branche vers l'entreprise ? Diversité des pratiques de pluralité des formes d'articulation entre entreprise et branche.* IRES.

Delahaie, N. & Vincent, C. (2021). The SMIC as a driver for collective bargaining. The interplay of collective bargaining and minimum wage in France. In Dingeldey I., Schulten T., & Grimshaw D (Eds.), *The interplay between minimum wage and collective bargaining in different sectors and regions on the world.* Routledge Editions.

Del Rey, S. (2012). Los principios de la estructura de la negociación colectiva tras la Ley 3/2012, de medidas urgentes para la reforma de mercado de trabajo, XXV Jornadas de Estudio sobre Negociación Colectiva. La reforma Laboral 2012, Madrid, 4 October 2012, 1–14.

Eurofound (2015). *Spain: A first assessment of the 2012 labour market reform.* Eurofound (europa.eu)

Eurofound (2022a). *Living and working in Spain.* https://www.eurofound.europa.eu/country/spain

Eurofound (2022b). *Living and working in France.* Eurofound (europa.eu).

Fernández Rodríguez, C., Rojo Ibáñez, R., & Martínez Lucio, M. (2014). The reform of collective bargaining in the Spanish manufacturing sector with reference to the metal and chemical sectors: Legacies and risks in the reform of regulation since 2008, Project 'The impact of industrial relations reforms on collective bargaining in the manufacturing sector (incorporating social dialogue in manufacturing during the sovereign debt crisis), University of Manchester.

Fernández Villazón, L. (2018). La prioridad aplicativa del convenio colectivo de empresa: Límites e incidencia sobre los fenómenos de descentralización productive. Revista General de Derecho del Trabajo y de la Seguridad Social, ISSN-e 1696-9626, Nº. 51, 2018: 166–197.

France Stratégie (2021). *Évaluation des ordonnances du 22 septembre 2017 relatives au dialogue social et aux relations de travail, Rapport 2021 du Comité d'évaluation*, décembre, Paris,

Freyssinet J. (2002). La réforme de l'indemnisation du chômage en France. *La Revue de l'IRES*, n° 38: 1–50.

Freyssinet, J. (2015). La modernisation du dialogue social. *Note Lasaire*, n° 46. Pages?

Giraud, B. & Signoretto, C. (2021). *Reconfiguration des usages et des pratiques du « dialogue social » en entreprise dans un contexte de changement socio-productif et institutionnel, Rapport pour la Dares, LEST*, Université Aix-Marseille.

Groux, G. (2010). Europe centrale et de l'est: une amplification de nouvelles pratiques de dialogue social de l'industrie ? *Travail et Emploi*, n° 123: 67–76.

Hege, A., Dufour C., & Kahmann M. (2015). La loi du 20 aout 2008 et les fondements de la représentation syndicale. *La Revue de l'IRES*, n° 87: 95–123.

Jobert, A., Reynaud, J-D., & Saglio, J. (1993). *Les conventions collectives de branche: Déclin ou renouveau?*, CEREQ.

Jobert, A. (2003). Quelles dynamiques pour la négociation collective de branche ? *Travail et emploi*, n° 95: 5–26.

Kahmann, M. & Vincent, C. (2022). Decentralised bargaining in France. CODEBAR project. https://aias-hsi.uva.nl/en/projects-a-z/codebar/codebar.html

Knegt, R., Ramos Martín, N. (2016). Clustering labour market reforms and social dialogue in nine EU Countries: Comparing responses to the economic crisis. DIADSE Project Overview Report, 11–40. https://aias-hsi.uva.nl/en/projects-a-z/diadse/reports/reports.html

Lahera Forteza, J. (2022). La negociación colectiva tras la reforma laboral de 2021, Tirant Lo Blanch, pp. 29–32.

Leonardi, S. & Pedersini, R. (2017). *Multi-employer bargaining under pressure: Decentralization trends in five European countries*. ETUI.

Leap, T. & Grigsby D. (1986). A conceptualization of collective bargaining power, *ILR Review*, 39 (2): 202–213

Marginson, P. (2015). Coordinated bargaining in Europe: from incremental corrosion to frontal assault?, *European Journal of Industrial relations*, 21 (2): 97–114.

Mercader Uguina,, J., Gómez Abelleira, F., Gimeno Díaz de Atauri, P., Muñoz Ruiz, A., & Pérez del Prado, D. (2016a). DIADSE: Dialogue for Advancing Social Europe, Country Report on Spain, p. 14. https://aias-hsi.uva.nl/en/projects-a-z/diadse/reports/reports.html.

Mercader Uguina, J., Gómez Abelleira, F., Gimeno Díaz de Atauri, P., Muñoz Ruiz, A. & Pérez del Prado, D. (2016b). DIADSE: Dialogue for Advancing Social Europe, Policy Paper Spain, pp. 2–3. https://aias-hsi.uva.nl/en/projects-a-z/diadse/reports/reports.html

Mercader Uguina, J. & De la Puebla Pinilla, A. (2021). *La Reforma Laboral de 2021: Elogio de la sensatez* (elforodelabos.es)

Mercader Uguina, J., (2021). El fin de la prevalencia del convenio de empresa en materia salarial: ¿punto de llegada o de partida?, *Labos Revista de Derecho del Trabajo y Protección Social*, 3, Número extraordinario 'La reforma laboral de 2021': 111–128 / doi: https://doi.org/10.20318/labos.2022.6643

Moll Noguera, R. (2018). La descentralización de la negociación colectiva en Portugal y España. Un breve estudio de derecho comparado, *Derecho de las relaciones laborales*, ISSN 2387–1113, Nº. 10, 2018: 1151–1162.

Muñoz Ruiz, A. (2014) . Problemas prácticos del convenio colectivo de empresa, Lex Nova; La prioridad aplicativa del convenio colectivo de ámbito inferior a la empresa respecto al convenio de sector: dificultades y propuestas de solución, *Revista Trabajo y Derecho: Nueva Revista de Actualidad y Relaciones Laborales*, nº 9, 2015: 29–126.

Muñoz Ruiz, A. & Ramos Martín, N. (2022). Decentralised bargaining in Spain. CODEBAR project. CODEBAR – AIAS-HSI – University of Amsterdam (uva.nl)

Müller, T., Vandaele, K., & Waddington, J. (2019). *Collective bargaining in Europe: Towards an endgame. Volume II.* ETUI.

OECD (2013). Estudio de la OCDE sobre la reforma laboral 2012 en España: Una evaluación preliminar, December 2013, pp. 1–5. http://www.oecd.org/fr/els/emp/OCDE-EstudioSobreLaReformaLaboral-ResumenEjecutivo.pdf

OECD/AIAS ICTWSS database, (2021). https://www.oecd.org/employment/ictwss-database.htm

Pérez Infante, J. (2003). La estructura de la negociación colectiva y los salarios en España, *Revista del Ministerio de Trabajo y Asuntos Sociales*, No. 46, 2003: 41–97.

Pernot, J.-M (2014). France and the European agenda: An ambiguous impact on industrial relations. In Rocha, F. (Ed.), *The new EU economic governance and its impact on the national collective bargaining system* (pp. 91–114). Fundación 1º de Mayo.

Pernot, J.-M (2017). French trade unions in the aftermath of the crisis. In Lehndorff, S., Dribbusch, H., & Schulten, T. (Eds.), *Rough waters: European trade unions in a time of crises* (pp. 37–60). ETUI.

Pose Vidal, S. (2009). La cláusula de descuelgue salarial en tiempos de crisis económica, *Actualidad Jurídica Aranzadi*, 784, 22 October 2009: 1–3.

Ramos Martín, N. (2012). Sector-level bargaining and possibilities for deviations at company level: Spain. EUROFOUND, 1–8, http://csdle.lex.unict.it/Archive/LW/Data%20reports%20and%20studies/Reports%20and%20studies%20from%20EUROFOUND/20110325-013630_Eurofound_Sector_level-barg_SPAIN_Feb11pdf.pdf

Rehfeldt, U. & Vincent, C. (2017). The decentralization of collective bargaining in France: An escalating process. In: Leonardi, S. & Pedersini, R. (Eds.).

Multi-employer bargaining under pressure: Decentralization trends in five European countries (pp. 151–184). ETUI.

SECAFI (2020). Les Accords de performance collective bousculent le dialogue social. *Traits d'union, n° 120*, Paris, SECAFI.

Sellier, F. (1993). Articulation des niveaux de négociation et construction des acteurs. In Jobert, A., Reynaud, J.-D., & Saglio, J. (Eds.). *Les conventions collectives de branche: Déclin ou renouveau?* (pp. 169–182). 169–182.

Sisson, K. (1987). *The management of collective bargaining: an international comparison.* Oxford University Press.

6. Does Decentralisation Lead to New Relationships between Trade Unions and Works Councils? Germany and the Netherlands Compared

Sophie Rosenbohm & Frank Tros

Abstract

A major trends in collective bargaining across Europe is decentralisation, involving a shift from multi-employer to single-employer bargaining. In this chapter, the authors address the question of how decentralisation affects the relationships between trade unions and works councils in dual channel systems of interest representation. The analysis focuses on Germany and the Netherlands, two countries with legally established dual-channel systems of employee representation, where trade unions and works councils play a role in both consulting and negotiating employment and working conditions at the company level. While similar statutory allocations and demarcations of powers between works councils and unions exist in both countries, company case studies reveal marked differences in how trade unions and works council cooperate in practice.

Keywords: collective bargaining, works councils, decentralisation, Germany, the Netherlands, dual channel systems

Introduction: Decentralisation in dual channel systems

One of the main trends in collective bargaining across Europe since the 1980s is decentralisation, involving a shift from multi-employer to single-employer bargaining. However, there are nuanced variations in national developments regarding the initiating actors and the intensity and patterns of decentralisation processes. As a consequence of decentralisation

Frank Tros (ed.). *Pathways in Decentralised Collective Bargaining in Europe.* Amsterdam: Amsterdam University Press, 2023
DOI 10.5117/9789048560233_CH06

of collective bargaining towards the company level, trade unions might meet other workers' representatives, such as works councils, at that level.

In this chapter, we address the question of how patterns of decentralisation affect the relationships between trade unions and works councils in dual channel systems of interest representation. Dual channel systems with trade unions and elected works councils alongside are typically marked by a specific divide in rights and responsibilities between trade unions and works councils. Moreover, both arenas – collective bargaining, on the one hand, and workplace employee representation, on the other – are usually separated by different spheres of conflict. But does this relationship fundamentally change during the process of decentralisation when competences are transferred from the industry level to the company or establishment level?

In the literature, it has been discussed whether patterns of decentralisation are dependent on the type of institutional channels of employee representation at the company and workplace level. In single-channel systems, where workplace representatives are elected and/or delegated by trade unions, unions can keep substantial control over decentralisation processes (Ibsen & Keune, 2018). Empirical evidence points to higher effectiveness of single-channel systems by better ensuring a process of organised decentralisation of collective bargaining (Traxler, 2008). This is confirmed by recent developments in coordinated decentralisation in Sweden (Rönnmar & Iossa, 2022). In dual-channel systems, where employees are not only represented by trade unions, but also by works councils, the relationships between sector and local negotiators might be weaker and more fragile, reducing the control of unions over decentralisation (Nergaard et al., 2009). In Germany and the Netherlands the dual representation is split over two levels: trade unions are then only active at the sectoral level while works councils are the only channel for employee representation at the company level (see also Chapter 3 in this book; Haipeter, Armaroli, Iossa, & Rönnmar, 2023). But these levels and channels can be blurred in practice: works council members can be members of the trade unions and works councils and trade unions can cooperate at the workplace and company level. Trade unions in dual-channel systems might use works councils as a power resource in collective bargaining at the company level. Trade unions can use the institution of works councils in their strategy for better engagement with workers and their needs within companies, to recruit more members and to unionise the councils (Haipeter, 2021). Works councils can use trade unions' competences in negotiating terms and conditions of employment within the company.

While some evidence and assumptions about the differences between single-channel and dual-channel systems with regard to decentralisation exist, we would like to adopt a slightly different perspective and focus on developments within dual-channel systems. It is still an empirical question how relationships between trade unions and works councils are affected by decentralisation within systems where the dualisation of employee representation is anchored in elaborate legislation. Against this backdrop, this chapter seeks to investigate the following questions: Do works councils become substitutes or partners of unions in decentralised bargaining? Do partnerships or conflicts arise between both actors? What does coordination between trade unions and works councils look like and how is it organised?

To give answers to the above-mentioned questions, we focus on Germany and the Netherlands, two countries with legally established dual-channel systems of employee representation where trade unions and works councils play both a role in social dialogue and negotiating employment and working conditions at the company level. We decided to concentrate on those countries where works councils have similar roles for workplace interest representation and where collective agreements with trade unions have legal primacy above workplace regulations with works councils. Fundamentally, collective bargaining and co-determination at the workplace level are separate legal fields. Only when collective bargaining parties give jurisdiction to works councils or if works councils are supported by trade unions (or vice versa) will both fields partly overlap. These more "pure" dual-channel systems in Germany and the Netherlands can be separated from the more "mixed-channel systems," somewhere between purely single and purely dual-channel systems in workers representation (in e.g., France, Italy, and Spain), where trade unions can have formally delegated members in bodies of employee representation within the companies (Kahmann & Vincent, 2022; Armaroli & Tamassetti, 2022; Muñoz Ruiz & Ramos Martín, 2022).

Thus, from a legal perspective Germany and the Netherlands share similar institutional features with regard to employee representation and formal relationships between the two representative bodies. This similar institutional context makes it interesting to analyse whether we can observe different actors' strategies – and maybe different organisational power resources of trade unions and works councils – to cope with decentralisation processes, and how this affects the relationship between works councils and trade unions. Against this backdrop and based on company case studies in these countries in manufacturing and retail, we will analyse the role that trade unions and works councils play when it comes to decentralisation. Moreover, we will investigate whether trade unions do see works councils as a power resource through (re)connecting to workers and for cooperation. Finally, we will explore how relationships between trade unions and works councils are shaped and if conflicts or cooperation emerge.

The chapter has been organised in the following way. The first section describes some stylised facts about the institutional features of the dual-channel systems in Germany and the Netherlands. After a brief discussion of the main decentralisation trends in both countries and their commonalities as well as differences, we present the empirical findings of our company case studies focusing on the impact of decentralisation towards works councils and their relationships with trade unions. The chapter concludes with a discussion of the relationships between trade unions and works councils in both countries, how (dis-)similarities between the two countries in this relationship might be explained, and gives a brief outlook for further studies.

The dual channel system of employee representation in Germany and the Netherlands

In both countries, employee interests are represented through two institutional actors, trade unions, which are in charge of collective bargaining, and works councils at the company and/or establishment level. Moreover, works councils in Germany and the Netherlands have a statutory basis. The first Works Councils Act ('Wet op de Ondernemingsraden') in the Netherlands dates back to 1950 and regulates the structures, rights, and elections of works councils within companies. The legal reforms of 1971 and 1979 strengthened the formal independence from the company (or public sector) director, and the rights to information, consultation, and co-determination. The functioning of works councils in the Netherlands further expanded in the 1980s and 1990s (Van het Kaar & Looise, 1999), but stabilised in recent decades (Tros, 2022). Currently, 95% of companies with more than 200 workers have established a works council in the Netherlands (Wajon, Vlug, & Enneking, 2017). Small- and medium-sized companies have lower establishment rates: around 60% of the companies have between 50 and 100 employees (Wajon, Vlug, & Enneking, 2017). Establishing a works council is obligatory for companies with more than 50 employees, but if the employees do not ask the employer to do so, the employer will not be sanctioned for not having installed such a body.

In Germany, the Works Constitution Act – the first version of which dates from 1952 and has been amended several times since then (1976, 1989, 2001, 2021) – regulates the structures and participation rights of works councils, which are elected by all employees in a workplace. Works councils can be elected in all establishments with more than five employees. The establishment of a works council is voluntary and at the initiative of the employees. Currently, a works council exists in around 8% of all establishments (Ellguth & Kohaut, 2021). However, coverage varies widely between smaller and bigger establishments. Prevalence of works councils remains at a consistently high level of 90% (of employees) and 85% (of establishments) in large establishments with more than 500 employees.

In addition, works councils are formally independent of trade unions and are elected by all employees at a workplace in both countries. In Germany, the Works Constitution Act sets out that works councils have a duty to maintain "industrial peace" and are obliged to act in the best interests of both the workforce and the establishment. This means that works councils in Germany may not call for industrial action, such as strikes. In a similar manner, works councils in the Netherlands have a dual aim according to the law: to act in the interest of the workforce in the context of the interests of the company. Trade unions in the Netherlands have always been ambivalent towards works councils as a consequence of this dual aim, and, moreover, because of the employers' generally friendly attitudes and behaviours towards works councils in the Netherlands. According to FNV (the largest trade unions confederation in the Netherlands), works councils cannot organise countervailing powers because works councils are expected to also represent the interests of the company and its management and because of missing the strike weapon.

Demarcation of powers

The dual-channel systems in both countries are marked by a specific demarcation of powers between works councils and trade unions (Jansen & Tros, 2022; Haipeter & Rosenbohm, 2022). In Germany, and in contrast to trade unions, works councils are not allowed to negotiate collective agreements. Works councils and management can, however, negotiate so-called workplace agreements (*Betriebsvereinbarungen*) on a range of issues. The relationship between workplace agreements and collective agreements is regulated by statutory law. In addition to the stipulations of the Collective Bargaining Act, the WCA specifies (in Section 77.3) that collective agreements have primacy. That is, pay or other working conditions that are actually or customarily regulated by collective agreements may not be determined by a workplace agreement unless the collective agreement expressly permits the conclusion of supplementary workplace agreements.

In contrast, trade unions in Germany have only a limited legal anchoring in the workplace, which is one reason why they have often moved to set up workplace trade union representatives' bodies in large companies (shop stewards), elected only by trade union members and designed to function as counter-organisations or supplementary to works councils. Unlike works councils, these have no legal independent co-determination rights. However, shop stewards serve as links between the trade union organisation, the workforce, and the works council in larger companies in Germany.

The demarcation of powers between works councils and trade unions in the Netherlands is similar to Germany. In the Netherlands, the powers of trade unions, on the one hand, and works councils, on the other hand, are delimited in the Works Councils Act in relation to the regulation of collective terms and conditions of employment (Jansen & Tros, 2022). The statutory allocation of powers means that the works council does not, in principle, have any powers in relation to primary terms of employment, such as fixing remuneration, the number of holidays, or working hours. It is also a consequence of the law that, if the collective agreement provides an exhaustive set of rules, the works council loses its power in relation to secondary and tertiary terms of employment. This is called the primacy of the collective agreement. Rules are regarded as exhaustive if a collective agreement offers no further scope for elaboration at the company level. The literature mentions that collective bargaining parties and works councils can often cross over into each other's domains because an agreement between a company and a works council can make arrangements on (primary) employment terms while collective bargaining parties are not obliged to confine themselves in collective labour agreements to the regulation of primary terms of employment. (Jansen, 2019: 204). In contrast to collective agreements, the principle in Dutch law is that arrangements with the works council on terms of employment do not automatically permeate to individual employment contracts. That said, there are ways to do so in practice. If collective bargaining parties agree in the collective agreement to grant authority to the works council and the employer to make arrangements for the further detailing of a particular topic, then those more detailed arrangements may permeate the employment contracts of all employees. We see such "decentralisation provisions" in several collective agreements in the Netherlands across different sectors.

Important in our analysis is that shop stewards in the Netherlands are almost non-existent. This can be understood in historical perspective. In the early 20th century – when industrial relations were further shaped – trade unions focused their activities on the sector and national levels; the economic crisis taught them that unemployment and problems of distributions and industrial production could be better solved at the sector levels, instead of the company levels (Windmuller et al., 1987: 73). The pragmatic reformist (rather than revolutionary) ideology among trade unions was strong. Furthermore, employers in the Netherlands were relatively more resistant to trade union activities within the companies (Windmuller et al., 1987: 81). This led to a central focus of the social partners in the Netherlands, further institutionalised and developed after the Second World War, when two national social dialogue institutions were established: the bipartite Labour Foundation (1945) and the tripartite Social-Economic Council (1950). Both these institutions became highly influential and part of an implicit trade-off that involved respecting the employers' "management prerogative" to organise their organisations in a capitalist social-economic system without direct co-determination rights for the trade unions in the organisation of work. In the 1960s and 1970s, some trade union networks (*bedrijfsledengroepen*) were installed within a number of large companies, but without much success. They experienced complicated relationships with trade unions at more central levels as well as with works councils that were considered too focused on harmony with the management (Kösters & Eshuis, 2020). Since the 1980s, the already limited numbers of union networks within companies have declined further. Shop stewards and union networks in companies seem to have been a temporary phenomenon in the Dutch industrial relations system in the extraordinary decades of the 1960s/1970s, although there might be good reasons nowadays for trade unions to organise actions at the workplace level (Bouwmans & Eshuis, 2018; Kösters & Eshuis, 2020).

Relationships between trade unions and works councils

Trade unions have no direct influence in works councils in either Germany or the Netherlands. They can influence things indirectly, however, to the extent that union candidates are works council members and, in turn, works councils ask advice from trade unions. In Germany, important links exist between both actors. Analysis of the German works council election results in 2018 show that just over two thirds of the members elected were members of trade unions affiliated to the German Trade Union Federation (DGB) (Demir et al., 2019).[1] In addition, an intensive division of labour has de-

---

1   Due to missing data or different data structures, these figures refer only to IG Metall, ver. di, IG BCE, and NGG.

veloped between trade unions and works councils in Germany. Trade unions have taken on the tasks of providing training for works council members and supplying expert advice as well as organising support when needed. They also provide organisational power to works councils as a strongly unionised workforce will bolster the works councils' hand in negotiations with management. Finally, by concluding collective agreements, they relieve works councils of the burden of having to negotiate on contentious issues, such as pay increases or the length of working hours, for which they are ill-equipped given that they lack the right to strike.

Conversely, works councils in Germany have a legal duty to monitor compliance with the provisions of labour law and the implementation of collective agreements at company and workplace level. Their focus is on specific problems concerning employment conditions at the company and/or workplace level that cannot be dealt with in the broader provisions of industry-level collective agreements. They can also support the mobilisation of workers for strike action during collective bargaining, provided they do not directly call a strike themselves. Finally, they undertake union recruitment in the workplace, an especially important task in workplaces where unions have not established their own representation in the form of shop stewards. For Germany, then, it can be concluded that both actors have a reciprocal and interdependent relationship.

In the Netherlands, too, trade unions have some indirect influence in works councils, albeit to a lesser extent than in Germany. A comparative study from WSI/Hans-Boeckler-Stiftung about works councils in Germany and the Netherlands estimates that almost 60% of Dutch works councils never, or hardly ever, receive advice from trade unions, compared with 28% of the works councils in Germany (Van den Berg et al., 2019). Compared to Germany, Dutch works councillors take more advice from (commercial) consultants, have poorer relationships with unions, and have relatively better relationships with management (Van den Berg et al., 2019). According to the earlier mentioned survey, the interactions of works councils in the Netherlands seems to be based on cooperation with management, social partnerships, and constructive dialogue with management more than they are in Germany (Sapulete, Behrens, Brehmer, & Van Witteloostuijn, 2016; Van den Berg, Grift, Sapulete, Behrens, Brehmer, & Van Witteloostuijn, 2019). Compared to the German Betriebsräte, works councils in the Netherlands seem to act in a less formal way (Sapulete et al., 2016; Van den Berg et al., 2019). These strong ties with management and weak ties with trade unions may also explain why trade unions in the Netherlands are hesitant about delegating negotiating powers to works councils.

Like in Germany, works councils in the Netherlands have a legal duty to enhance compliance of the stipulations in collective agreements within the companies and they can ask for trade unions to get involved if an employer refuses to abide by the collective agreements.

Perforated systems

It is important to note that not all employees in Germany are encompassed by this "dual system" of industrial relations (collective bargaining and works councils). Only 30% of employees are currently covered by both a works council and a collective agreement. Compared to the early 2000s, this represents a decline of 13% points. Accordingly, the proportion of employees outside the scope of collective bargaining and not represented by a works council has risen sharply (Figure 6.1.). In this respect, it can be argued that different "worlds of industrial relations" or "parallel universes of collective bargaining" exist within the German system (Schröder, 2016; Müller & Schulten, 2019).

Figure 6.1. Share of employees with works councils (WC), industry collective bargaining (IC), company collective bargaining (CCB), and collective bargaining (CC) in the private sector in Germany, 2000–2020

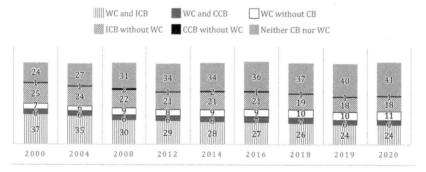

Source: IAB-Establishment Panel; authors' illustration.

In the Netherlands, the coverage rate of collective bargaining is higher and stable,[2] but here, too, not all companies – and in particular SMEs – have established such councils in their organisations, despite a legal obligation to do so. Figure 6.2. shows considerable sectoral variation in this: from just 50%

2   This stability refers to "coverage"; trade union involvement is less stable (fewer signings of collective agreements by FNV, the largest trade union confederation in the Netherlands).

in the trade sector to 99% in the public sector. Trade is also the sector with the lowest trade union memberships (9.5% in 2021, compared to 30.4% in the public sector). This suggested positive correlation between trade union membership and establishment levels of works councils, is not evident for all sectors: private service companies in the Netherlands often install a works council, but their workers are relatively organised at low levels. There is also large variety in the establishment of works councils between firm size categories: from 54% in companies with 50–75 employees to 95% in 200+ companies (Wajon et al., 2017). This is another reason for trade unions being hesitant to decentralise powers to works councils.

Figure 6.2. **Share of establishments with works councils by sector, companies with more than 50 employees (2017, the Netherlands)**

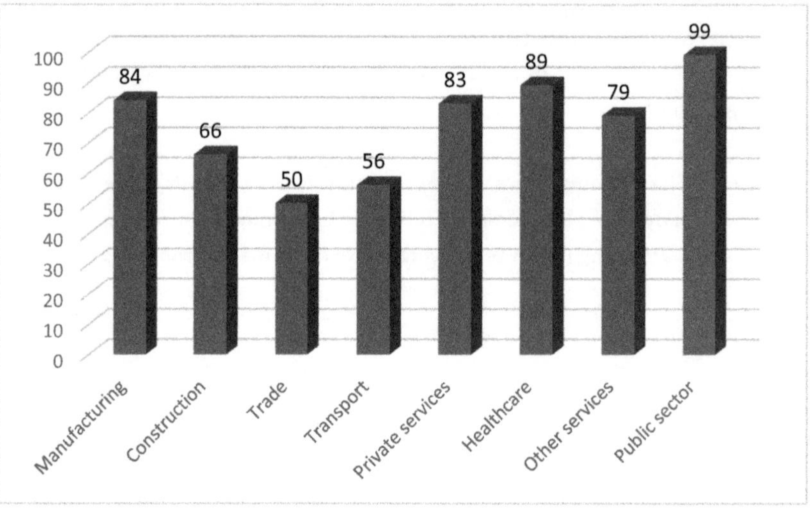

Source: Wajon et al., 2017.

In sum, in both countries national legislation strictly demarcates the rights and powers between trade unions and works councils. In Germany, trade unions have more interactions with works councils than in the Netherlands, which might be explained by the Dutch trade unions' strategies on establishing an influential position in national and sectoral dialogue, instead of organising workplace representation in the 20th century. However, there are higher rates of works councils being established in the Netherlands. The works councils' coverage rate in Germany has fallen slightly, but the proportion of employees who are neither covered by a works councils nor a collective agreement has risen sharply.

Decentralisation within dual-channel systems of employee representation

Before turning to the case studies, which describe the role of trade unions and works councils in decentralisation in detail, it is important to first give a short, more encompassing picture of decentralisation in Germany and the Netherlands.

Germany: All types of decentralisation

While the legal basis and main features of the German dual system of industrial relations remains largely unchanged, considerable changes within the system have taken place in recent years with decentralisation being the most relevant development. Decentralisation has taken different forms ranging from wild decentralisation to controlled decentralisation (Haipeter & Rosenbohm, 2022). In general, the erosion of collective bargaining coverage constitutes the main threat to the German model. Over the last 20 years, collective bargaining coverage has decreased considerably. Currently, only 51% of employees are working at a workplace that is covered by a collective agreement. Moreover, collective bargaining coverage varies widely depending on establishment size and sector. In 2020, 84% of West German (and 72% of East German) establishments with more than 500 employees were covered by collective agreements; by contrast, for workplaces with 10–49 employees, the coverage rate was just 36% in West Germany and 26% in the East. Coverage rates (by employees) also varies between sectors, ranging from 98% in the public sector to 13% in the information and communication sector (Ellguth & Kohaut, 2021). The decline in collective bargaining coverage is an expression of uncontrolled decentralisation as it is mainly driven by two processes: that of firms leaving employers' associations (or opting for an "agreement free" status within them); and that of firms that never join associations in the first place.

At the same time, however, more organised forms of decentralisation have become apparent within the German system of industrial relations. One form of coordinated decentralisation includes the shift of regulatory competences from the actors at industry level to the actors at company level. This development constitutes a process of layering, in which new elements and new competencies are added to existing institutions. It is coordinated in the sense that the collective bargaining actors themselves define the norms and have the possibility – at least in principle – to redefine them at any time. Thus, it does not (automatically) lead to lower importance of institutions at the sectoral level. In Germany, this process originates in the late-1980s, with the delegation of authority over the organisation of working time. Thus, this process includes a transfer of responsibilities from the field of collective bargaining to that of co-determination and the regulatory zone of the Works Constitution Act. This shift in the locus of regulation to the workplace requires works councils to address new topics and take on new responsibilities (Haipeter & Rosenbohm, 2022).

Another type of decentralisation, and, in terms of its repercussions on industry collective bargaining, the more important form of coordinated decentralisation, concerns the use of derogation clauses. Trade unions and employers' associations may agree to such clauses within collective agreements, which then allow deviations at company level, even if they suspend, delay, or undercut collectively agreed standards at sectoral level. In Germany, the demands for such decentralisation arose during the early 1990s, when a public debate about the system of collective bargaining and whether and how it should be reformed arose – mainly triggered by an economic crisis, the transformation of the economy in East Germany, and challenges posed by globalisation. From the employers' side, collective agreements were increasingly depicted as a rigid corset, clamping down on companies' freedom of manoeuvre in this debate. Moreover, this was complemented by companies leaving the employers' associations – and thus withdrawing from collective agreements – or informally circumventing collectively agreed provisions. In the early 2000s, the whole debate about decentralisation gained importance due to political pressure from the federal government and the threat to amend the law to allow company pacts, which would permit the undercutting of collective agreements by the workplace parties. The response of the collective bargaining parties, especially in manufacturing,[3] was to develop controlled forms of decentralisation by introducing "opening clauses," starting with the introduction of hardship and restructuring clauses (see also Haipeter, 2021; Haipeter & Rosenbohm, 2022; Müller & Schulten 2019). In the metalworking industry, the conclusion of the so-called Pforzheim Accord in 2004, significantly widened the scope for such derogations since it contained, for the first time, a general opening clause. Derogations are now permitted for a wide variety of reasons where this can be shown to improve competitiveness, innovation, and the safeguarding of employment. Chapter 3 in this book also concludes that the German manufacturing sector ticks all the boxes of decentralisation pathways (Haipeter et al., 2023).

It is important to note that the existing agreement regulating derogations in the metalworking and electrical industry stipulates that derogations can only be negotiated by recognised collective bargaining parties – the trade

---

3   Up until now, there have been hardly any general opening clauses allowing for derogations from collective agreements in retail.

union and either the individual employer or the employers' association. This means that works councils in the metal working industry are not in charge of negotiating those derogations. This underlines that this type of decentralisation does not include a shift from the field of collective bargaining to the regulatory zone of the Works Constitution Act. However, shortly after the Pforzheim Accord was signed, some instances occurred in which works councils nevertheless agreed to management's demands before the trade union had even become involved (e.g., Bahnmüller, 2017; Haipeter, 2021). As a consequence, in 2005, IG Metall drew up a set of coordination guidelines in order to ensure effective control centred on the following points. Firstly, applications to negotiate agreements on standards below the industry norms had to be submitted to the union's area headquarters (Bezirke), the organisational equivalent of the regional employers' associations, and required approval by officials at that level after considering extensive information about the company in question. Secondly, area officials could give local union branches authority to conduct negotiations. Thirdly, negotiations were to be supported by firm-level collective bargaining committees, whose role was to ensure that union members took part in the negotiations, were informed, and could participate in decision-making. In these instances, it is the union that checks company applications for derogation, establishes and leads the collective bargaining committees, negotiates with management, and organises membership participation and membership recruitment.

Overall, the practice of decentralisation varies considerably across sectors in Germany. Especially the use of derogation clauses, allowing for company-level derogations, varies substantially across industries (see also Müller & Schulten, 2019). While the decentralisation of collective bargaining in the German metalworking industry has been characterised by a complex interplay of "wild" and controlled decentralisation – with the latter entailing both a shift to the establishment as well as derogations from industry agreements – decentralisation in retailing has mainly been of the wild variety. Ending the extension of collective agreements and introducing scope for association membership without collective bargaining coverage – triggering a sharp decline in organisational density at the employers' associations that applied collective bargaining – has led to an enormous shrinkage of collective bargaining coverage in the German retail sector.

The Netherlands: Less decentralisation

In contrast, in the Netherlands, collective bargaining coverage is still high, at a level of 80% of the employees in the private sector. Sector agreements remain dominant and still cover almost 90% of the workers under collective bargaining. The numbers of collective agreements at the company level have been stable in recent decades: around 500 agreements, covering 11% of the total employees under collective bargaining. The Dutch collective bargaining regime is not really multi-layered: a company is covered by a sector agreement or has its own company agreement. Sector bargaining parties have the authority to give dispensation to a company from coverage under the sector agreement if it concludes its own collective agreement. In response to the "threat" that a big company might exit the sector institutions, in 2021 the social partners in the metal- and electrotechnical industry clarified three dispensation conditions. The first condition is that the same trade unions that bargain at the sector level must be involved in company-level bargaining. Second, the terms and conditions of employment in the company agreement must be of "equal value." The third condition is that the company keeps its obligations in terms of contributing to sector funds for pensions, training, and labour market policies. Collective bargaining parties have some scope for deviations at the company level but only above the minimum standards, so there are no negative derogations options as we see in Germany. Some sector agreements, such as in the metal and electro-technical industry, contain "decentralisation provisions," where works councils have the power to agree tailor-made regulations on working hours and holidays and unions on pay systems at the company level (but not on collective wage increases). This modest trend of coordinated decentralisation is limited in all sectors because of the resistance of trade unions to give power to works councils and because a large proportion of the employers (especially SMEs) do not want to bargain twice about employment terms and conditions with trade unions (Jansen & Tros, 2022). In sum, we see a trend of cautious organised decentralisation and limited wild organisation in the Netherlands. Together with the full use of legal extension mechanisms, the strategy of wage moderation might also explain why bargaining coverage remains robust in the Netherlands (Ibsen & Keune, 2018). The collective bargaining system is still going strong, but it should also be noted that trade unions in the Netherlands struggle to negotiate good agreements for workers (e.g., in the retail, hospitality, and healthcare sectors).

Since the mid-2010s, there has been debate about greater works council involvement in company regulations on terms and conditions. The employers' association AWVN[4] sees collective agreements with trade unions as the most obvious and efficient method to regulate employment terms

---

4   AWVN is an employers' association at national level and is involved in the making of over 450 collective agreements in many sectors.

and conditions. In their view, collective bargaining with trade unions at sector as well as at company level better serves industrial peace, prevents competition in employment terms and conditions, and fosters sustainable relationships in social dialogue and employment relations. Nevertheless, somewhat ambiguously, AWVN *also* sees regulations on employment terms and conditions in co-determination with works councils (and without trade unions) as a good method. The most important criterion, in AWVN's view, should be the level of support among the workers in the companies for trade unions or for works councils acting as their representative body. FNV is strongly against this "alternative" pathway to agreeing company regulations about primary terms and conditions of employment with the works council. They point to councils' and councillors' dependencies on their employers, the lack of a strike weapon, and works councils' lower expertise and negotiation skills in collective bargaining.

There is no empirical research about the numbers of collective regulations with works councils in the Netherlands. It can be assumed that the proportion of workers under such a regime is at least lower than the share of employment not covered by collective agreements because of the legal primacy of collective bargaining by unions (so less than 20%).

In sum, when we compare both countries, we see a far stronger erosion of collective bargaining coverage in the last decades in Germany than in the Netherlands. This has also led to significant variation in organised and wild forms of decentralisation between sectors in Germany. In the Netherlands, however, we see a less sharp decentralisation trend, as a result of more cautious sectoral collective bargaining parties and their supportive legal framework that makes sector agreements generally binding for all companies within the sector (including unorganised employers).

Case studies on relationships between trade unions and works councils in decentralisation processes

Germany: Insights from case studies in the metalworking and electrical industry

In the following, we will shed light on what role the relationship between trade unions and works councils plays during decentralisation processes. Both case studies from the metalworking and electrical industry in Germany relate to controlled decentralisation and the use of derogations. Focusing on the metalworking and electrical industry is particularly interesting since the trade union IG Metall has developed specific procedures for safeguarding coordination and for preventing unauthorised derogations as well for regulating concessions.

Case study Germany: Metal Forming[5]
Metal Forming is a medium-sized company with around 400 employees at its headquarters. The company makes parts for applications in the automotive industry, such as components for car bodies and powertrains. The case study investigates a derogation agreement that the company concluded with IG Metall in 2019, following a similar agreement negotiated the previous year. The company had been experiencing liquidity problems and had undergone a change in ownership.

There were several key points in the negotiations of the derogation agreement that both parties insisted on. According to the works council's expert, the management's main focus was on the savings to be made and on the scope for reducing employee numbers. Job security was a "red line" issue for the employee representatives, and they were not prepared to agree to both concessions and headcount reductions. In addition, there were a number of other important concerns, such as whether monetary concessions would be repaid if the business situation improved, and the number of apprenticeships. In the end, both parties achieved an agreement that comprises a mixture of material concessions by employees and quid pro quos from the company on job security, investment commitments, repayments of missed income, and information and monitoring rights. A conflict arose over the question of a bonus payment for union members only; in this case, these bonus payments were intended – as they were generally in the metalworking industry – to offset union dues, strengthen member loyalty, and create incentives to join the union. For these reasons, the employers' associations in the metal industry have decisively rejected any such arrangements, and this was also the case at Metal Forming. IG Metall subsequently concluded an agreement on this only with the company and without the consent of the employers' association, as an addendum to the derogation agreement.

Case study Germany: Lights[6]
Lights is a medium-sized company with about 5,500 employees worldwide, with around 1,500 employees at the German headquarters. The company

---

5   For the whole case study, see Haipeter & Rosenbohm, 2022: 47–53.
6   For the whole case study, see Heipeter & Rosenbohm, 2022: 53–60.

produces light fixtures and offers lighting system solutions. In 2021, the company concluded a derogation agreement with IG Metall.

In late 2019, however, management approached the works council and IG Metall with a request to negotiate a derogation agreement. The works council and union then undertook a quick check of the company's situation and realised that management's request was not without foundation.

The employers' side entered the negotiations with two main demands: firstly, to extend weekly working time without pay compensation; and secondly, to postpone the industry-level collectively agreed pay increases and not implement a new element in the industry collective agreement, an annual one-off payment that can also be converted into additional time off. Of these, employee representatives were more willing to agree to longer working hours than to a reduction in pay. However, this was only on the condition that this would also promote the harmonisation of working time standards between the company's various parts. Negotiations were not limited to these points, however, and were broadened, not least due to the demands raised by the employee side. Apart from the central issue of job security, the employee side demanded investment commitments and wanted to enforce extension of the scope for co-determination by the works council. In this regard, it was demanded that the works council gets involved in outsourcing decisions ("make-or-buy") earlier, in order to be able to influence product development at the gestation stage. In addition, employee representatives requested the establishment of a joint task force with management to solve operational problems. This was supplemented by demands for an increase in the apprenticeship quota, an extension of part-time work for older workers, the conversion of temporary workers' contracts into unlimited contracts, a guarantee that the company would become full members of the employers' association, and the payment of a bonus for union members. As in the Metal Forming case, this latter payment became a bone of contention between the negotiating parties, especially given the resistance of the representative from the employers' association. Although employee representatives realised that their chances of winning this were slim, it offered helpful leverage to push through other demands.

In the end, a derogation agreement was concluded comprising a mixture of material concessions by employees and quid pro quos from the employer. It includes, for instance, the postponement of agreed industry-level pay increases, a convergence of working times, but also a commitment to investments and rules regarding the monitoring of those investments by the trade union and the works council, with the possibility of a sanction for any shortfall. Among other things, it excludes compulsory redundancies and ensures that the works council participates in make-or-buy decisions at an early stage and stipulates the establishment of a task force consisting of management and the works council to jointly work out solutions for any operational problems.

Case studies in the Netherlands

To illustrate the relationships between trade unions and works councils and their positions and strategies in decentralised collective bargaining in the Netherlands we go more in-depth in two case studies. The first case reflects the traditional roles of trade unions and works councils in the Netherlands (DSM, manufacturing). The second case relates to uncoordinated (or "wild") decentralisation by breaking traditions in collective bargaining and co-determination (supermarket).

Case study the Netherlands: DSM[7]

From century-old roots as the Dutch State Mines, DSM has evolved into a multinational company numbering 23,000 people worldwide and around 3,800 people in the Netherlands, specialising in food, chemicals, and bioscience. DSM has its own company agreement, negotiated with four trade unions (FNV, CNV, De Unie, and VHP). There is no sector agreement in DSM-related sectors in the Netherlands. The advantage that DSM has from having a company agreement is that it is able to control its labour cost developments and to follow its own policies in e.g., sustainable employability and variable pay. At plant and business unit level, DSM has six works councils, all under the umbrella of one works council at the central level (the *centrale ondernemingsraad*, Central Works Council).

The main conclusion of the case study is that the roles and activities of trade unions and works councils are clearly divided. Some years ago, there was a discussion among DSM's Supervisory Board, its Company board, and the Central Works Council, questioning a larger role for works councils in the traditional trade union field of employment terms and conditions. This discussion led to the conclusion that works councils have less knowledge about wages, other payments, and collective bargaining processes than trade unions. Secondly, works council members are more dependent on DSM as their employer than professional negotiators paid by trade union organisations. Although they have demarcated powers, trade unions and works councils profit from reciprocal communications. Firstly, DSM's works councils see a role in keeping close control over the fulfilment of DSM's

7   For the whole case study, see Jansen & Tros, 2022: 29–33.

collective agreement and, for example, the detailed implementation of working hours schedules within the standards set out in the collective agreement. Many works councillors, including the chair of DSM's Central Works Council, are members of one of the trade unions (in this case, FNV). Moreover, the recent "triangle" project group involved in making a teleworking arrangement during the COVID-19 pandemic is an example of communicated trade unions and works council activities (unions agreed on payments, works councils on organisational conditions at the same social dialogue table with the employer).

Sometimes, there are frictions between the three stakeholders (employer/governor – trade union – works council) when they want to enter the other's field. The FNV union wants to be involved earlier in reorganisation and transfer plans in order to have more influence in earlier stages of the plans themselves and their effects on DSM's personnel and loss of employment in the region. According to DSM and its Central Works Council, information and consultation about reorganisation are tasks for the works councils, as they are regulated in the national Works Councils Act. As regulated by national law, announcements of collective dismissals have to be made to the trade unions, but they can only negotiate about the terms and conditions of those involved in collective dismissals or those threatened by job losses and not about the justification of the reorganisation itself or other organisational impacts. DSM prefers to have a long-term Social Plan with the unions about these terms and condition to prevent social unrest in every restructuring plan (there is now a five-year Social Plan). The chair of the Central Works Council points to the negative side effects when trade unions want to be involved too early in consultation rounds: "fighting can lead to less willingness by DSM's management to give information about reorganisations, what is needed for the works councils."

A recent case involving DSM's sale of a small company offers another example of the tensions and lack of cooperation that arises between the two bodies. The works council gave its approval on condition of agreeing a good "transfer collective agreement" (*transfer cao*) with the trade unions. When DSM could not come to an agreement with trade unions, the works councils did not withdraw their approval of the transfer.

Case study the Netherlands: Supermarket[8]
This case is an example of uncoordinated or disorganised decentralisation, where the workers' representation changed from trade unions to the works

---

8   For the whole case study, see Jansen & Tros, 2022: 36–39.

council in the distribution centres (supply chain) of a large supermarket in the Netherlands. In response to strikes and conflicts with the trade unions in 2017, the employer stopped bargaining with the trade unions – which were asking for a wage increase of 2.5% and fewer temporary jobs and more standard employment contracts. The employer initiated consultations with the supermarket's central works council and the works council for the distribution centres about a company regulation – a so-called *arbeidsvoorwaardenregeling* (AVR) – regarding the same topics that were traditionally regulated in the collective agreement with the trade unions. The supermarket's works councils did not ask the employer to restart the collective bargaining with the trade unions, despite the fact that around 700–800 distribution workers are trade union members. The representativeness of the council members is disputed by the unions and the interviewed works councillor. In early 2018, the works council gave its consent to the AVR proposed by the management, for a period of five years. Management gave every individual worker in the logistics departments a choice, although it was pressing for them to sign the AVR in a context of social unrest with resistance from trade union members in the workplaces. The FNV negotiator in this case is not only highly critical of the way the employer bypassed and overruled the trade unions in collective bargaining, but is also fundamentally against AVRs as a way of regulating employment terms and conditions. According to him, workers' interests when it comes to primary conditions, such as wages and bonuses for inconvenient working hours, etc., should not be represented by works council members who have no expertise in bargaining, who are too dependent on their employer, and who cannot use the strike weapon. "In fact, an AVR is a one-sided regulation by the employer," in his view. This case has three main effects. Firstly, compared to the former collective agreement, the lower labour standards that are regulated in the AVR are actually resulting in lower earnings for new logistic workers in standard employment, as well as employees on flexible labour contracts – including many temp agency workers. It has led to a divide between the older "expensive" workers and the new "cheaper" workers, with a financial incentive to replace older employees with younger (often migrant) workers. The second effect is a further polarisation between the employer and the trade unions. The trade unions felt undermined by their replacement with workers councils and met a closed door. FNV's trust in the employer has also been damaged by what they saw as "aggressive behaviour from the company in pressing the employees to sign the new AVR in 2018 and excluding workers who did not want to sign from a collective wage increase." A third effect is related to the functioning of the works councils in the supermarket, now with more trade union members but also with lower trust in the management.

Discussion based on the case studies

Cooperation among works councils and trade unions in decentralisation

Case studies in Germany
Overall, evidence from the German metalworking and electrical industry highlights that, in the case of the decentralisation via derogation clauses, trade unions are still the most important actor in bargaining at establishment or company level, since they check any applications by companies seeking to derogate from industry standards, set up and lead bargaining committees and negotiate with management, and organise membership participation and recruitment. Although derogations in the metalworking and electrical industry clearly fall within the scope of action of the collective bargaining parties, the cooperation between the union and works councils is highly relevant for negotiating and implementing such provisions. Works councils usually play a central role on negotiating committees, they are the experts in their own companies, and their approval is vital, as no viable agreement can be reached without their involvement and consent. In the case of Metal Forming, the bargaining committee not only consisted of an experienced collective bargaining official from IG Metall, but also of unionised works councillors and shop stewards from different departments in the company, enabling information and concerns to flow in both directions between the committee and individual departments. Similar to the case of Metal Forming, the union and the works council in the case of Lights were anxious to make the composition of the bargaining committee as broad as possible and to represent as many company affiliates, departments, and employee groups as they could. This body then appointed a smaller negotiating committee, led by IG Metall but also including six works councillors from different areas of the company, who were also trade union members.

In the case of Metal Forming, the link between the works council and the trade union was also highly relevant when the derogation process started. The whole process started with the management's announcement that it would shut down an essential part of the establishment. In line with the Works Constitution Act, the works council was informed about this alteration to operations. The works council immediately informed the IG Metall's local administrative office and used its network to locate and engage legal advice. Talks then began with the company that revealed that there was a major liquidity problem that could not be dealt with by closing the tool shop alone and that further measures would be necessary, which would include seeking a derogation from the industry agreement.

This underlines that close cooperation between the trade union and works councils is crucial for successful coordination of collective bargaining at company level. In our case studies, this is mainly ensured by a high organisation rate of works council members. Several aspects are important in this regard. Firstly, the union needs to ensure that works councils are not too willing to concede when faced with employer pressure. Secondly, having the union take the lead in contested negotiations can be a great help for works councils, relieving them of the challenge of facing management, who will have to sit down with the union's typically highly experienced negotiators, and allowing them to benefit from the power resources that the union can mobilise during the negotiation process. Moreover, negotiations on these issues can also enhance works councils' capabilities, as they will be provided with comprehensive business information by the employer that they would not otherwise have received in such a detailed form, despite their statutory right to such information in the normal course of co-determination (Haipeter, 2010).

Moreover, works councils need trade unions, both to provide professional support when engaging in the new tasks devolved to them and to back them up with organisational and bargaining power to enable them to negotiate fair derogation deals with management. The Lights works council has benefited greatly from the close cooperation it has enjoyed with IG Metall in implementing the agreement. One important factor in this is the importance of the company to the local union administration; Lights is the second largest company in the area and the chairman of the works council sits on the executive board of the local union office. This form of networking between the union and the works councils at large companies has existed for a long time. However, it has been recently complemented by the involvement of works councils in union projects to support and activate works councils that go beyond the well-rehearsed patterns of union support on specific enquiries and problems. For instance, an important building block in the context of the derogation agreement at Lights was the participation of the works council and the company in a trade union project aimed at strengthening the competences of both employee representatives and employers in dealing with digitalisation. Within the framework of the Work 2020 project, an "Agreement for the Future" was concluded between IG

Metall and the company. This was not a collective agreement in the formal sense, but rather a form of workplace agreement, concluded at company level, which focused on improvements in training opportunities for employees and included provisions on obligatory discussions on training between employees and supervisors and digital skills surveys to be conducted, if desired, by the works council.

In both German cases, established relationships between the works council and the union were crucial during the negotiation phase and formed an important resource for the employee representatives. Not only are all the members of the Metal Forming's works council in the union, but there are also close ties between the works council and the local union administration. Works councillors regularly attend union training sessions and seek union advice if problems arise.

In the case of derogations from industry agreements, trade unions need works councils as these represent the link to both workforces and management and are indispensable for monitoring how derogations are implemented at workplace level. Moreover, a core element of derogations in the metalworking and electrical industry is participation by union members. Indeed, the trade union included this as a requirement in its 2005 coordination rules. It is intended to foster a closer relationship between the union and its members, as well as employees more generally, when it is engaged in negotiations over derogations, given that, in contrast to bargaining over pay increases, these can entail a lowering of terms and conditions, at least temporarily. In the case of Metal Forming, the works council and trade union also played an important role in informing the workforce. Works councillors and shop stewards frequently went to departments to talk to workers in person and explain the risks posed to the whole workforce from closing the toolroom, helping strengthen employee unity. This approach also helped to increase union membership within the workforce. Both the works council and the union attribute this to intensive communication, the negotiation of the union membership bonus and, importantly, the legal protection offered by membership – an important argument for joining the union in view of the threat of job cuts. In the case of Lights, the union and the works council also made great efforts to create incentives for employees to join the union. Firstly, they provided comprehensive information; and secondly, only union members had a right to vote on the outcome of the negotiations. Both of these are typical incentives used by IG Metall in negotiations on derogations. However, a further instrument was added at Lights. In the questionnaire sent out at the beginning of negotiations to ask employees about their priorities, employee representatives also asked about union membership and enclosed a piece of paper asking if employees would like to have a say in the negotiations. As a result, the union was able to recruit up to 80 new members.

In the case of Lights, the IG Metall and trade union members of the works council invited the IG Metall members among the employees to a membership meeting, to vote on whether or not negotiations should be initiated. Negotiations for a derogation agreement had been held twice before – the last time only a year previously – and on both occasions without a result. In the previous year, union members at an IG Metall membership meeting had decided to break off negotiations. In any event, the breakdown of talks in the preceding dispute proved helpful in obtaining a mandate to start discussions again in the general meeting held to discuss fresh negotiations. IG Metall and the works council were able to argue that they would adopt a tough stance and would not hesitate to break off negotiations if necessary.

Case studies in the Netherlands

Where we see trade unions in the German cases being the bargaining actors, together or at least in active cooperation with works councils, we see far less overlapping of roles in both Dutch cases. Either it is "only trade unions" (as in DSM) or "only works councils" (as in the supermarket). For the Dutch manufacturing sector, then, we can conclude that is only trade unions that bargain on wages and other material compensations (see also Chapter 3 in this book; Haipeter et al., 2023). Remarkably, and also in the DSM case, trade unions leave the implementation of such decisions entirely to management and the works councils, without their involvement. The DSM case clearly reflects the aims and functioning of the Dutch legal system: collective bargaining on employment terms and conditions is for trade unions and co-determination on organisational and non-wage HR issues is for works councils. This case study mirrors the regulation and practices in other manufacturing sectors in the Netherlands where trade unions have decentralised the issue of flexible working hours (by day, month, and year) towards works councils, without any formal involvement of trade unions. The cooperative practices between unions and councils of the type seen in the German cases, do not exist in the Netherlands. Not even in the DSM case, where we would expect such strategic partnerships due to the combination of DSM's collective bargaining at the company level (instead of the dominant sectoral level in the Dutch regime) and relatively well-developed co-determination practises by works councils. The company has continued these demarcated practices in recent issues, such as teleworking, COVID-19 measures, and restructuring. In their own way, both case studies in the

Netherlands confirm and perfectly illustrate the dual-channel system in the Netherlands of separated juridical competences and demarcated positions of trade unions and works councils. In the supermarket case, where trade unions have been entirely replaced by works councils, this separation is absolute. At DSM, both bodies of workers representation communicate what they are doing in their own field, although the unions prefer to be more involved in organisational development issues than the employer and the works council allow for. In the supermarket case, the employer strategically replaced trade unions' collective bargaining with works council involvement, without coordination between the two bodies of workers representation and, consequently, it undermined the position of the trade unions. However, both cases show, albeit in different ways, that trade unions might benefit from greater cooperation with works councils in their negotiations with individual employers to prevent further decentralisation in negotiating employment terms and conditions and decentralisation of social dialogue towards works councils.

Trade union presence at the workplace

Crucial differences exist between the German and Dutch cases with regard to trade union presence in the workplace. While IG Metall uses different means in the workplace when it comes to derogations, ranging from being present and leading the bargaining committee and organised works council members to shop stewards, similar activities are not observed for the Dutch cases. In both German cases, the majority of works council members are organised within the trade union and thus form a hinge between the workplace level and trade union activities. This is supplemented by separate workplace trade union representatives' bodies (shop stewards), which are elected by trade union members. Although, those shop stewards have no legal co-determination rights, they nevertheless open up a direct link between the workforce and the trade union. For the union, such bodies are indispensable for staying in control of derogation processes and monitoring their implementation.

As described earlier, trade unions in the Netherlands are traditionally not present at workplace level (with some exceptions). Moreover, works councillors are less likely to be trade union members than in Germany. Nevertheless, the DSM case shows that works councils in business units with higher union memberships are more oriented towards the unions' agendas and policies than works councils in less organised business units (overall estimates of trade union memberships vary from 25% to 40%). It also helps communication between unions and councils when (chairs of) works councils are members of trade unions. But the difference is that in the Dutch manufacturing sector, neither bodies cooperate other than giving each other information and perhaps discussing certain issues. Respect for each side's own, separate roles is seen as crucial for the functioning of both collective bargaining as well as consultation and co-determination. The DSM case also shows that the proper functioning of this dual-channel model in this company is challenged by several factors. The continuity of collective bargaining by trade unions is dependent on union membership among new generations of workers. Younger workers are less unionised in the Netherlands, and that is also the case at DSM. The actual good communications and relations between the two bodies are partly based on the unions' having members on the works councils, but this factor also gives no guarantee for the future. Frictions and tensions remain and will require the right responses from all stakeholders in terms of their respect for the different roles and positions of the two bodies of workers' representation. Trade unions' presence in the workplace and involvement in the functioning of works councils is quite different than in the German cases where they operate together when it comes to derogations from collective agreements. The supermarket case in the Netherlands is illustrative of the isolation of both workers' representation bodies. It is difficult to imagine that trade unions would have been replaced by works councils if there had been more trade union members in the works councils and trade unions had had more communications with the works councils. Furthermore, dissatisfaction among employees around the replacement of the collective agreement by company regulations (AVR) has led to the election of new, more unionised works council members in the company. The new works council seems to adopt a more proactive approach, but, at the same time, more unionisation of the councils seems to lead to lower trust in the relationship between the management and the works councils. Following this experience, FNV is aiming for closer cooperative relations with the supermarket's works councils, including new communications and face-to-face meetings in order to support them in providing information, consultations, and expertise.

Conclusion

We see similar statutory allocations and demarcations of powers between works councils and unions in both countries. There is no formal difference between the two countries in the opportunity for works councils to be involved in negotiations at the company level if the collective bargaining parties give them a role. We also see debates in both countries about giving works councils more involvement in negotiating collective terms and conditions of employment at the company or even workplace level. However, there are some key differences between the two countries that have an impact on the role of works councils in shaping decentralisation and on the new relationships between trade unions and works councils. Firstly, there is more "effective" pressure from German employers to decentralise. Secondly, trade unions in the Netherlands are traditionally weaker and less present in the workplace than in Germany. Thirdly, in Germany, works councils are more influenced by trade unions as a result of consultation and unionised councillors. How can this be explained?

In Germany, there is more experience and evidence of factual decentralisation practices towards works councils. Contrary to the Netherlands, in some German industries there are general derogation clauses within collective agreements, which allow deviations at company level, even if these suspend, delay, or undercut collectively agreed standards at sectoral level. In addition, we also observe a shift in regulatory competences from the actors at industry level to the actors at company level; especially with regard to flexible working time arrangements. However, both forms can be regarded as controlled forms of decentralisation as they are defined through norms set by the bargaining actors at sectoral level. Controlled decentralisation through agreed derogations from industry-level collective agreements or in the form of shifting competencies to the workplace level does not, however, lead to a general erosion of the dual system of interest representation in Germany. Our empirical evidence underlines that when effective coordination is in place, works councils do not become substitutes for trade unions. However, the opposite might be true as well: when there is no coordination, employers might be able to bypass trade unions. Nevertheless, in Germany, the relationship among those actors changes considerably and the previously clear division of labour within the dual system becomes much more blurred. Works councils in Germany are getting involved, alongside the trade unions, in collective bargaining, and trade unions are much more actively involved in company affairs (see also Haipeter, 2021).

It is worth mentioning that organised decentralisation within the German metal and electrical industry rests upon a close articulation between works councils and the trade union and a strong union presence in the workplace (see also Müller & Schulten, 2019). In the growing segment where the institutions and actors of the dual system are absent (see Figure 1), meaning that neither collective agreements nor works councils are in place, no such coordinated process of decentralisation is feasible in Germany. For instance, in industries like retail, where trade unions are much weaker and works councils are less widespread, such mutual reinforcement is much rarer.

Much more than in Germany, trade unions in the Netherlands are very prudent and hesitant to give works councils a role in bargaining on primary working conditions, such as wages and working hours. Negative derogations are not possible. Positive derogations can be done unilaterally by employers without the involvement of any workers' representatives, unless it is explicitly agreed in the collective agreements, e.g., with respect to working time (but definitely not in wages). The case study of the Dutch supermarket illustrates that, in practice, the employer can bypass the trade union by making agreements with the works council, even in a context of rather high trade union membership. This is a possibility within the Dutch law. Although hard evidence cannot be given that such uncoordinated, wild decentralisation practices are growing in the Netherlands, debates and awareness about this issue have grown in recent years. More than in the past, some employers and their associations are seriously considering the pathway of making company agreements with works councils instead of collective agreements with trade unions. One of the unintended effects might be that works councils become more unionised, as we have seen in the supermarket case, which might also affect the traditional consensual model of co-determination in the Netherlands. In general, social partners in the Netherlands do not see trade unions and works councils cooperating in collective bargaining as a real option (again, a difference with Germany).

Our case studies suggest that trade unions and works councils are more collaborative in Germany. This might be explained by the strategic trade union response to the employers' push towards decentralisation. In Germany, this push from the employers' side has more power and impact, while in the Netherlands sector bargaining is more supported by legislation on the extension of sector agreements, which gives companies very low escape options in the direction of works councils (with exceptions of sectors like IT). To put it in other words, many German employers can directly profit from "opting-out" of employers' associations, while unorganised employers in most of the sectors in the Netherlands remain covered by sectoral agreements. During derogation negotiations in Germany, works councils, workplace union representatives, and the union itself – as negotiation leader – must coordinate their interests and develop common negotiating aims and strategies much more closely than usual in the normal operation of the dual system. The success of any derogation process very much depends on the presence of union officials, who are skilled in collective bargaining, and on works councils, which are able and willing to collaborate with the union. The clearer separation of activities of trade unions and works councils in the Netherlands is not only shaped by Dutch labour law, but also by less need of trade unions to connect to works councils in a stable collective bargaining regime, consisting of sector agreements without derogation opportunities. Trade unions in the Netherlands therefore have less experience in collaborating with works councils, do not see them as a power resource in decentralisation, and continue their strategy of "no decentralisation to works councils." At the same time, in the quite stable context of the Netherlands, works councils do not build up negotiation skills and capacities in the same way as German councils in manufacturing do. Then we come to a "chicken-and-egg" discussion to explain the councils' passivity in collective bargaining in the Netherlands or to a self-fulfilling prophecy of incapable works councils. No derogation leads to low experience among councils, and low experience leads to an unwillingness among collective bargaining parties to delegate to these unexperienced councils. Given the stricter functioning of the dual-channel structure in the Netherlands, which assigns a very limited role to works councils in co-negotiating and in the implementation of collective agreements, one might also say that Dutch trade unions are missing the opportunity to (re-) connect with workplaces and to deepen or widen their rank and file. By not advising or collaborating with works councils, trade unions risk becoming powerless in future cases of "wild" decentralisation in which employers initiate regulation of collective terms and conditions of employment with works councils.

Finally, we would like to make the comment that work councils in Germany and the Netherlands are both confronting big challenges today and in the near future. They might be increasingly involved in consultations and co-determination about organisational developments and its effects on jobs, skills, and quality of work, as a result of the anticipated digital and "green" transitions in companies. When done right, this might lead to further growth of the functioning of the institution of works councils in many companies in both countries. The possible trend of broadening and deepening the agenda for co-determination and works councils in organisational transitions might result in a further decentralisation in labour relations, while it can be assumed that, at the same time, these issues can limit influenced at sectoral level. In turn, this requires new strategies from trade unions to set the rules in collective agreements and to consider greater involvement in the functioning of works councils.

References

Armaroli, I. & Tomassetti, P. (2022). Decentralised bargaining in Italy. CODEBAR-project. CODEBAR – AIAS-HSI – University of Amsterdam (uva.nl)

Bahnmüller R. (2017). Von der Erosion des Flächentarifvertrags zur Chance gewerkschaftlicher Erneuerung. In Schulten, T., Dribbusch, H., Bäcker, G., & Klenner, C. (Eds.), *Tarifpolitik als Gesellschaftspolitik: Strategische Herausforderungen im 21. Jahrhundert* (pp. 34–47). VSA.

Bouwmans, S. & Eshuis, W. (2018). *Positie en strategie vakbeweging. Beschouwingen, analyses en voorstellen.* De Burcht.

Demir, N., Funder, M., Greifenstein, R., & Kißler, L. (2019). *Trendreport Betriebsratswahlen 2018 – Entwicklungstrends der betrieblichen Mitbestimmung.* Universität Marburg, FB 03 Gesellschaftswissenschaften und Philosophie, Institut für Soziologie. https://nbn-resolving.org/urn:nbn:de:0168-ssoar-65151-3

Ellguth, P. & Kohaut, S. (2021). Tarifbindung und betriebliche Interessenvertretung: Ergebnisse aus dem IAB-Betriebspanel 2020. *WSI-Mitteilungen*, 74(4): 306–314.

Haipeter, T. (2010). *Betriebsräte als neue Tarifakteure: zum Wandel der Mitbestimmung bei Tarifabweichungen.* Edition Sigma.

Haipeter, T. (2021). Between industry and establishment: Recent developments in German collective bargaining and codetermination. *Labour & Industry: A journal of the social and economic relations of work*, DOI: 10.1080/10301763.2021.1901333

Haipeter. T. & Rosenbohm, S. (2022). Decentralised bargaining in Germany. CODEBAR-project. CODEBAR – AIAS-HSI – University of Amsterdam (uva.nl)

Haipeter, T., Armaroli, I. Iossa, A., & Rönnmar, M. (2023). Decentralisation of collective bargaining in the manufacturing sector. In F. Tros (Ed.), *Pathways in decentralised collective bargaining in Europe* (pp. 73–112). Amsterdam University Press.

Hassel, A., Von Verschuer, S., & Helmerich, N. (2018). *Workers' voice and good corporate governance.* Institute of Economic and Social Research (WSI) of the Hans-Böckler-Foundation.

Jansen, N. & Tros, F. (2022). Decentralised bargaining in the Netherlands. CODEBAR-project. CODEBAR – AIAS-HSI – University of Amsterdam (uva.nl)

Kahmann, M. & Vincent, C. (2022). Decentralised bargaining in France. CODEBAR – AIAS-HSI – University of Amsterdam (uva.nl)

Kösters, R. & Eshuis, W. (2020). *De vakbond en de werkvloer, op zoek naar nieuwe relaties.* De Burcht.

Müller, T. & Schulten, T. (2019). Germany: Parallel universes of collective bargaining. In Müller, T., Vandaele, K., & Waddington, J. (Eds.), *Collective bargaining in Europe: Towards an endgame. Volumes I, II, III and IV* (pp. 239–265). ETUI.

Muñoz Ruiz, A. & Ramos Martín, N., (2022). Decentralised bargaining in Spain. CODEBAR-project. CODEBAR – AIAS-HSI – University of Amsterdam (uva.nl)

Nergaard, K., Dølvik, J.E., Marginson, P., Arasanz Díaz, J., & Bechter, B. (2009). Engaging with variable pay: A comparative study of the metal industry. *European Journal of Industrial Relations*, 15(2): 125–146.

Rönnmar, M. & Iossa, A. (2022). Decentralised bargaining in Sweden. CODEBAR-project. CODEBAR – AIAS-HSI – University of Amsterdam (uva.nl)

Sapulete, S., Behrens, M., Brehmer, W., & van Witteloostuijn, A. (2016). Gebruik van invloedtactieken door de OR: Duitsland en Nederland vergeleken. *Tijdschrift voor Arbeidsvraagstukken*, 32 (2): 157–176.

Traxler, F., Arrowsmith, J., Nergaard, K., & Molins López-Rodó, J. (2008). Variable pay and collective bargaining: A cross-national comparison of the banking sector. *Economic and Industrial Democracy*, 29(3): 406–431.

Tros, F. (2022). Innovating employee participation in the Netherlands. *Industrielle Beziehungen. Zeitschrift für Arbeit, Organisation und Management (The German Journal of Industrial Relations)*, 29 (1): 3–24.

Van den Berg, A., Grift, Y., Sapulete, S., Behrens, M., Brehmer, W., & van Witteloostuijn, A. (2019). Works councils in Germany and the Netherlands compared: An explorative study using an input-throughput-output approach. *WSI-Studien*, 2019 (17): 1–36.

Van het Kaar, R. & Looise, J. (1999). *De volwassen OR. Groei en grenzen van de Nederlandse ondernemingsraad.* Samsom.

Wajon, I., Vlug, P., & Enneking, E. (2017). *Naleving van de Wet op de Ondernemingsraden. Stand van zaken begin 2017.* Vlug Adviseurs en Onderzoeksbureau EVA.

Windmuller, J., de Galan, C., & van Zweeden, A. (1987). *Arbeidsverhoudingen in Nederland.* [6th edition based on J. Windmuller, *Labour relations in the Netherlands* (Cornell University Press, 1970)]. Het Spectrum.

7. Trade Union Participation and Influence in Decentralised Collective Bargaining

Mia Rönnmar, Marcus Kahmann, Andrea Iossa, Jan Czarzasty,[1] Valentina Paolucci

Abstract

The aim of this chapter is to analyse the role of trade unions in decentralised collective bargaining, specifically regarding trade union and works council participation in and influence on the processes and outcomes of collective bargaining at company level. To identify and explain differences and similarities in trade union and works council practice regarding company-level collective bargaining, the authors use an analytical framework based on the power resources approach and focus on structural, associational, and institutional power. The analysis suggests a degree of interchangeability in these power resources. Structural power resources are, for example, important for the outcomes of company bargaining, however, institutional and associational power resources may complement the lack or presence of such structural power resources.

Keywords: trade unions, works councils, collective bargaining, decentralisation, worker participation, power resources

Introduction

There is a general trend in many EU member states towards decentralisation in collective bargaining, as introduced in Chapter 1 of this book. The aim of

1   The Polish contribution to this chapter is published as part of an international research project co-financed by the Ministry of Science and Higher Education in Poland, under the "PNW" scheme in 2020–2022, under agreement no 5159/GRANT KE/2020/2.

Frank Tros (ed.). *Pathways in Decentralised Collective Bargaining in Europe.* Amsterdam: Amsterdam University Press, 2023

DOI 10.5117/9789048560233_CH07

this chapter is to analyse the role of trade unions in decentralised collective bargaining. More specifically, we take an interest in trade union and works council participation in and influence on the processes and outcomes of collective bargaining at company level.

A comparative approach is adopted, and the chapter contributes to the discussion on trade unions and decentralised collective bargaining through an analysis of similarities and differences across countries, sectors, and companies.

To identify and explain differences and similarities in trade union and works council practice regarding company-level collective bargaining, we use an analytical framework based on the power-resources approach (Lèvesque & Murray, 2010; Schmalz, Ludwig, & Webster, 2018). This approach is used as a filter for understanding whether and to what extent trade unions have been able, or willing, to mobilise certain power resources to impact the process and outcomes of company-level collective bargaining (see also Müller & Platzer, 2018). The power-resources approach has been frequently used in industrial relations research over the last decade, but its operationalisation for the comparative analysis of decentralised bargaining has been limited.

Labour power is unevenly structured and distributed in different national and sectoral contexts. However, from the extensive literature on power resources, it is possible to identify four commonly recognised forms through which it proceeds: structural; associational; institutional; and societal power resources. We consider that all of them have a potentially prominent role in shaping and influencing the dynamics and modalities of decentralised collective bargaining. The relationship between these forms is complex, sometimes conflicting, and not simply an add-on (Schmalz, Ludwig, & Webster, 2018). In our analysis of company cases, we found no significant mobilisation of societal power resources by trade unions and works councils. Therefore, the analytical framework in this chapter focusses on the following three forms of power resources:

a) *structural power* refers to the bargaining power of the workforce derived from its location in the labour market as well as in the production process (Wright 2000). Marketplace bargaining power derives from scarce skill or competences that make them valuable to their employer and difficult to replace. Workplace bargaining power is based on workers occupying strategic positions in production, such that disruptive action will impose highs costs on the employer. In industries with high productivity and highly integrated production, workers' bargaining power is particularly elevated as the impact of work stoppages goes far beyond the workplace.

b) *associational power*, unlike structural power, relies on the formation of collective actors (political parties, works councils, trade unions). It can partly compensate for the lack of other types of power resources (Hyman & McCormick, 2013). Union membership and voter approval in works council elections are common indicators for associational power. However, they are insufficient as a base. To become effective, numerical strength must be combined with other factors such as membership activism and participation, adequate infrastructural resources, and internal cohesion (Lévesque & Murray, 2010).

c) *institutional power* refers to the institutional and legal supports that bolster – and restrict – union action. It may provide a substitute for dwindling associational and structural power (Hyman & McCormick, 2013). Institutional power is distinctive in that it is relatively independent of the business cycle and short-term political change (Schmalz & Dörre, 2014). It includes institutions of economic and welfare governance that impact the unions' capacity to represent workers, but also their position in tripartite arrangements, collective bargaining, and workplace representation. Labour law and industrial relations systems are crucial sources of institutional power.

The content and outline of the chapter are as follows. In a first step, the chapter discusses a selection of key aspects related to trade union participation in and influence on the processes and outcomes of decentralised collective bargaining at company level from a cross-country and cross-sectoral comparative perspective. Firstly, we present an analysis of the institutional and legal framework of trade unions and decentralised collective bargaining, which is of great importance for institutional power. Secondly, we provide an analysis of trade union coordination and social partnership, which are of great significance for generating and maintaining associational and institutional power. Then, we discuss and analyse trade union membership, organising, and participation as a crucial resource of associational power.

In a second step, and in light of the discussion in the previous sections, this chapter provides a comparative company case studies analysis, utilising the power-resources approach, and presents an analysis of company-level trade union practices, processes and outcomes of decentralised collective bargaining. The final section contains some concluding remarks.

This chapter discusses developments in eight EU member states, i.e., France, Germany, Ireland, Italy, the Netherlands, Poland, Spain, and Sweden. These countries represent an interesting institutional diversity, which can be discussed in terms of comparative typologies, such as *varieties of capitalism* and liberal market economies (LMES) and coordinated market economies (CMES) (Hall & Soskice, 2001), *varieties of unionism* (Kelly & Frege, 2004), and *varieties of labour law and industrial relations systems* (Hepple & Veneziani, 2009; Finkin & Mundlak, 2015; Barnard, 2012; Marginson & Sisson, 2004; and Bamber et al., 2021). Although these comparative typologies contain elements of simplification, they still fulfil valuable pedagogical and analytical functions. The comparative case studies analysis in this chapter focuses on company case studies in France, Germany, and Ireland. The chapter builds on materials, analysis, and conclusions produced within the framework of a joint European-comparative research project (Tros, 2022).

Institutional and legal framework of trade unions and decentralised collective bargaining

This section analyses the institutional and legal framework of trade union rights and activities and decentralised collective bargaining, which constitutes a primary source for trade unions' institutional power. The discussion focusses on the national level and cross-country comparison.

Industrial relations and institutional framework

The countries subjected to study represent the Anglo-Irish, Continental European, Eastern European, Nordic, and Southern European labour law and industrial relations systems, as well as the common and civil law distinction. The variety of labour law and industrial relations systems manifests itself in differences as regards, for example, the importance of constitutional principles, the balance between legislation and collective bargaining, the degree of state influence or voluntarism, the role of the courts and case law, the degree of trade union organisation and collective bargaining coverage, and forms of employee representation and influence.

Labour law and industrial relations in Ireland, Italy, and Sweden reflect a particularly strong emphasis on voluntarism, collective autonomy, and contractual regulation of terms and conditions of employment through collective agreements and employment contracts (Paolucci et al., 2022; Armaroli & Tomassetti, 2022; Rönnmar & Iossa, 2022). For example, in Sweden, most of an employee's terms and conditions of employment, including wages, are set by collective agreements, and there is no minimum wage legislation or system for extension of collective agreements. Autonomous collective bargaining is complemented, and strengthened, by statutory regulation on trade unions, collective bargaining, and employee influence, including information, consultation, and co-determination. In addition, most statutory regulation is 'semi-compelling', and provides room for deviations by way of collective agreements.

In France, as in Spain, labour law and industrial relations are character-ised by a legalistic tradition, extensive statutory regulation in working life and on trade unions, collective bargaining, and employee influence, and state intervention in industrial relations (see further Chapter 5; Muñoz Ruiz et al., 2023). In France, there is minimum wage legislation, and a statutory system for extending collective agreements, resulting in an almost complete collective bargaining coverage. In recent years, state intervention and statutory reform, for example, the "Macron Ordinances" have reframed the system of employee representation and influence and introduced a compulsory division of collective bargaining topics among levels (Kahmann & Vincent, 2022).

In Germany, labour law is influenced by a legalistic tradition and charac-terised by an elaborate constitutional and statutory framework for collective bargaining and employee influence and workplace co-determination. At the same time, there is strong emphasis on collective autonomy and collective bargaining. There is a system in place for extending collective agreements, but in recent years fewer collective agreements have been declared generally binding. Minimum wage legislation was introduced in 2015, in response to an "erosion of collective bargaining" (Haipeter & Rosenbohm, 2022).

In Poland, finally, labour law and industrial relations have been influ-enced by the processes of democratic transformation, EU enlargement, and marketisation, resulting inter alia in fragmented collective bargaining (Czarzasty, 2022).

The interplay between legislation, collective bargaining, extension of collective agreements, and minimum wage regulation is at the core of the labour law and industrial relations system, and of importance for the processes and outcomes of company-level collective bargaining. Further-more, the adversarial or cooperative character of social partner relations, the organisation of the labour market, trade union structures, such as trade union pluralism and trade union demarcations (e.g., industrial or craft trade unions, blue-collar, white-collar, or general trade unions, and political or religious affiliations of trade unions), and the degree of trade union organisation impact on the role and influence of trade unions.

The national systems for employee representation and influence differ. In single-channel systems, employee influence is channelled only through trade unions. In Sweden, for instance, trade unions both negotiate and conclude collective agreements on wages and other terms and conditions of employment at cross-sectoral, sectoral, and local level, and take part in information, consultation, and co-determination at workplace level. In dual-channel systems, e.g., in France, Germany, the Netherlands, and Poland, employee influence is channelled both through trade unions and works councils. France has witnessed a recent statutory reform of employee representation and works councils (Kahmann & Vincent, 2022), and in Poland, the impact and activities of works councils are limited (Czarzasty, 2022). In countries with well-established dual-channel systems of employee influence, like Germany and the Netherlands, the relation between trade unions and works councils at company-level can differ and be characterised either by collaboration or by competition and conflict. This, in turn, may impact on trade union activity and strength, and company-level collective bargaining (see further Chapter 6; Rosenbohm & Tros, 2023).

Multi-level legal framework of trade unions and decentralised collective bargaining

As EU member states, the countries subjected to study in this chapter are covered by a common international and EU/European legal framework, which interplay with national regulation on trade unions and collective bargaining.

At *international and European level*, a number of legal sources, including ILO Conventions No 87, 98, and 154 and the revised European Social Charter, entail a legal recognition of fundamental trade union rights, such as the freedom of association, right to collective bargaining, and right to collective action. According to the European Court of Human Rights, the freedom of association, as protected by Article 11 of the European Convention of Human Rights, also comprises the right to bargain collectively and the right to industrial action.[2] Furthermore, fundamental rights protection is provided by Article 28 of the EU Charter of Fundamental Rights on the right of collective bargaining and collective action.

In the EU, the European social dialogue, a collective route to legislation at EU level involving the European social partners, takes place at both cross-sectoral and sectoral level (cf. Articles 152 and 154–155 TFEU) (Welz, 2008; Marginson & Sisson, 2004). EU labour law clearly emphasises employee influence and aims for a partial harmonisation of regulation on

---

2   See, for example, the cases of *Demir and Baykara v Turkey*, judgement of 12 November 2008, and the case of *Enerji Yapi-Yol Sen v Turkey*, judgement of April 2009.

information, consultation, and employee participation. The fundamental right to information and consultation is afforded protection by Article 27 of the EU Charter of Fundamental Rights, and extensive regulation on this topic is found inter alia in the Directives on transfers of undertakings, collective redundancies, European Works Councils, and a general framework of information and consultation.[3]

The (2020/2041/EU) Directive on adequate minimum wages in the EU has implications for national labour law and industrial relations, and trade unions and company-level collective bargaining (COM (2020) 682 final). The aim of the Directive is to establish a framework for setting adequate levels of minimum wages, and access of workers to minimum-wage protection, in the form of wages set out by collective agreements or, where it exists, in the form of a statutory minimum wage. The Directive also includes provisions on measures to promote collective bargaining.[4]

In the EU law context, fundamental trade union rights and freedom of association, collective bargaining, and collective action have also been challenged. In the much-debated *Viking* and *Laval* cases,[5] the Court of Justice of the EU held that the exercise of the right to collective action constituted a restriction on the freedom of establishment and freedom to provide services, respectively, and needed to be justified.

Fundamental trade union rights and collective bargaining can also be challenged by "states of emergency," such as economic crises and pandemics. During the global financial crisis, many EU member states put crisis-related measures in place, and subsequently the "eurozone" and sovereign debt crisis resulted in far-reaching austerity measures and deregulatory labour law and industrial relations reforms in many member states. These developments, and the role played by the "Troika" (the European Commission, the European Central Bank, and the IMF) and bail-out packages, have been criticised, and legally challenged at several levels, in national constitutional courts, in the Court of Justice, and before international human rights bodies, such as the ILO and the Council of Europe (Deakin & Koukiadaki, 2013; Kilpatrick, 2014).

---

3   Directives 2001/23/EC, 98/59/EC, 2009/38/EC, and 2002/14/EC.
4   The Directive includes guarantees for national systems of industrial relations built on autonomous collective bargaining (cf. Article 1.1.–1.3.). Still, the proposal has been strongly and jointly opposed by, for example, the Swedish social partners, who see it as posing a fundamental threat to the Swedish autonomous collective-bargaining system and key principles of wage formation and mechanisms for wage-setting. In October 2022 the Directive (2022/2041/EU) was adopted.
5   See Case C-438/05 *Viking* and Case C-341/05 *Laval*.

The COVID-19 pandemic has challenged the foundations of EU integration, and principles of human rights, democracy, solidarity, and free movement, and also resulted in economic crisis and urgent tasks for labour markets and social welfare systems. At the same time, in several member states, collective bargaining between social partners has played an important role in handling the pandemic. In Sweden, for example, quick and flexible adaptations to national, sectoral collective agreements were made, thousands of local collective agreements on short-time work were concluded, and crisis management agreements were put in place in the public healthcare sector (Rönnmar & Iossa, 2022; ILO, 2022: 139 ff.).

At *national level*, key issues related to trade unions, collective bargaining, and employee influence are regulated by a multitude of legal sources, including constitution, legislation, collective bargaining, and case law, depending on the characteristics of the labour law and industrial relations system. This legal framework is of great importance for trade union activities and strength, and company-level collective bargaining.

Regulation on trade unions includes issues of freedom of association, formation, and representativeness of trade unions, and internal affairs of trade unions. The representativeness of trade unions can be the subject of statutory regulation, as in France (Kahmann & Vincent, 2022). Instead, in Sweden, there are minimal formal requirements for forming a trade union, and recognition of trade unions is automatic. There are no statutory or case law-based procedures or criteria for determining the representativity of trade unions. All trade unions enjoy the same basic statutory rights to freedom of association, general negotiation, collective bargaining, and collective action, and further rights are afforded to "established trade unions," i.e. trade unions that are currently or customarily bound by a collective agreement (Rönnmar & Iossa, 2022). Furthermore, regulation on rights to time-off, training, and practical facilities for trade union representatives is important support for trade union activities.

Regulation on collective bargaining includes the right to – and sometimes obligation of – collective bargaining, and provisions on actors, processes, and outcomes of collective bargaining. The definition and legal effects of collective agreements are key and vary between the countries subjected to study. In Germany and Sweden, for example, collective agreements are legally binding, both for the contracting parties and for their members. A collective agreement has both a normative and mandatory effect. In Sweden, an employer bound by a collective agreement is obligated to apply this agreement to all employees, irrespective of trade union membership. Furthermore, unless otherwise provided for by the collective agreement, employers and employees being bound by the agreement may not deviate from it by way of an individual employment contract. In Germany, deviations from the collective agreements are permissible if they are favourable to the employee (Haipeter & Rosenbohm, 2022; Rönnmar & Iossa, 2022). Many sector agreements in the Netherlands are "minimum agreements," which allow for deviations to the benefit of employees but without related bargaining rights for trade unions at the company level (Jansen & Tros, 2022). In contrast, in Ireland, a collective agreement is not legally binding (Paolucci et al., 2022). Systems for extension of collective agreements are established by way of statutory regulation in, for example, France, the Netherlands, and Germany.

The legal scope for company-level collective bargaining and its size, as well as the relation between collective agreements at different levels, is of key importance for the development of decentralised collective bargaining and the role and activities of trade unions at company-level in this context. The relation between collective agreements and other workplace agreements are determined by way of statute, collective bargaining, or case law on, for example, principles on the binding effect of the collective agreement, favourability, opening clauses, and derogations.

Regulation on employee influence includes rights to information, consultation, and co-determination, and the interplay between EU and national law. The content of the regulation also differs depending on the single- or dual-channel system of employee representation in place, and the functions and activities of trade unions and works councils, respectively.

Trade union coordination and social partnership

This section deals with issues of trade union coordination and social partnership in the context of increasingly decentralised (and in some cases like Poland, even disintegrating) collective bargaining. In this context, trade unions' mobilisation of associational and institutional power resources is of particular importance. The discussion focusses on developments in Ireland, France, Germany, Poland, and Sweden.

Trade union strategies towards collective bargaining vary, depending on the institutional context of the industrial relations system at the national level and sectoral specifics at the industry level. As a result, there are different approaches to coordination and social partnership. This is also conditioned by state policies and attitudes of employers.

In the case of Ireland and Poland, two countries with a pluralist type of industrial relations system (even though one belongs to the Anglo-Irish system, and the other to the Eastern European one), collective bargaining is substantially decentralised, and confined to the company-level with single-employer collective agreements dominating. Absence of sectoral (industry-level/multi-employer) bargaining has been compensated by the presence of tripartite institutions engaged in social dialogue, although its trajectories have differed substantially.

In Ireland the social partnership system, involving the state, central-level business associations, and the Irish Trade Union Congress was established with the conclusion of the Programme for National Recovery in 1987. The system, based on a principle of a trade-off between wage and tax moderation, survived for twenty years but collapsed following the 2008 crisis. The collapse of social partnership appears to be a pivotal point for Irish industrial relations. In the post-crisis years, "the Irish Congress of Trade Unions and the Irish Business and Employers' Confederation agreed a 'protocol' to guide collective bargaining in private and commercial state-owned firms that prioritised job retention, competitiveness, and orderly dispute resolution" (Paolucci et al., 2022).

In Poland, tripartite institutions were established in the 1990s as a part of the *aquis* in course of preparations for EU membership (Vaughan-Whitehead, 2000) but their development was flawed by subsequent crises (leading to a de facto demise of the central tripartite body in 2013, re-established in 2015) and persistent internal imbalance of power (weak social partners versus dominant government), a phenomenon labelled "illusory corporatism" (Ost, 2011). The only substantive prerogative of tripartite bodies through which trade unions can exercise wage moderation are national minimum wage negotiations, yet since the adoption of the Minimum Wage Act of 2003 they have rarely succeeded.

Besides certain similarities, there are substantial differences between the two countries. While in Poland there is no bargaining coordination, either vertically or horizontally, it is present and quite vibrant in Ireland. Coordination in Poland is arguably hindered by the advanced pluralisation (three national-level confederations with various political leanings), decentralisation, and fragmentation of trade union movement, while in Ireland trade union federations like SIPTU (pharmaceutical sector), Madate (retail sector), and FSU (financial sector), "[i]n the absence of centralised collective bargaining...resorted to their own organisational resources to empower shop stewards and revitalise their company-level representation structures" (Paolucci et al., 2022: 70). Vertical coordination in the private sector is informal, yet relevant. Horizontal coordination is observed, albeit not in all sectors. It is, for example, non-existent in the food processing industry. In the dynamic perspective, it seems that following the demise of the social partnership system, Ireland has moved away from the neo-corporatist paradigm (although the Irish model, even in its prime, received criticism for its ambiguous character, and was called "neoliberal corporatism", see Boucher & Collins, 2003) towards a self-regulating system, which encourages comparisons with Sweden.

Sweden epitomises the Nordic system, and yet shares certain similarities with Germany, through a strong tradition of corporatism, which sets them the apart from the superficial neo-corporatist arrangements in Ireland and Poland. Thus, absence of tripartism in Sweden can be explained by a robust tradition of autonomous (bipartite) regulation of the labour market and industrial relations, with little interference by the state. This is reflected in the strategies of trade unions, which are focused on negotiating with employers at sectoral level but leave room for "organised decentralisation" via successful negotiation and practical implementation of local collective agreements. Extensive employee representation and information, consultation, and co-determination at local level are also of great importance (Rönnmar & Iossa, 2022). In Swedish case studies from the manufacturing and retail sectors, the white-collar trade union Unionen emphasises two important strategic choices made in the mid-1990s: to strive for national, sectoral collective agreements with substantive regulation on terms and conditions of employment, and to prioritise collective bargaining before legislation. The blue-collar trade union IF Metall emphasises the importance of creating fruitful conditions for local collective bargaining and setting obligatory minimum standards, and using fallback clauses to safeguard the level of wages and terms and conditions of employment and counteract potential inequality in bargaining power (Rönnmar & Iossa, 2022). As for coordination, a meaningful illustration of cross-sectoral coordination is provided by the formation of the Swedish Unions within Industry (*Facken inom Industrin*) by blue-collar and white-collar/professional–university graduate trade unions in the private industry sector in 1996 (Rönnmar & Iossa, 2022). Swedish trade unions perceive the two dimensions of collective bargaining (national, sectoral, and local) as complementary. Furthermore, the Swedish cross-sectoral, social-partner agreement on security, transition, and employment protection, which was concluded in 2020 and 2021, and also resulted in legislative reforms, can be seen as a strengthening of social partnership and autonomous collective bargaining (Rönnmar & Iossa, 2022).

While sharing some characteristics with Sweden, in terms of tripartism being largely missing from the national system of industrial relations (arguably due to the federal state structure where locus of control is mainly laid at the level of a constituent state, i.e., Land), Germany presents a case of a dual-channel system. Employees are indeed represented by both representative channels of trade unions and works councils, but the main purpose and focus of trade unions is collective bargaining at sector and (centralised) company level, while it is the works councils that operate at workplace level. Collective bargaining and workplace co-determination involve different actors on the employee side, and constitute two levels of labour regulation (see also Chapter 6; Rosenbohm & Tros, 2023). This is a key factor, determining the strategies of trade unions. Trade unions, on the one hand, retain a monopolistic position in collective bargaining, while works councils, on the other hand, are responsible for the implementation of collective agreements at the workplace level. Thus, the two types of bodies ought to cooperate. Facing decentralisation of collective bargaining, trade unions have chosen to get involved in the process rather than to stay out of it, reasoning that organised decentralisation is better than an uncontrolled ("wild") one. As a result, they have engaged in number of endeavours in partnership with works councils, the meaningful example of which is derogation from the sectoral agreement in the metalworking industry, where the works council and IG Metall acted together at company level in implementing the agreement derogating from the industry-level agreement (Haipeter & Rosenbohm, 2022). German unions have also been forced to respond to the employers' strategy of opting-out of collective bargaining by creating a special membership status of employer associations (OT – *ohne Tarifbindung*). The trade unions' strategic responses involve primarily union organising and new forms of member participation (Haipeter & Rosenbohm, 2022).

France represents a specific variation of the Continental European system, due to a long tradition of state involvement in industrial relations that can be traced back to the dirigisme paradigm in public policy (see also Chapter 5; Muñoz Ruiz et al., 2023). As a result, the national system of industrial relations in France is often labelled statist/*étatist*. This played a decisive role in promoting collective bargaining and sustaining it at industry-level with the "favourability principle" playing a major part. Tripartism has been present in France since the early post-war years. With one of the lowest density rates in the EU, French trade unions' legitimacy is largely facilitated by their bargaining activities. Since 2017, coordination of bargaining between levels is no longer based on the "favourability principle," but rather on the complementarities of bargained topics (Kahmann & Vincent, 2022). As exemplified by the electrical sector, the "role of the industry federation in company level bargaining may vary to some extent from one trade union confederation to another, but the general picture is that of a loose coupling between union actors at both levels" (Kahmann & Vincent, 2022: 31). The picture is similar for the metal and retail sector. Inter-union coordination, given the pluralisation of union movement, is weak but may vary contextually (at company level).

Trade union membership, organising, and participation

Recruiting members, developing them into new activists, and encouraging participation at different levels are at the heart of trade unions' associational power. This section analyses the role of trade union membership, organising and participation in the context of decentralised collective bargaining in a cross-national perspective. It focuses on the evolution of union density and the renewal of union approaches to collective bargaining.

Cross-country differences in trade union membership

Despite cross-country differences in meaning and significance of union membership, a common rule applies: the likelihood of successful worker representation increases with the degree of organisation of workers (Schmalz & Dörre, 2014). To measure and compare workers' associational power, union membership, and, in particular, membership density is an important, yet imperfect, indicator.

Table 7.1. presents trade union density for the eight countries under study. Variation is considerable. Union density reaches from 10.8% in France to 65.2% in Sweden. While density has been on the decline almost everywhere in Europe since the 1980s, its rate differs significantly across countries. It is strongest in Ireland and Germany, where it has more than halved since 1980. Spain is the only country in the panel data in which density has remained stable, albeit at a low 12.5%. It remains highest in Sweden at 65.2%. Despite declining union density, collective bargaining structures have remained largely in place in continental (Western) Europe, albeit at the price of introducing considerable flexibility. Except for Ireland, Germany, and Poland, coverage rates have resisted decline and remained high over the last two decades (Table 7.1.).

Table 7.1.   Trade union density and bargaining coverage in eight EU-countries

	Union density		Bargaining coverage
	1980	**Most recent**	**Most recent**
France	18.6	10.8	98
Germany	34.9	16.3	54
Ireland	57.1	26.2	34
Italy	49.6	32.5	100
Netherlands	34.8	15.4	75.6
Poland	–	13.4	13.4
Spain	13.3	12.5	80.1
Sweden	78.1	65.2	87.7

Source: OECD/AIAS/ICTWSS database, based on national sources (Visser, 2021).

It is noteworthy that membership decline has been uneven also across sectors, occupations, and companies. In Germany, for example, the auto-motive industry managed to keep union density at high levels of over 50%, whereas in retail it strongly declined after several well-organised chains went bankrupt. Membership is still significant in the privatised postal, telecommunication, and transport services, but unions fail to reproduce this pattern amongst new market competitors (Dribbusch & Birke, 2019). The increase in the proportion of women in union membership has not been sufficient to offset the effects of the loss of male members in terms of density.

Most analyses of union density have focussed on economic factors such as the level of (un)employment or movements in prices and wages (see Hyman & McCormick, 2013). However, such approaches fail to explain the often counter-cyclical trends in Northern Europe that can be best explained by the unions' key role in the administration of unemployment benefits. Hence, institutional factors are also important, and many comparative analyses have indeed highlighted the legal framework and government policy as well as general support for union security as determinants of union density. Clegg (1976) insists on the significance of the specific industrial relations institutions, namely, the structure of collective bargaining. Membership density is high where the extent of bargaining – the proportion of workers in a plant, industry, or country covered by an agreement – is high. But, if there is membership decline, do union approaches to bargaining have a role in this? And, if these are a relevant factor, is it possible to adapt them and use them as an opportunity to revitalise unions and works councils, thereby potentially compensating for the loss of institutional and structural power resources in bargaining?

Trade unions' organisational responses to the decentralisation of collective bargaining

The discussion about the role of membership and activism in a changing context for collective bargaining first came to the fore in the 1990s when certain US unions saw the "organising model" as a response to persistent membership decline, contrasting it starkly with the dominant "servicing model" to collective bargaining (Voss & Sherman, 2000). In European trade unions, this debate was received selectively or did not filter through from academia (Thomas, 2016). Trade unions have generally hesitated to review their practices with regard to membership in the context of decentralised bargaining. Germany and Ireland are an exception to this rule in that they developed distinctive participative approaches.

Membership participation and organising: An uneven situation
Trade unions share an ethos of internal democracy that extends to collective bargaining. It supposes a bidirectional relationship between union negotiators and members. Ideally, union members participate in the formulation of claims, the ratification of draft agreements, and their follow-up. They may also participate in negotiation processes, be it through adjusting claims or industrial action. Beyond such an ethos, however, there is significant variation in trade union approaches to collective bargaining and democracy, between countries but also sectors and unions. Such variation highlights differences in social relationships between the constituent parts of the union (members, activists, lay officers, full-time officials). Müller et al. (2018), e.g., make an analytical distinction between managerial, professional, and participative relationships in bargaining.

Of these three ideal-types, only the "participative relationship" considers members as potentially active participants in collective bargaining alongside professional union staff and leaders. Participative relationships tend to be well represented in countries with a strong union tradition in collective bargaining (Müller et al., 2018: 650). However, despite the persistence of such traditions in Italy (Armaroli & Tomassetti, 2022), Sweden (Rönnmar & Iossa, 2022), or France (Kahmann & Vincent, 2022), membership participation and organising have not been prominent in redefining trade union strategies in relation to decentralised bargaining in any of these three countries.[6] To be

---

6   This is not to say that problematic evolutions in terms of membership and bargaining coordination cannot be identified. By negotiating alongside the workplace representation bodies, local (and sometimes national) Italian trade unions have maintained a degree of control over company

sure, such approaches are not easy to implement since they can question the union's traditional role in industrial relations (Rehder, 2008) and require the restructuring of organisational resources. Moreover, decentralised union democracy has been discussed as precluding overall strategic direction and potentially detrimental to union efficiency (see Hyman & McCormick, 2019). Maybe more fundamentally, unions may not feel an urgency to develop membership and activism as they see themselves in a situation of relative institutional security, be it in the form of high bargaining coverage or above-average union density.

Still, innovative approaches to membership and activism can be identified in Ireland and Germany, two countries that have been hit particularly hard by the transformation of collective bargaining. These approaches can be characterised as participative as they share an emphasis on strengthening the participation of membership throughout the different phases of the decentralised bargaining process and rely on robust feedback mechanisms between members, activists and union leaders. However, unlike more "radical," bottom-up approaches to organising, union staff retains the leading role in coordinating action between levels and actors.

The remainder of this section focuses on these approaches. Both converge in that they conceive the decentralisation of collective bargaining as an opportunity for strengthening union and works council vitality at company level. Yet, the rationale underlying the decision to develop such an approach varies, reflecting profound differences in collective bargaining context. In Germany, IG Metall promotes extended membership participation to assure, first and foremost, the quality and legitimacy of derogatory deals with management. In Ireland, SIPTU's efforts to reinforce membership participation in company bargaining represent a response to the breakdown of national social partnership and a condition for establishing pattern bargaining.

IG Metall: Assuring the quality of derogatory deals

In the German metalworking and electrical industry, the decentralisation of collective bargaining mainly involves derogations from regional sectoral

---

bargaining. The lack of bargaining depth at this level as well as increased competition with 'outsider' unions may however be perceived as a problem (Armaroli & Tomassetti, 2022). In large French business groups, company union delegates enjoy much autonomy from their union, resulting in low levels of union information and control over company bargaining. Activism and membership are often limited to elected worker representatives, feeding into the much-observed poverty of company bargaining (Kahmann & Vincent, 2022). In Sweden, unions largely oversee what is negotiated at company level. Union density stands at about 65%, but there are signs that the weakening of local union clubs entails problems for the pursuit of company bargaining (Rönnmar & Iossa, 2022).

agreements. Already in the late 1990s, IG Metall, Germany's largest industrial union with 2.2 million members, began experimenting with increased membership participation in local negotiations with management over deviation (Turner, 2009). As derogation can entail a lowering of terms and conditions, at least temporarily, the core idea of the new approach is that members would be more receptive to such an outcome if they were involved in the process.

Three forms of participation characterise IG Metall's approach to negotiating derogations (Haipeter & Rosenbohm, 2022): ongoing information of trade union members through meetings during negotiations; member participation in company-level union bargaining committees; and, crucially, votes by members on whether to start negotiations and whether to accept a negotiated outcome. Experience has shown that members who are involved are much more likely agree with the outcome of the process. There has also been a further, and largely unexpected, effect, however. In many cases, the union has been able to recruit new members as employees have wanted to participate and have a voice (Haipeter, 2010). Given these unexpected results, in 2006 the union's district organisation in North Rhine-Westphalia demanded that certain benefits should be available for union members only.

In retrospect, experiences with derogations were the starting point for a "member-oriented offensive strategy" that IG Metall developed in the early 2010s (Haipeter & Rosenbohm, 2022). This involved tying the budgets of IG Metall's organisational units to income from membership dues, underpinned by annual operational objectives and target membership figures. Member orientation thus became a cross-sectional strategy and a benchmark for measuring success across the full spectrum of the union's activities, a process in which the experiences of negotiating derogations played a decisive role (Hassel & Schroeder, 2018). This strategy can boast some success. Unlike most other unions affiliated to DGB (*Deutscher Gewerkschaftsbund*), IG Metall has consolidated its membership levels over the last decade.

SIPTU: *Rebuilding bargaining strength from below*
Since the collapse of national social partnership in 2009, the main levels at which collective bargaining takes place in Ireland are the company and the plant levels. The breakdown of centralised bargaining triggered SIPTU (Services Industrial, Professional and Technical Union; general union), Ireland's largest affiliate to the ITUC (Irish Trade Union Congress) with 180,000 members, to strategically target strongly unionised companies in commercially buoyant export sectors, such as the pharmaceuticals, chemicals, and medical sectors. A main objective of the renewed approach to collective bargaining was the coordination of the bargaining system "from

below" (Paolucci et al., 2022). It was intended that the pay deals reached in strongly unionised firms in these sectors would set the trend for the restoration of collective bargaining on pay rises after a period of widely pervasive concession bargaining.

The participation of union members in decentralised bargaining is key to SIPTU's strategy (Paolucci et al., 2022). Targeting companies characterised by favourable conditions, both in terms of workers' structural power and established union presence, facilitates officials' work towards re-engaging union members at the workplace level. Meetings with members are organised to discuss issues of concern and shape the bargaining agenda. These are followed by regular surveys to assess workers' priorities over time. In some rare instances, small campaigns, involving overtime bans and work-to-rules – whereby workers refused to give their input into companies' teams and structures – are organised. Meanwhile, SIPTU used its internal training structures to prepare sector-level officials and shop stewards for company-level bargaining by enhancing their negotiating skills. To assure coordination between companies, union officials, each specialised in a specific company, collaborate daily, primarily by sharing information on the status of pay talks in relevant workplaces.

At workplace level, the renewed approach to bargaining has led to rebuilding organisation and representation at the firm level and the revitalisation of membership participation after 22 years of centralised tripartite bargaining (Paolucci et al., 2022). These days, all major Irish unions soon have accepted the return to decentralised pay bargaining as an opportunity to reconnect with members and to demonstrate unions' effectiveness in gaining pay rises.

Company-level trade union practices, and processes and outcomes of decentralised collective bargaining: Examples from France, Ireland, and Germany

This section analyses how, at company level, trade unions and works councils deal with the evolving environment of collective bargaining. What practices can be observed? What power resources do they rely on and combine? How do they impact bargaining outcomes and processes at this level? To answer these questions, this section pursues a cross-industry and cross-country analysis of three companies, building on the conceptual tools and analyses developed in the preceding sections. To capture the variety of company bargaining, it was decided to vary sector (pharmaceutical and manufacturing industries) as well as type of market economies: the three company cases belong to the liberal (Ireland), coordinated (Germany), and (post-) statist (France) variants of capitalism. In all of them, company bargaining is significant and occurs either constantly or irregularly. The respective material is taken from Paolucci et al. (2022), Haipeter and Rosenbohm (2022) as well as Kahmann and Vincent (2022). The main aim of this section is to demonstrate the usefulness of a power resources-based approach as a research heuristic in comparative studies.

Electric: The weight of statutory prescriptions

Electric is a French multinational that is a global leader in the provision of electrical energy and automation solutions for private homes, buildings, and industry. It employs 130,000 people worldwide and 15,500 in France. Its internal bargaining structure is complex. Other than at group-level, bargaining also takes place at intermediate (individual subsidiaries or their regrouping) and local (plant) levels. Bargaining activity is intense. Between 2019 and 2021, some 160 company agreements were signed. There is also the sectoral agreement in manufacturing, but its significance is limited for management and company union delegates, except for the sector's generally binding job classification scheme. At European level, there is a framework agreement on the anticipation of organisational change.

Reflecting the traditionally strong role of interventionism in French industrial relations, the (multi-) annual statutory obligations for collective bargaining channel and set the pace for trade union activity at Electric. They cover a wide array of topics such as wages, equal opportunities as well as workforce management and career trajectories. This requires specialist negotiating skills. The five representative unions at Electric have supported the development of company-specific resources to deal with bargaining imperatives. The agreement on union rights goes beyond the legal require-ments in terms of time-off, number of union representatives, and union budget. Electric management also provides specific training for union negotiators, including a private business school degree co-designed by the company. The wealth of company specific resources contrasts with those of the sectoral unions. Their ties with the unions at Electric are weak and there is very little coordination between company and sectoral bargaining.

Unions at Electric – and to some extent also management – find it difficult to take some distance from the bargaining agenda determined by public policy. Considerations of compliance tend to dominate over the search for company-specific solutions. The group level agreement on strategic workforce planning (Gestion prévisionnelle de l'emploi et des compétences; GPEC) is a case in point. Initially adopted by the HRM department of Electric as an ambitious social partner tool to prevent social plans, its development has progressively come to a standstill since the statutory obligation in 2005 to negotiate such agreements. The tendency towards formalism in bargaining also links to the scarcity of unions' associational power resources at Electric. Data on union membership are unavailable, but interviewees believe that it has been declining over time. Activism tends to be restricted to members who hold a representative mandate. Industrial action is limited to plant closures and the partial centralisation of collective bargaining at group level, endorsed by the unions, has further contributed to pacifying industrial relations.

Bargaining processes and outcomes appear satisfying to the unions at Electric. Terms and conditions are much better than those fixed by the sectoral agreement, even if the unions underline a tendency towards the individualisation of wage rises. Workers' favourable structural power resources are key to management's longstanding investment in collective bargaining: most workers at Electric are highly qualified engineers and managerial staff (cadres) who operate in high autonomy working environments. As the labour market for such personnel is tight and organisational restructuring is frequent, management uses collective bargaining to guarantee worker satisfaction and social peace.

PharmCo: Regaining local bargaining power and skills

The mobilisation of power resources in decentralised bargaining reveals quite distinct patterns at PharmCo site in Ireland. It produces food chemicals and comprises three plants. The diversified, and vertically integrated, organisational structure has sheltered this PharmCo facility from the threat of relocation and contributed to an increase of its workforce. The site employs over 600 workers.

The company recognises trade unions and meaningful collective bargaining is in place, despite the lack of strong institutional support mechanisms. Most unionised workers in the production plants– around 260 laboratory and quality control workers, supervisors, operatives, and warehouse workers – are represented by SIPTU (Services Industrial, Professional and Technical Union), while 50 craft workers are Connect members. Union density amounts to over 50%, well beyond the standards at *Electric*. Up to 2016, pay deals at PharmCo were comparable to median pay rises in the sector. However, in the case of the agreement negotiated in 2018, the 3.6% pay agreement negotiated by unions at PharmCo significantly exceeded the 2.5% median rise in the wider chemicals, pharmaceutical and medical devices sector – a trend not repeated in the 2020 pay agreement. Due to the company's remarkable financial performance, a main challenge faced by the union is to temper members' expectations regarding pay increases. Given these difficulties, the union has sought to improve the overall reward package by negotiating new items, such as extra paid holidays and additional health insurance benefits.

SIPTU's bargaining tactics at the site are strongly marked by the strategy developed by SIPTU at national level as a reaction to the loss of institutional power resources linked to the collapse of the social partnership. It evolves around re-engaging union members at the workplace, assessing workers' bargaining priorities as well as rebuilding local negotiating skills. The benefits of such an effort to strengthen associational power resources are apparent at PharmCo, where a formal workplace representation structure called the "Committee" has been established. It comprises 10 shop stewards, each representing a specific division of the company. It is led by a chairman, who is elected by the members, and by a sector-level trade union official, external to the company, who is directly employed by SIPTU. The Committee is the locus for all the discussions that are relevant to collective bargaining. While the Committee defines a shared bargaining agenda, considering the view of all the members previously surveyed, only the Chairman and the Sectoral Official sit at the actual bargaining table. The role of local negotiators has dramatically changed as bargaining activity intensified and shop stewards directly regulate the terms and conditions of employment. To strengthen shop stewards' bargaining power, SIPTU has also invested significant resources in developing their negotiating skills through training.

Given the significance of the company in terms of union density, size, and profitability, SIPTU considers PharmCo a pattern setter in collective bargaining. Coordination with wider sectoral bargaining activities is strong. The Chairman and the union official at PharmCo rely on the SIPTU sector-specific pay target that is then communicated to all union members, along with other potential issues for collective bargaining. Meanwhile, the Chairman and the sectoral official evaluate the financial position of the company. If PharmCo rejects SIPTU's pay proposal, it must bring evidence of its inability to afford the pay increase. If the company refuses to provide evidence, the LC (Labour Court) might get involved. Its recommendations are not binding, but PharmCo has generally accepted them.

Lights: A sectoral agreement that constitutes the frame for derogation

Lights is a medium-sized company with about 5,500 employees worldwide, of which around 1,500 are employed at the German headquarters. Out of these, about 800 are blue-collar production workers, the remaining workers are white-collar employees working in administration, development, and sales. The company produces luminaires and offers system solutions for lighting. It has both industrial and private customers and is represented by sales subsidiaries almost worldwide. Unlike the French and Irish cases, decentralised bargaining is not the rule at Lights, but limited to instances of derogation from the sectoral agreement to which the company is bound via its membership in the employer association Gesamtmetall.

In late 2019, Lights management approached the works council and IG Metall with the request to negotiate a derogation agreement. The demand occurred against the background of the company's struggle with the transformation of the lighting industry. The technological conversion to LED luminaires had resulted in specific long-term challenges: a high volume of investment that delivered only weak returns over a sustained period, an increased need for additional skills, and the digitalisation of production and products. Unlike instances of "wild decentralisation," management's request was formulated in the institutional framework of the "Pforzheim agreement" that regulates derogations from industry agreements in the metalworking and electrical industries. This collective agreement guarantees workers representatives information rights vis-à-vis management and the place of the union as a bargaining partner. Worker representatives checked the company's situation and realised that management's request was not without foundation. They believed that the associational power resources in the company were sufficient to justify the launch of a bargaining process that would be meaningful for workers, too.

Building on IG Metall's guidelines on worker participation and organising in bargaining over derogation, the union and the works council then invited the union members to vote on whether negotiations should be initiated. By underlining their open-ended nature (previous derogation negotiations had come to nothing on two occasions), they gained the support of well over 90% for opening negotiations. To start with, worker representatives formed a collective bargaining committee. This body then appointed a smaller negotiating committee, led by IG Metall but also including six works councillors from different parts of the company. Prior to this, the committee and the local union administration had produced an employee questionnaire to gauge the workforce's bargaining priorities.

Negotiation over derogation took place between the negotiating committee, Lights management as well as a representative of the regional employers' association. In line with IG Metall's recommendations, workers' access to information played a strategic role in the negotiation process, although it was severely hampered by the pandemic. The union and works council used digital communication channels to disseminate information on the progress of negotiations. As production workers do not have access to digital information at the workplace, worker representatives also placed emphasis on providing information via leaflets and letters to members. In the end, union members voted in favour of the agreement by a clear majority. Its duration is limited to five years. It exchanges the convergence of working-time between different groups of workers and the postponement of agreed industry-level pay increases against, amongst other things, investment commitments, an apprentice quota, the waiver of compulsory redundancies, the participation of the works council in make-or-buy decisions as well as the establishment of a joint task force supervising the implementation of the agreement.

Case comparison

In all three company cases, decentralised bargaining occurs in the context of the change and weakening of bargaining structures at sectoral level. It is either limited to incidences of derogation (Lights) or a continuous and long-standing practice (Electric; PharmCo).

In all three cases, its outcomes are judged satisfying by worker representatives. At PharmCo and Electric, the relative scarcity of qualified staff comforts the workforce's structural power and accounts for management's view on collective bargaining as a tool to improve the company's attractiveness as an employer and to guarantee social peace and productivity. At PharmCo, the combination of structural power with the mobilisation of associational power resources allows for stronger dynamics in bargaining and the positioning of the site as a pattern setter in collective bargaining. Enhancing union negotiators' skills, membership participation and cross-company coordination by the union are key to this. The relative wealth of institutional resources at Electric indicates that the mobilisation of equivalent associational power was not necessary to achieve comparable outcomes in terms of bargaining satisfaction. The derogation agreement at Lights suggests that the works council and the union partly made up for the workforce's lack of structural power by effectively threatening management to refuse one-sided concessions. Similar to SIPTU, information, membership participation, and organising were crucial for this relative success.

Bargaining processes, on the other hand, vary considerably between the cases. Differences in institutional power resources seem to play a major role in this. Decentralised bargaining at Electric is strongly marked by the prescriptions of public authorities and therefore tends towards formalism. This contrasts notably with bargaining processes at PharmCo which are more contingent due to the absence of such institutional prescriptions. At Lights, the bargaining process is to some extent framed by the provisions contained in the sectoral framework agreement on derogation, while remaining open about the issues which are addressed. In both the Irish and the German cases, union efforts to strengthen their organisational power levers in decentralised bargaining have entailed the strengthening and streamlining of internal deliberative processes in company bargaining.

Concluding remarks

This chapter analyses the role of trade unions in decentralised collective bargaining, and trade union participation in and influence on the processes and outcomes of collective bargaining at company level. The analysis is based on developments in eight EU member states and highlights a multitude of similarities and differences at national, sectoral, and company levels regarding trade union access to and mobilisation of structural, associational, and institutional power resources in the context of collective bargaining decentralisation. The collective bargaining focus on the company level, including specific strategies and practices in the analysed company case studies, reveals current and future challenges as well as potential for innovation in decentralised collective bargaining. This study and analysis is exploratory and does not aim at building, developing, or testing theory. This chapter contributes to the research discourse on decentralised collective bargaining in a novel way through its operationalisation of the power resources approach to company-level collective bargaining.

The analysis of the *institutional and legal framework of trade unions and decentralised collective bargaining* highlights that *international and EU* labour law provide a strong legal recognition for fundamental trade union rights, including freedom of association and the right to collective bargaining. However, trade unions' access and possibility to mobilise institutional power resources, not least in company-level collective bargaining, depend to a large extent on the *national* institutional and legal context. Thus, the characteristics of the national labour law and industrial relations system, which vary greatly among the countries studied, create institutional power resources of various strength, that the trade unions can – and do – mobilise in order to influence the processes and outcomes of company-level collective bargaining. Key aspects in this regard are, for example, the interplay between EU law and national labour law, the balance between legislation and collective bargaining, the degree of state influence or industrial relations voluntarism, the forms of employee representation and influence, and the legal regulation of trade unions and collective bargaining.

Trade union coordination and social partnership are important in collective bargaining. Trade unions' capacity to coordinate across levels of collective bargaining and establish social partnership relations with employers are related to their successful mobilisation of institutional and associational power resources. These power resources partly stem from the characteristics and traditions of national industrial relations systems. The analysis shows that trade union coordination and social partnership (in an autonomous, bipartite form) are frequent in, for example, Germany and Sweden, where the institutional and legal frameworks for industrial relations enable trade unions to achieve the objective to coordinate and establish partnerships. The result is trade unions' influence on the processes and outcomes of company-level collective bargaining. In national industrial relations contexts marked by disorganised decentralisation and lower degrees of coordination (or lack thereof), for example, in Ireland and Poland, trade unions can mobilise associational and structural power resources to achieve a certain degree of coordination and social partnership and compensate for a lack of institutional and legal support. In national industrial relations contexts characterised by state intervention, for example, in France, trade unions can rely on relatively strong institutional resources that may compensate for a lack in structural and associational power to achieve extensive coverage and effective enforcement of collective bargaining, wherefore trade union strategies and activities of coordination and social partnership are less developed.

The analysis of *trade union membership, organising, and participation* illustrates that despite the overall decline in trade union density and the increasing importance of guaranteeing the coordination of collective bargaining across units and levels, relatively few national trade unions have developed membership-focussed approaches as a response to the decentralisation of collective bargaining. Such limited engagement has many sources, one of them being perceived institutional security in the form of high trade union density, extensive collective bargaining coverage together with a strong legal framework. Conversely, incidences of innovation in membership approaches have occurred where the unions' decline of institutional power has been pronounced, resulting from the erosion of centralised coordination in collective bargaining. Where trade unions took on the challenge of organisational change, they conceived decentralisation as an opportunity to consolidate and even improve their power position. Evidence points to converging benefits in the form of renewed deliberative vitality, new members, and a reinforced coordination capacity.

The case-based discussion on *company-level trade union practices, processes and outcomes of decentralised collective bargaining* emphasises the importance of structural power resources for the outcomes of company bargaining, but also shows that institutional and associational power resources may complement the lack or presence of such structural power resources. Thus, it suggests a degree of interchangeability of structural, associational, and institutional power resources. It shows that the mobilisation of associational power in company bargaining, at least under otherwise favourable structural conditions, has the potential to offset the effects of a loss of institutional power in terms of social partnership regulation. In turn, evidence suggests that the relative abundance of institutional power resources at company-level may disincentivise the development of associational power, thereby hampering the unions' capacity of cross-company bargaining coordination.

Overall, trade unions are key actors in decentralised collective bargaining. Despite a strong European trend towards decentralised collective bargaining, sometimes in disorganised and fragmentised forms, the company case studies and the analysis show that trade unions have access to, and can mobilise, structural, associational, and institutional power resources. As a result, they can influence the processes of company-level collective bargaining and achieve quality outcomes.

References

Armaroli, I. & Tomassetti, P. (2022). Decentralised bargaining in Italy. CODEBAR-project. CODEBAR – AIAS-HSI – University of Amsterdam (uva.nl)

Bamber, G. J. et al. (2021). *International & Comparative Employment Relations. Global Crises and Institutional Responses* (7th edn.). Sage.

Barnard, C. (2012). *EU Employment Law* (4th edn.). Oxford University Press.

Boucher, G. & Collins, G. (2003). Having one's cake and being eaten too: Irish neo-liberal corporatism. *Review of Social Economy*, 61(3): 295–316.

Clegg, H. (1976). *Trade unionism under collective bargaining: A theory based on comparisons of six countries*. Basil Blackwell.

Czarzasty, J. (2022). Decentralised bargaining in Poland. CODEBAR-project. CODEBAR – AIAS-HSI – University of Amsterdam (uva.nl)

Deakin, S. & Koukiadaki, A. (2013). The sovereign debt crisis and the evolution of labour law in Europe. In Countouris N. & Freedland M. (Eds.), *Resocialising Europe in a time of crisis*. Cambridge University Press.

Dribbusch, H. & Birke, P. (2019). *Gewerkschaften in Deutschland. Herausforderungen in Zeiten des Umbruchs*. Friedrich-Ebert-Stiftung.

European Commission (2020), Proposal for a Directive of the European Parliament and of the Council on adequate minimum wages in the European Union, COM (2020) 682 final.

Finkin, M. W. & Mundlak, G. (Eds.) (2015). *Comparative labor law: Research handbooks in comparative law.* Edward Elgar.

Haipeter, T. (2011). Works councils as actors in collective bargaining: Derogations and the Development of codetermination in the German chemical and metalworking industries. *Economic and Industrial Democracy*, 32(4): 679–695.

Haipeter, T. & Rosenbohm, S. (2022). Decentralised bargaining in Germany. CODEBAR-project. CODEBAR – AIAS-HSI – University of Amsterdam (uva.nl)

Hall, P. A. & Soskice, D. (Eds.) (2001) *Varieties of capitalism: The institutional foundations of comparative advantage.* Oxford University Press.

Hassel, A. & Schroeder, W. (2018). *Gewerkschaften 2030: Rekrutierungsdefizite, Repräsentationslücken und neue Strategien der Mitgliederpolitik.* WSI Report, No. 44.

Hepple, B. & Veneziani, B. (Eds.) (2009). *The transformation of labour law in Europe: A comparative study of 15 countries 1945–2004.* Hart.

Hyman, R. & McCormick, R. (2013). *Trade unions in Western Europe: Hard times, hard choices.* Oxford University Press.

Hyman, R. & McCormick, R. (2019), Democracy in trade unions, democracy through trade unions? *Economic and Industrial Democracy*, 40(1): 91–110.

ILO (2022). *Social dialogue report 2022: Collective bargaining for an inclusive, sustainable and resilient recovery.*

Jansen, N. & Tros, F. (2022). Decentralised bargaining in the Netherlands. CODEBAR-project. CODEBAR – AIAS-HSI – University of Amsterdam (uva.nl)

Kahmann, M. & Vincent, C. (2022). Decentralised bargaining in France. CODEBAR-project. CODEBAR – AIAS-HSI – University of Amsterdam (uva.nl)

Kelly, J. & Frege, C. (Eds.) (2004). *Varieties of unionism: Strategies for union revitalization in a globalizing economy.* Oxford University Press.

Kilpatrick, C. (2014). Are the bailouts immune to EU social challenge because they are not EU law? *European Constitutional Law Review*, 10: 393–421.

Lévesque, C. & Murray, G. (2010). Understanding union power: Resources and capabilities for renewing union capacity. *Transfer*, 16(3): 333–350.

Marginson, P. & Sisson, K. (2004). *European integration and industrial relations: Multi-level governance in the making.* Palgrave MacMillan.

Müller, T., Vandaele, K., & Waddington, J. (Eds.) (2018). *Collective bargaining in Europe: Towards an endgame. Volume III.* ETUI.

Müller, T. & Platzer, H. (2018). The European trade union federations: Profiles and power resources — changes and challenges in times of crisis. In Lehndorff, S., Dribbusch, H., & Schulten, T. (Eds.) *Rough waters: European trade unions in a time of crisis.* ETUI.

Muñoz Ruiz, A. & Ramos Martín, N., (2022). Decentralised bargaining in Spain, CODEBAR-project. CODEBAR – AIAS-HSI – University of Amsterdam (uva.nl)

Muñoz Ruiz, A., Ramos Martín, N., & Vincent, C. (2023). Interplay between state and collective bargaining, comparing France and Spain. In F. Tros (Ed.), *Pathways in decentralised collective bargaining in Europe* (pp. 143-178). Amsterdam University Press.

Ost, D. (2011). Illusory corporatism ten years later. *Warsaw Forum of Economic Sociology*, 2 (1): 19–49.

Paolucci, V., Roche, W. K., & Gormley, T. (2022). Decentralised bargaining in Ireland. CODEBAR-project. CODEBAR – AIAS-HSI – University of Amsterdam (uva.nl)

Rehder, B. (2008). Revitalisierung der Gewerkschaften? Die Grundlagen amerikanischer Organisierungserfolge und ihre Übertragbarkeit auf deutsche Verhältnisse, *Berliner Journal für Soziologie*, 18(3): 432–456.

Rönnmar, M. & Iossa, A. (2022). Decentralised bargaining in Sweden. CODEBAR-project. CODEBAR – AIAS-HSI – University of Amsterdam (uva.nl)

Rosenbohm, S. & Tros, F. (2023). Does decentralisation lead to new relationships between trade unions and works councils? Germany and the Netherlands compared. In F. Tros (Ed.), *Pathways in decentralised collective bargaining in Europe* (pp. 179-209). Amsterdam University Press.

Schmalz, S. & Dörre, K. (2014). Der Machtressourcenansatz: Ein Ansatz zur Analyse gewerkschaftlichen Handlungsvermögens. *Industrielle Beziehungen*, 21(3): 217–237.

Schmalz, S., Ludwig, C., & Webster, E. (2018). The power resources approach: Developments and challenges. *Global Labour Journal*, 9 (2):113–134.

Thomas, A. (2016). The transnational circulation of the "organizing model" and its reception in Germany and France. *European Journal of Industrial Relations*, 22(4): 317–333.

Tros, F. (2022). Comparisons in decentralised bargaining: Final report CODEBAR-project. CODEBAR – AIAS-HSI – University of Amsterdam (uva.nl)

Turner, L. (2009). Institutions and activism: Crisis and opportunity for a German labour movement in decline. *Industrial and Labor Relations Review*, 62 (3): 294–312.

Vaughan-Whitehead, D. (2000). Social dialogue in EU enlargement: Acquis and responsibilities. *Transfer: European Review of Labour and Research*, 6(3): 387–398.

Visser, J. (2021). OECD/AIAS ICTWSS Database. Detailed Note on Definitions, Measurement, and Sources. https://www.oecd.org/els/emp/Methodological-Note-OECD-AIAS_ICTWSS.pdf

Voss, K. & Sherman, R. (2000). Breaking the iron law of oligarchy: Union revitalization in the American labor movement. *American Journal of Sociology*, 106(2): 303–349.

Welz, C. (2008). *The European Social Dialogue under Articles 138 and 139 of the EC Treaty.* Kluwer Law International.

Wright, E. (2000). Capitalist-class interests, and class compromise. *American Journal of Sociology*, 105(4): 957–1002.

Authors

Dr Ilaria Armaroli is research fellow at ADAPT (Italy). She obtained a PhD in Human capital formation and labour relations and is mainly publishing about industrial relations, collective bargaining, and employee voice. ilaria.armaroli@adapt.it

Dr Jan Czarzasty is head of the Economic Sociology Unit in the Institute of Philosophy, Sociology and Economic Sociology at SGH Warsaw School of Economics (Poland). He holds a PhD in Economics. His main research interests include industrial relations, also at cross-national level, comparative studies of modern capitalism, and economic sociology. jczarz@sgh.waw.pl

Prof. Thomas Haipeter is head of the research department "Working Time and Work Organisation" of the Institute Work, Skills and Training at the University of Duisburg-Essen (Germany). His main research area is labour relations and labour regulation in national, comparative, and transnational perspectives. thomas.haipeter@uni-due.de

Dr Andrea Iossa is senior lecturer in labour law at Kristianstad University (Sweden). He holds a PhD in labour from Lund University and works on topics related to European and comparative labour law and industrial relations, collective bargaining, and labour mobility. andrea.iossa@hkr.se

Dr Niels Jansen is assistant professor at the Faculty of Law, and social-legal researcher AIAS-HSI, at the University of Amsterdam (the Netherlands). He obtained his PhD in 2018 about the representativeness of trade unions. n.jansen@uva.nl

Dr Marcus Kahmann is sociologist and researcher at IRES, Institute for social and economic research (France). He is experienced in, among others, trade union organisations, labour relations in international perspectives, and labour migration. marcus.kahmann@ires.fr

Prof. Ana Belén Muñoz Ruiz is associate professor in the Area of Labour Law and Social Security of Universidad Carlos III de Madrid (Spain). She has written several papers on the Spanish model of collective bargaining and is member of the Observatory of collective agreement of Fundación 1º de Mayo (CCOO). In addition, she is mediator of national collective disputes at Fundación del Servicio Interconfederal de Mediación y Arbitraje FSP (SIMA-FSP). abmunoz@der-pr.uc3m.es

Dr Valentina Paolucci is assistant professor in Management, Organisational Behaviour and HRM at Maynooth Business School (Ireland). She holds a PhD in Comparative Employment Relations from the University of Warwick. Her research interests lie in the area of trade union revitalisation, precarious work, and collective bargaining in multinationals. valentina.paolucci@mu.ie

Dr Nuria Ramos Martín is assistant professor in international and European Labour Law at AIAS-HSI, University of Amsterdam (the Netherlands). She has been project manager/co-coordinator of several international research projects and contributed as an expert to several reports for the European Commission and the European Parliament on telework, precarious work in Europe, platform work, and transparent and predictable working conditions in the EU. n.e.ramosmartin@uva.nl

Prof. Mia Rönnmar is a professor in private law at the Faculty of Law at Lund University (Sweden). Her main research areas are Swedish, comparative, and EU labour law and industrial relations. mia.ronnmar@jur.lu.se

Dr Sophie Rosenbohm is a post-doctoral researcher at the Institute for Work, Skills and Training (IAQ) at the University of Duisburg-Essen. Her research interests include (transnational) industrial relations, sociology of work, and qualitative research methods. sophie.rosenbohm@uni-due.de

Dr Frank Tros is senior researcher at AIAS-HSI, University of Amsterdam (the Netherlands). He is experienced in labour relations, collective bargaining, social dialogue, and co-determination in the Netherlands and in cross-country comparisons. He initiated and coordinated the research project Comparisons in Decentralised Bargaining (CODEBAR), co-financed by the European Commission (2020–-2022). f.h.tros@uva.nl

Dr Catherine Vincent is senior researcher at IRES, Institute for social and economic research (France). She is experienced in industrial relations, collective bargaining and vocational training in France and in Europe and in social dialogue in the public services. catherine.vincent@ires.fr

List of Tables and Figures

Index